Modern Capitalism

ITS GROWTH AND TRANSFORMATION

Modern Capitalism

ITS GROWTH AND TRANSFORMATION

John Cornwall

Professor of Economics, Dalhousie University

M.E. Sharpe INC.

ARMONK, NEW YORK

Reprinted by arrangement with St. Martin's Press, Inc.

Library of Congress Cataloging in Publication Data

Cornwall, John.
Modern capitalism.
Reprint. Originally published: New York: St. Martin's Press, 1977.
Includes bibliographical references and indexes. 1. Economic History—1945- . 2. Economic development. 3. Capitalism. I. Title.
[HC59.C727 1982] 330.12′2 82-5490
ISBN 0-87332-222-3 (pbk.) AACR2

Printed in the United States of America

Contents

Preface

In the not-too-distant future, when economists and economic historians have had the opportunity to reflect on and evaluate the importance of those stages that seem to highlight the evolution of market capitalism, the quarter of a century following World War II will surely stand out as one of the most dramatic. Economists today, partially aware of what transpired during this period, have tended to express this insight in terms of the rapid rates of growth of economic activity by so many different economies. However, this way of viewing the period tends to understate the magnitude and the scope of the developments. For what took place during this era, and continues to a lesser extent today, was a transformation of modes of production, consumption and distribution, a reallocation of labor and capital between firms, industries and nations, and a revolution in 'life styles' the extent and rapidity of which has never been equaled historically. Economies grew rapidly, to be sure, but they grew rapidly in a very special unbalanced way that resulted in an ever-changing composition of output, industrial distribution of employment and spatial distribution of economic activities. Without too much exaggeration, it could be said that the structure of the different economies by the mid-1970s would not have been recognizable a quarter of a century earlier.

During much of this period economic theorists were intensely involved in developing models of economic growth suggesting that the events of the time posed a challenge for economists that they, quite understandably, were only too willing to take up. What better way to emphasize and establish the explanatory power of economic theory than to apply it to the spectacular economic events currently unfolding? Unfortunately, as any follower of the developments of macrodynamic theory during this time can attest, the concern of growth theory was not primarily or even secondarily to explain why growth or transformation rates differed so greatly in this period from any other or in one country compared with another: rather, the main concern of growth theory centered on a selection of problems that dealt with such matters as the stability and existence of an equilibrium in highly simplified mathematical models. Economists specializing in other branches of the discipline who might have chanced to survey the main developments of growth theory during this period must have been bewildered, indeed, at the lack of concern by growth theorists with the explanatory power of their theories. For if macrodynamic theory is about anything at all, it is about the macrodynamics of output (and price), in particular why output grows more rapidly at one period of time than another and why some economies grow more rapidly than others during the same period.

This anomaly is indeed hard to grasp.[1] And in trying to account for a lack of concern with the more basic problems of the macrodynamics of output, there is little evidence of a consensus that events of the postwar period were in some sense inexplicable. More serious, in retrospect there is every indication that the necessary 'building blocks' for constructing a theory of why growth rates did and will differ were there, if growth theorists had only chosen to use them. One of the main arguments of the present study is that economic theory in general and macrodynamic theory in particular are not logical systems concerned only with internal consistencies, technical 'niceties' and providing a rationalization for capitalism. Much of economic theory is quite frankly little more than this, but intermixed with the frivolous in economic theory can be found any number of useful hunches, theories, insights and models. These can be refined and synthesized into a coherent whole with an aim toward explaining one of the more fascinating developments in the history of capitalism, that which has taken place in the past quarter of a century. The central task of this study is to provide such an explanation.

The method of analysis chosen in the pages to follow was dictated by two strong convictions, both of which owe much to the writings of Schumpeter. First, while there may be some justification for trying to explain economic growth and transformation primarily in terms of economic events, there is very little excuse for economists attempting to explain these events by limiting their analysis to the various elements that compromise what has come to be thought of as 'growth theory.'[2] There was never a moment during the course of writing the book that I felt an investigator could get to the heart of the matter of why growth rates differ without integrating many areas of economics that have become artificially separated. As a result, important developments in areas other than traditional growth theory were utilized in order to make a point, and this necessitated something of a compromise in terms of the analytical approach adopted. On the one hand, nothing much was to be gained by adopting the approach of those who had already given us an outline of the broad sweep of capitalist development, together with some highly suggestive notions as to the prime factors explaining this development.

[1] Unfortunately the history of economic thought reveals this is not an isolated instance. And surely, much of the attack on economic theory today, an attack on its relevance and even its objectivity, must stem from the fact that such anomalies are not isolated instances in an otherwise steady accumulation of ever better, more encompassing theories that enrich our understanding of the real world.

[2] The main thrust of traditional growth theory is well summarized in F. Hahn and R. Mathews, 'The Theory of Economic Growth: A Survey,' *Economic Journal*, December 1964, and G. Harcourt, 'Some Cambridge Controversies in the Theory of Capital,' *Journal of Economic Literature*, June 1969. An advance text covering 'growth theory' is E. Burmeister and R. Dobell, *Mathematical Theories of Economic Growth*, MacMillan, New York, 1970.

On the other hand, a journal article writ large, that detailed the vast amount of very specialized work accumulated in fields such as labor, demography, trade and information theory, to name but a few, as well as traditional growth theory would have been unmanageable. What was possible, and hopefully was successful, was an approach that attempted to bring together the main thrusts of important theoretical and applied work in these various, diverse fields in an effort to explain the important trends in market capitalism during the postwar period. Quite naturally, this also involved supplementing these studies at various points along the way with ideas of my own.

For example, as will soon become clear, it was literally impossible to explain why the pace of growth and transformation differed without incorporating some of the findings of labor economics. Growth theorists in the past did not address this particular area because they assumed away the frictions, uncertainties and monopoly elements of the real labor markets by adopting the competitive model. But, as will be argued below, it was the ability of some economies to overcome to a large extent these market imperfections and a singular inability of others to do the same that does much to explain the differences in performance during the period. Numerous other examples could be cited. Indeed, it was the belief that differences in market imperfections between periods and across countries are the stuff that makes for differences in economic performances that largely forced the present study to delve into various branches of economics.

The approach adapted here naturally involved a certain amount of arbitrariness in the sense that many important studies had to be overlooked or treated in a most summary way. But this was inevitable, given the conviction that our understanding of what took place had to focus on some of the important institutional factors that gave rise to these market imperfections. It was also made inevitable by the simple fact that this study concerned itself with developing a model that had some claim to generality in the sense that it hoped to explain growth and transformation in a wide number of market economies. This required the compilation and use of data covering many countries in order to support the theory and, here again, space limitations required a good deal of selectivity.

Besides the strongly felt belief that many different areas in economics had to be integrated in order to tell the whole story, it was also felt that a deliberate integration of historical, theoretical and econometric methods was required. The complexity of the economic world being what it is, no other approach seemed tenable. For example, as in an earlier book (*Growth and Stability in a Mature Economy*), the method of analysis placed heavy reliance on econometrics, incorporating studies of other investigators as well as the testing of new models. But in no sense was it ever felt that some kind of global, dynamic, econometric model could have been constructed that captured the workings of any of the market economies discussed here. Certainly, in principle, the model developed below can be characterized as one composed of a system of equations, a set of endogenous and predetermined variables and a resulting recursive structure that determines a path for the endogenous variables over time. But the events to be explained, their interactions and internal dynamics, simply proved to be much too complex to be summarized explicitly in such a tidy fashion. While a firm understanding of what did take place was very much dependent upon the results of various econometric works, these were constantly supplemented by theoretical, institutional and historical considerations.

From what has just been said it is clear that little reliance was placed on the neoclassical method of analysis. Neoclassical analysis has not developed in such a way as to be able to handle the frictions and market imperfections of real life except in a rather artificial way. But there are other difficulties. For example, in Chapter IV it is argued that the allocative features of labor markets cannot be described in terms of the neoclassical precepts. Labor moves between firms and industries not so much in response to changes in relative wages as in response to changes in vacancies, relative wages remaining constant. This does not mean that labor markets never function according to the neoclassical views; rather it means that all theories involve simplifications and the essence of the manner in which market economies allocate labor can be captured only by emphasizing other kinds of 'signals' than changes in relative wages.

Or take the matter of explaining patterns of trade. The neoclassical view has been developed with skill and detail in what has come to be known as the Heckscher–Ohlin theory of trade and comparative advantage. But, as an increasing body of trade theorists have pointed out, the Heckscher–Ohlin theory is rather ill-suited not only to handle economic problems that involve uncertainty and other market imperfections, but also to handle elements of real change. Thus, given very special kinds of production functions, given tastes and given perfect certainty about current and future events, it is certainly possible to derive a process of gradual specialization and trade. To this very limited extent, neoclassical trade theory can deal with change. But the postwar period in fact was a period of radical and continuous transformation in production functions, in the kinds of goods traded and in consumer tastes. There was never a moment in this period when events indicated that trade and development patterns could ever be approximated in terms of the textbook convergence of economies to some fixed specialization and trade position. Because of this, and because of the need to incorporate developments in foreign trade in the analysis in later chapters, emphasis was placed on what has come to be known as the neotechnology theory of trade and comparative advantage.

To put the matter somewhat differently, what is downgraded in the pages to follow is the view that economic events are the outcome of some invisible hand guiding an economy through time in some predetermined way, with the outcome depending only upon some assumed initial conditions. On the contrary, what is argued below is that the historical path each capitalist economy took (and is now taking) in the postwar period was and is the outgrowth of events over which the economic actors of the various countries had some control. The Japanese economy modernized and grew rapidly because Japanese entrepreneurs, workers, bankers and civil servants wanted the Japanese economy to grow rapidly and were prepared to make the decisions and the sacrifices that were necessary to achieve this end. Technological progress did not fall like manna from heaven more heavily and rapidly in Japan than, say, in Britain or America; rather, the collective efforts of the different groups just cited allowed a more rapid absorption of new technologies in Japan than elsewhere and this was translated into relatively rapid rates of growth of labor productivity and output.

What will soon become apparent is that the model developed here allows for this 'human element.' Moreover, the non-neoclassical approach adopted has a benefit that is first set out in Chapter IV. It allows the investigator to bridge the gap that now exists between the study of growth in developing and in developed economies. What is argued in the pages to follow is that (until very recently, at least) much the same kind of model can be used to explain the growth process in semi-industrialized and industrialized nations.

Finally, an apology will be extended at this point and once more at the conclusion of the study. As suggested, macrodynamics is the study of the macrodynamic of output and price. But by far and away the more important social, political and economic issues facing capitalism today arise from the perverse behavior of prices. The advent of double-digit inflation during the latter part of the postwar period in most of the countries studied here raises the possibility that the kind of market capitalism described may not survive to the end of the present century. For this reason alone, an apology is in order to any investigator who chooses to study the macrodynamics of output before that of price. In defense let it be repeated that earlier explanations of the growth and transformation record of the market economies have been quite inadequate. Given the scope and speed of this transformation, such an explanation is clearly an interesting scientific problem demanding further analysis. Second, as argued in Chapters IX and X, the same forces that led to rapid growth in the postwar period led to successful export drives. Without the latter, periodic deflationary policies were required by different countries under the prevailing system of relatively fixed exchange rates. A discussion of the causes of slow or rapid growth can, therefore, be of some use in determining the conditions necessary for a successful implementation of full employment policies. But a further, more convincing, defense of the study undertaken here is also available. The advent of widespread inflation is one of the more important elements differentiating the period beginning roughly in the early 1970s from that of the early 1950s until the early 1970s. In trying to understand how to cope with inflation and other problems now facing capitalism, it would seem to be absolutely essential that we first understand the workings of market capitalism in a period largely free of these problems.

In general terms, the intellectual debts here are primarily to Schumpeter and Svennilson among an earlier generation and to Kaldor and Kindleberger, economists of a more recent vintage. The influence of these economists on the present work will soon be plain enough. For his help I would specifically like to thank Paul Herrington. In addition, appreciation must be extended to Ronald Britto, Michael Hodson, Jerry Hollenhorst, Paul Huber, Lord Nicholas Kaldor, Charles Kindleberger, Barry Lesser, Michael Shields, Charles Stalon, Ronald Tracy and Brendan Walsh, several of whom took strong exception to parts of what is to follow. I would also like to thank Research and Projects at Southern Illinois and Tufts University and Dalhousie University Research Development Committee, Humanities and Social Sciences for financial aid and assistance as well as the National Institute of Health for financial support under Research Grant No. 5-R01-HD-07645-02. Parts of Chapters IV and V were originally published in the *Economic Journal*, June 1976, and *Kyklos*, No. 1, 1977.

for Anne, Paula and Morgan

Chapter I Growth as a Transformation

A. Svennilson and Schumpeter on Growth

Ingar Svennilson's *Growth and Stagnation in the European Economy*[1] was published early in the post-World War II period. Largely neglected, it attempted to explain the development patterns of the industrialized, market economies of Europe between 1913 and 1938. From today's perspective, Svennilson's theoretical approach stands in stark contrast to the kinds of theorizing that were about to become so popular with economists, especially that propounded by the neoclassicists.[2] For example, the latter, when allowing for more than one sector in a model, tended to deal only with 'balanced growth' processes whereby each sector grew at the same rate equal to the overall growth rate. As a result, such important historical processes as 'industrialization,' 'modernization,' 'consumerism' and 'post-industrial' development could not be handled at all well. In contrast, Svennilson placed great emphasis on the notion of a transformation or unbalanced growth of market economics as evidenced by such events as a continuous shifting of the composition of output, a rise and subsequent decline of individual industries (as technology and consumer tastes changed or were modified), and the redistribution of labor and capital across industries and regions. In Svennilson's analysis the notion of transformation included:

> A change of production methods, mainly in the direction of more advanced mechanization;
> A change of input–output relations between raw materials and end-products;
> The development of new end-products, and shifts in the distribution of consumption between various products;
> Changes in exports and imports in relation to the output of domestic industry;
> A redistribution of manpower between different industries and occupations.[3]

[1] I. Svennilson, *Growth and Stagnation in the European Economy*, Economic Commission for Europe, Geneva, 1954.
[2] See the references in footnote 2 in the Preface.
[3] Svennilson, op. cit., p. 7.

Any attempt to explain the process of growth without stressing these aspects of unbalanced growth could only be considered 'as a highly abstract and theoretical conception.'[4]

There were other important contrasts between his approach and the theorizing in macrodynamics that was to follow. Svennilson perceived economic change as an interaction between the various forms of transformation just mentioned and the growth of national income and output. For example, as a result of discoveries and innovations, changes in technology and production through their impact on costs and prices strongly affected the rate of growth of output. Sectoral shifts in the distribution of capital and labor also had a pronounced impact on growth rates because of differences in sector levels and rates of growth of factor productivities. But in addition the rate of growth of the economy affected the nature and speed of the transformation since rising incomes generated shifts in the distribution of final demand and output, demands for intermediate goods, labor and capital, and influenced the rate and incidence of technological progress itself.

A key to understanding differences in rates of growth and transformation was the rate of growth of factor supplies, especially capital, in certain key sectors. Thus, unlike neoclassical analysis, the rate of capital formation was critical in determining the long-run growth rate and this was very much related to the unbalanced nature of the growth process. Given the specificity and immobility of capital goods and labor, the development of new goods, new techniques, new industries and firms and new locations of economic activities required new kinds of capital goods and a redistribution of the labor force. Growth of factor supplies at the margin in key industries became a critical feature in determining the speed and scope of the growth and transformation process. To put Svennilson's argument somewhat differently, one could not explain why growth rates differed both over time and across countries without taking account of differences in the 'flexibility' between economies arising from differences in the rate at which capital and labor were augmented in the 'industries of the future.'

In addition to the ordinary capacity effect of investment and its influence on capacity in new industries and areas, investment played the traditional and critical multiplier role in Svennilson's analysis of determining the level of aggregate demand. More to the point, without a level of investment that maintained high levels of demand – high enough to strain the productive capacity of the economy – growth and transformation would be slowed down. This stemmed from such factors as the stimulating effects of high and rising aggregate demand on the rate of innovation, technological progress and productivity and the greater adaptability of labor, as well as on management's greater willingness to innovate when unemployment was low and capital utilization high. Thus, Svennilson argued that the role of demand was critical in the sense that the rate of growth and transformation was not independent of

[4]ibid.

the level of demand. In this sense alone much of modern growth theory, with its assumption of continuous full employment, would have been considered question-begging and even irrelevant.

The writings of Schumpeter on growth have much in common with those of Svennilson.[5] The marked contrast with the neoclassical method of analysis is just as dramatic and, in addition, the common stress of the two economists on the unbalanced nature of the growth process stands out. 'Qualitative change' as an integral part of the growth process is but Schumpeter's expression for 'transformation.'

Qualitative change is introduced in the growth process by 'innovations' in the form of new production functions designed to produce new goods or to produce existing products better. This dramatic, almost autonomous, source of change is first implemented by the 'heroic entrepreneur.' Indeed, innovation and entrepreneurship go hand in hand in the Schumpeterian scheme of things, since without innovations there remains only a small role for the entrepreneur to play in the workings of the capitalist system: that of the coordinator of the factors of production as in neoclassical analysis.

Svennilson, in contrast to Schumpeter, viewed innovations more as endogenous phenomena than as partly autonomous factors appearing during certain phases of the business cycle. A reasonable interpretation of Svennilson's views is that innovations are but the natural consequence of rising per capita incomes and differing income (or growth) elasticities of demand. The discussion of innovations in Chapters VI and VII will indicate a weakness in Svennilson's analysis in its failure to stress sufficiently the importance of entrepreneurship. But the views of the two economists are anything but inconsistent, and the common stress on the importance of investment in instituting qualitative change or transformation is more important than any difference in emphasis they might have had.

B. Growth and Transformation in the Interwar Period

Both Schumpeter and Svennilson saw 'model-building' as essentially a means for explaining certain key periods in the history of capitalism. Thus, Schumpeter's analysis of capitalist development can be viewed as an attempt to explain the workings of capitalism before it had become 'trustified' and 'laboristic.' One of Svennilson's chief hopes was that his study would link up the important events of the early period of industrialization in the various economies with the course of their development in the post-World War II period. By developing a model that would explain events of the interwar period, this link was also to function as a means of promoting better understanding of what was about to take place in the post-World War II period.

[5] See especially J. Schumpeter, *The Theory of Economic Development*, Oxford University Press, New York, 1961.

Thus, the view of the development of market economics as an interaction of the growth of aggregate output and different aspects of transformation, where rates of growth and transformation depended on the rates of growth of factor supplies in certain key sectors, and ultimately strong (and growing) demand pressures, provided a framework for Svennilson's explanation of the slowness of the growth and transformation process in the interwar period. The year 1913 marked the culmination of an extended period of rapid, relatively uninterrupted, growth in Europe. By the outbreak of World War I the industrial complexes of the United Kingdom, France and Germany had grown so rapidly they dominated European industry. The expansion of the capital goods industries was especially pronounced, induced somewhat by the length and strength of the preceding period of growth, making these countries the 'workshops of the world.' For example, together these three economies supplied sixty per cent of the world's exports of manufactured goods and seventy-five per cent of European exports.

Svennilson viewed World War I as a profound shock, drastically interrupting the workings of this growth and transformation process. By the end of the war industrial production and per capita output of most European economies including the big three were below their prewar level, as much of the prewar capacity of Europe, measured in terms of capital equipment and manpower, was lost as a result of the war. By way of contrast, the American economy grew during this period, emerging from World War I with a vastly enlarged industrial base.

In the meantime, three important changes developed during the war and immediately thereafter, partly a result of the war, partly a result of other factors. The first was the development of a new technology based on new applications of electricity and the combustion engine. Svennilson attributed their main significance to the manner in which they revolutionized the creation of mechanical motive power for transport, agriculture and industry. While the innovations in these fields had developed before the war, the cumulative impact of technical progress along these lines resulted in radical new possibilities for transformation of production and, eventually, demand. More particularly, a radical change in the degree of mechanization of agriculture and industry (especially in the capital goods industries) was now possible along with dramatic innovations in the fields of transportation and distribution.

The second and most important change singled out by Svennilson was the altered economic position of the European economy vis-à-vis the rest of the world which was attributed to three different influences: stagnation in the volume of world trade; the changing commodity composition of world demand for manufactured goods; and the rising competition from overseas industrial powers, especially the United States and Japan.

Svennilson attributed the decline in the volume of world trade largely to the decline in growth in the European economies. This led to a decline in imports into Europe, especially of primary products, which led in turn to a fall in the proceeds of primary-producing countries, thereby lowering their demand for European exports. In addition, the primary goods producers had been stimulated to become more self-sufficient by the war, which further reduced their demands for European exports. This rising economic independence of primary goods producers led to a shift in the commodity composition of foreign demand for manufactured goods, away from the traditional exports of the industrialized economies of Europe. Third, the rapid industrialization of Japan and the United States was stimulated by the war, adding an additional burden to postwar development of European productions and exports.

The final important change was the relatively rapid growth of population in the less developed, capital-poor countries of Europe coupled with an inability of the developed portion of Europe to supply capital to these countries. The resulting 'factor proportions' problem kept the poorer regions from developing along lines that might have increased intra-European trade, thereby stimulating growth all around.

All three changes – the revolution in technology, the changed international relationship between Europe and the rest of the world and the factors retarding the development of the less developed areas of Europe – in Svennilson's views required profound adjustments on the part of the European economies if growth and transformation in the interwar period was to proceed at their pre-World War I rate. The fact that the adjustments were so feeble was Svennilson's explanation of stagnation in Europe during the interwar period.

Rapid and sustained growth following World War I would have been, in Svennilson's view, possible only if a heroic response to these three changes had been made. This, in turn, required a transformation of the economic structure of the European economies through the joint efforts of business and government. Since the economic climate of the 1920s was still dominated by the notions of laissez-faire capitalism, most of the burden of responding to these changes and transforming the economies fell on the business community. In Svennilson's view the response was most inadequate. Moreover, when governments did intervene, as in the 1930s, 'it was the explicit purpose of economic policy for social reasons to soften and delay the effects of new development.'[6]

C. The Impact of Aggregate Demand

The economic conditions of the interwar period differed in many important respects from that before World War I. Svennilson singled out several factors that were important but his emphasis of the difference in the level of aggregate demand stands out. The interwar period was a period of high unemployment during booms and as well as recessions. Related to this is the fact that this

[6] Svennilson, op. cit., p. 38.

period was one of feeble recoveries of short duration from previous recessions. As a result the impetus to transformation, for introducing new, more efficient, capital-intensive techniques, or of channeling capital and labor into new industries whose products would later be revealed as those with high income elasticities of demand, was lacking. Rapid transformation and growth required sustained demand pressures that squeezed capacity and reduced the macro-risks involved in the innovative and risky investment ventures, and these pressures never developed. To express the same notion in Schumpeterian terms, there was a singular lack of quality entrepreneurship that would lead to the introduction of innovations in the industries of the future.

A large part of this lack of sustained demand pressures could be traced to the unwillingness of business to transfer resources into the production of those goods that would find receptive domestic and foreign consumers; i.e., a version of the familiar bootstrap operation whereby, if business in the aggregate would only undertake large-scale investment programs, the multiplier effect would generate enough demand to justify the expansion of capacity. But, in addition, a good part of the problem was the preoccupation of European governments (and business leaders) with currency problems and with driving down costs and prices instead of helping to transform the economy. Both factors, however, greatly depressed the rate of investment and therefore demand and prevented the exploitation of new techniques and potential markets.

> What was needed in order that economic growth could be resumed was a complete transformation of the economic structure, including a development of new industries, and a modernization of stagnating industries in order to squeeze out resources, including labor, that could be used more effectively in new fields. This transformation could not be completed overnight. The task was so great and the resistance to change in stagnating industries so strong that a considerable time would in any case be needed in order to carry transformation to a satisfactory end.
>
> The pace at which this transformation took place was, of course, dependent on the general monetary policy of the respective countries. High and stable employment without excessive inflationary tendencies might have speeded up the process. But the ideas and techniques of a balanced high-employment policy had not yet been developed and long-term progress was stranded on the rocks of inflation and deflation.[7]

Growth rates accelerated in capitalist countries shortly after the end of hostilities of World War II and continued at a rapid rate until the very recent period. As will be argued throughout the pages to follow, not the least of the causes of rapid growth following this war has been the high levels of aggregate demand, a factor so important in Svennilson's explanation of rapid growth before World War I. In large measure the high levels of demand and the resulting superior growth record could be attributable to the relatively high

[7] ibid., p. 46.

proportion of output devoted to investment.[8] But to a large extent the performance following World War II was the commitment to full employment by virtually every government in the various market economies.

Furthermore, in the concluding chapters of the book it will be argued that the unwillingness of governments resolutely to pursue full-employment policies beginning in the 1970s, largely because of a fear of rapid inflation, raises problems for the future with regards to both growth and stability. The shocks experienced by capitalism in the early 1970s, and the structural changes that were building up before these events and have continued since, suggests a comparison with the period following World War I.

D. Scope of the Present Study

As just mentioned, the interwar period stands in marked contrast not only to the pre-World War I period but to the resurgence of the developed market economies following World War II. As pointed out in the Preface, one of the main tasks of this study is to develop an understanding of the main macro-developments of the period since World War II. Not only is this study intended to explain the pervasiveness of this resurgence of market capitalism, compared with the performance of the various economies in earlier periods, but it attempts to explain why growth rates differed across countries in the post-World War II period (hereafter referred to as the 'postwar period'), a much more complicated task.

Instead of concentrating on what was contained within the boundaries of Europe of the interwar period, the analysis will be both broadened and narrowed. It will be broadened to include some of the more important market economies outside of Europe, in particular Canada, Japan and the United States; it will be narrowed, quite naturally, to exclude those countries in Europe that can no longer be considered market economies. In addition, little will be said with regard to countries such as Ireland, Spain, Portugal and Greece. While the model developed below is relevant for analyzing countries such as these, the analysis will be limited basically to the developed OECD market economies. This is primarily the result of a lack of comparable data for the former group. For the same reason, Sweden and Switzerland will not receive the attention they deserve.

The period to be covered runs from the beginnings of the 1950s until the present. This means that the model to be developed will attempt to explain a period of uninterrupted growth that lasted almost a quarter of a century. It also means that the analysis will have to at least try to deal with the impact of an accumulation of shocks that hit market capitalism toward the end of the present period. Thus, the oil crisis of 1973 together with the various implications for future energy sources, and the spread and persistence of

[8] See R. Mathews, 'Why has Britain had Full Employment Since the War?' *Economic Journal*, September 1968.

double-digit inflation beginning in the late 1960s, can be viewed as disturbances to market capitalism today that are analogous to the affect of World War I on the interwar period. Whether the cumulative impact of the more recent disturbances, including the increasing lack of confidence in capitalism itself, will be as great for modern capitalism in the future as World War I was for an earlier epoch remains to be determined.

As already stressed, if macrodynamics is about anything at all, it must be a study of why rates of growth of output (and prices) in some aggregate sense vary. This requires that model-builders address themselves to the question of why growth rates have differed and do differ over time and across countries. Yet as shall be argued in Chapter III, with few exceptions, growth theorists have directed their attention to vastly different kinds of problems. As a result, there has not developed the body of knowledge one would have expected, given that 'growth theory' has been one of the more popular fields in economics in recent times, from which to build on in an undertaking such as this.

Fortunately, Schumpeter's and Svennilson's studies, which stand out in contrast to the general course of development of postwar growth theory, suggest an approach that promises real insights into the question of why growth rates differ. Only a cursory look at some of the 'stylized facts' of the postwar period as outlined in Chapter II is necessary to show that these two, as few others, came to grips with the basic nature of the process of growth, i.e. that of a transformation or qualitative change, and succeeded in formalizing it into a very workable point of departure for analyzing the transformation of capitalism in the postwar period. The manner in which the analysis will build upon the works of these two is outlined in the second half of Chapter III. As will be clear in succeeding chapters, their views strongly influenced each stage of the present analysis.

E. An Outline of What is to Follow

Chapter II presents a short statistical summary of some of the more important aspects of Svennilson's and Schumpeter's transformation process bringing together comparable data for a wide number of market economies in order to show the important common trends. The chapter is also intended to suggest the method of analysis that must be adopted if these important trends are to be adequately explained. Chapter III is quite simply a discussion of the most popular form of dynamic analysis developed in recent times. Some of the serious shortcomings of this kind of analysis for explaining macrodynamic developments are discussed with a view toward developing a more fruitful framework.

Chapter IV marks the first stage in the development of an alternative framework. Here, the model of the 'dual economy' is discussed and developed further with a view toward showing that, when properly formulated, it is a powerful instrument for analyzing developments of modern capitalism. As such, it is a model with a 'sense of history.' It is argued in Chapter IV that this class of growth models can very well explain the growth process in both developing and developed economies. Chapter V discusses the response of labor to demand pressures with particular attention given to the kinds of movements of the labor force between sectors induced by a strong and growing aggregate demand for labor. The chapter also addresses itself to the question of whether or not certain market economies were hampered in their transformation process by a shortage of labor in the high-wage, high-productivity sectors in the postwar period. To anticipate the conclusions, evidence suggests that throughout the postwar period these sectors were able to find labor whenever their demands for labor were strong.

In Chapter VI an attempt is made to explain the rate of growth of manufacturing output. The importance of 'borrowing' technologies from the industrial leaders is stressed at this point. The borrowing of inventions and innovations developed first in other countries is an aspect of entrepreneurship overlooked by Schumpeter and Svennilson. Chapter VII analyzes the important role that manufacturing plays in the growth process. Chapter VIII attempts to tie together many of the ideas of the earlier chapters by estimating and simulating a simple econometric model. Chapters IX and X deal with the interrelationships between economic growth and international trade. Here it is argued that the same factors that cause economic growth and transformation to proceed at a rapid pace also lead to successful and imaginative export drives. As also mentioned in the Preface, this connection gives added importance to the achievement of a decent growth record. It is to be hoped that from these chapters there emerges a convincing view of the determinants of competitive advantage in manufacturing exports in a world of constant change in the commodity composition of trade and output. Nevertheless, if the reader is willing to accept the arguments of the previous chapters, Chapters IX and X may be skipped.

Chapter XI brings the analysis up to date with a discussion of market capitalism since 1973. It is argued that events of the time have very likely permanently altered the structure of capitalism. Chapter XII is a summing-up with a view to convincing the reader that a study of the quarter of the century following World War II is a very useful way to begin a study of the causes and consequences of the rather traumatic events of today.

Chapter II Some of the 'Stylized Facts' of Market Capitalism

A. Introduction

The main purpose of this chapter is to sketch the broad outlines of the process of transformation and qualitative change that took place in the postwar period. Whenever possible, comparisons are made with earlier periods of capitalist development by extending the data as far back in time as possible. Beginning with some comparative data on growth rates between countries and historical periods in Section B, the emphasis shifts in Sections C and D where data are used to bring out the unbalanced nature of growth. Svennilson's view of growth as a transformation and Schumpeter's notion of qualitative change are revealed here in terms of the pronounced differences in sectoral rates of growth of output, employment and productivities. Section E contains data on unemployment rates illustrating quite well the depressed economic conditions of the interwar period, conditions that retarded growth and change in the different market economies. Then, in Section F, some very general measures of the degree of flexibility afforded the different economies are given. Section G contains the conclusions.

B. Comparative Growth Rates

The postwar period saw a resurgence of the developed market economies that was exceptional both in terms of the rate at which the different economies grew and in terms of the large number of economies that experienced especially rapid growth rates. Table 2.1 gives comparable figures for a number of economies covering approximately one hundred years. The interwar period has been broken down in such a way that the depression-ridden 1930s is separated from the 1920s. Figures for rates of growth of aggregate economic activity, ($\dot{Q}$), are given along with rates of growth of output adjusted for labor input, ($\dot{q}$), all figures in constant prices. The acceleration in growth rates is particularly noticeable when the postwar period is compared with the pre-1913 period. In every country except the United States there has been an acceleration in growth rates, comparing the postwar period with the period prior to 1913, whether measured in terms of aggregate output or output per worker. When comparison is made with the 1920s, the record of the most recent period is still quite exceptional. In every country except France, the United States and Germany there has been an increase in the rate of growth of output per worker, compared with the 1920s, and usually a pronounced increase.

Table 2.1. Annual rate of growth of GNP or GDP (Q) and GNP or GDP per worker ($\dot{q}$)

	Earliest year	Up to 1913 $\dot{q}$	Up to 1913 $\dot{Q}$	1922[a]–29[b] $\dot{q}$	1922[a]–29[b] $\dot{Q}$	1929[b]–37[c] $\dot{q}$	1929[b]–37[c] $\dot{Q}$	1951–73 $\dot{q}$	1951–73 $\dot{Q}$
		%	%	%	%	%	%	%	%
Japan	1880	3.4	4.3	5.9	6.5	2.4	3.6	8.0[d]	9.5[d]
Sweden	1863	2.4	3.1	3.3	3.9	1.9	2.3	n.a.	n.a.
United States	1871	2.2	4.5	2.1	4.8	0.4	0.1	2.0	3.7
Canada	1872	1.9	4.0	2.1	5.1	−0.9	−0.3	2.2	4.6
Denmark	1872	2.1	3.2	2.1	3.6	1.1	2.0	3.3[e]	4.2[f]
Norway	1865	1.3	2.1	3.1	3.9	2.0	2.5	3.9	4.2
France	1855	1.5	1.6	5.8	5.8	−1.3	−2.1	4.8[e]	5.0
Germany	1853	1.5	2.6	6.0	5.7	2.1	2.8	4.7	5.7
Italy	1863	0.7	1.3	2.2	2.3	1.6	1.9	4.6	5.1
United Kingdom	1857	1.6	2.6	1.6	2.7	1.6	2.3	2.5	2.7
Netherlands	1900	0.7	2.2	2.0	4.0	0.3	0.2	4.0	5.0

[a] From 1925 for Germany and from 1923 for Sweden
[b] Or year of onset of depression if other than 1929
[c] 1938 for Japan
[d] 1953–73
[e] 1957–73
[f] 1954–73

Source: D. C. Paige, 'Economic Growth: The Last Hundred Years,' *National Economic Review*, July 1961; T. Cripps and R. Tarling, *Growth in Advanced Capitalist Economics 1950–1970*, Cambridge University Press, 1973; *National Accounts of the OECD, 1962–1973, Vol. I and II*, OECD, Paris; and *Labour Force Statistics, 1962–1973*, OECD, Paris. The figures used by Cripps and Tarling and the OECD are for GDP.

There is the possibility that events of the postwar were dominated by a tendency for economies to make up for the interruptions of the growth process caused by the depression of the 1930s and World War II. Thus, it can be argued that the exceptionally rapid rates of growth in the postwar period are temporary in nature and that a return to something more closely resembling the 1920s or even the period before 1913 is to be expected. If this were the case, it might be expected that a slowing down of growth rates during or toward the end of the postwar period would be discernible. This is certainly not the case up until the 1970s as borne out by the data in Table 2.2, where rates of growth of GDP per worker, ($\dot{q}$), and rates of growth of output per worker in manufacturing, ($\dot{q}_m$), the more important measures in this context, are shown. Beginning with a boom year in the early 1950s, growth rates are computed from that year until the next peak in economic activity. Growth rates so computed are listed under the column heading 'First Boom.' Growth rates from the second to third peak in economic activity for each country are then given under column heading 'Second Boom,' etc. Belgium, Canada and the United States underwent only three booms, so measured, during the whole period and are listed at the bottom of the table. If there is any trend at all in the output figures adjusted for labor input it is upward with only one country, Canada, showing a steady decline in growth rates from one sub-period to the next. Thus, the data up until the early 1970s cannot be used as evidence that the historically rapid rates of growth in the postwar period can be attributed simply to recovery from the 1930s and World War II.

Table 2.2. Annual average rates of growth of GDP per worker ($\dot{q}$) and GDP per worker in manufacturing ($\dot{q}_m$) selected periods, peak-to-peak in economic activity, 1950–70

	First boom 1950		*Second boom*		*Third boom*		*Fourth boom* 1970	
	$\dot{q}$	$\dot{q}_m$	$\dot{q}$	$\dot{q}_m$	$\dot{q}$	$\dot{q}_m$	$\dot{q}$	$\dot{q}_m$
	%	%	%	%	%	%	%	%
Japan	5.38	7.54	9.20	8.96	8.50	7.27	8.64	10.40
Germany	5.60	5.48	4.80	5.06	4.32	4.37	4.66	4.88
Italy	3.58	5.95	4.56	5.09	4.47	4.31	5.41	5.63
France	n.a.	4.37	4.40	4.03	5.27	4.68	4.88	5.42
Netherlands	3.75	4.32	3.78	4.65	3.60	3.94	4.73	7.19
Denmark	n.a.	n.a.	3.51	2.64	3.88	4.62	3.03	3.05
United Kingdom	1.95	2.59	2.09	2.08	2.18	2.79	2.81	3.71
Austria	n.a.	5.09	4.20	3.44	4.27	4.04	6.79	7.30
Norway	3.81	3.13	3.44	3.57	4.17	4.15	3.34	3.06
	First boom		*Second boom*		*Third boom*			
Canada	3.67	3.83	1.78	2.50	1.11	1.99		
Belgium	2.72	3.22	3.35	4.95	3.56	4.73		
United States	1.88	1.85	2.57	3.20	1.08	1.74		

Source: Cripps and Tarling, op. cit.

The most recent data available allow the period to be extended to 1973. Growth rates from 1969 or 1970 (depending upon whether the last peak recorded in Table 2.2 was 1969 or 1970) to 1973 show a more mixed pattern. In general, the countries of rapid growth, taking the postwar period as a whole (e.g. France, Germany and Italy together with Denmark), experience a slowdown in growth rates of both output per worker overall and in manufacturing in the early 1970s. On the other hand, the United Kingdom, Canada and the United States, along with Austria, Belgium and the Netherlands, experience an increase in the rate of growth of output per worker in manufacturing and for the whole economy, compared with earlier periods in each country. Unfortunately, some of the figures for the 1970s may reflect cyclical influences.[1] The possibility that the early 1970s marks a transitional period between an era of accelerating growth rates and one of slower or decelerating growth is discussed in Chapter XI.

C. The Transformation of Output

The data in Table 2.1 measure only the growth of certain aggregates and, therefore, fail to capture the various aspects of transformation that were occurring during the postwar period. A moderate amount of disaggregation is thus required. For example, data in Table 2.3, by breaking down the aggregate

Table 2.3. Annual average rates of growth of GDP and gross product in agriculture, industry and services in constant prices, 1955–73

		Annual average rates of growth		
	GDP	*Agriculture*	*Industry*	*Services*
	%	%	%	%
Canada	4.7	2.1	5.6	4.4
United States	3.8	1.8	3.8	3.9
Japan[a]	14.0	6.8	15.4	14.8
France[b]	5.5	1.5	6.6	5.1
Germany	5.2	1.9	6.0	3.8
Italy	5.2	2.2	6.4	6.2
United Kingdom[c]	2.6	2.9	2.7	2.4
Belgium	4.4	1.5	5.2	4.0
Denmark	4.7	1.0	5.8	4.7
Netherlands[d]	5.1	2.7	6.1	4.7
Norway[b]	4.3	−0.5	4.1	5.3
Sweden	4.2	0.7	5.5	4.0
Austria	5.1	1.4	5.8	5.5

[a]Current prices. Transportation and communication are included in industry.
[b]1955–69
[c]1955–72
[d]1955–68

Sources: *National Accounts of OECD Countries, 1950–1968, 1953–1969 and 1962–1973*, OECD, Paris.

[1] Figures for output per worker in Japan and Norway are not available for the 1970s. Rates of growth of total GDP (or GNP) and total manufacturing output do not show a pattern of accelerated growth up to the end of the 1960s. If anything, the more common trend is downward for rates of growth of both aggregate variables beginning with the subperiod that ends in 1969 or 1970. This is especially true for manufacturing output. Data for the 1970s were taken from *National Accounts of the OECD Countries, 1962–1973*, Vols. I and II, OECD, Paris.

output figures only slightly, indicate clearly the very unbalanced nature of growth during this period. In every economy listed in Table 2.3 except the United Kingdom, the rate of growth of agricultural output was less than rates of growth of output overall and growth rates in industry and services. The growth of industry output exceeded the growth of total output in every country and exceeded the growth of output of the service sector in every country except the United States and Norway. Figures for growth rates in manufacturing relative to GDP and the other sectors resemble those for industry as a whole.[2]

Table 2.4. Annual average rates of growth of the major categories of consumption, 1955–69

	Annual average rates at 1963 prices					
	Total	*Food*	*Clothing*	*Rent*	*Durable goods*	*Other*
Canada[a]	4.5	2.9	2.8	5.6	5.7	5.0
United States	4.1	2.3	4.1	4.9	5.7	4.3
Japan	8.7	5.7	9.1	6.3	12.9	
France[b]	5.7	3.7	5.5	6.0	9.7	6.4
Germany[c]	4.5	2.8	4.4	6.1	5.5	
Italy	5.6	5.1	5.3	3.3	9.0	6.1
United Kingdom	2.8	1.3	2.8	2.8	5.4	3.1
Belgium	3.4	1.9	3.2	2.0	7.0	3.8
Denmark	4.4	2.6	4.0	3.8	8.1	4.2
Netherlands	5.2	3.2	5.0	2.8	10.3	5.8
Norway	3.9	2.6	3.4	3.5	8.3	4.1
Sweden[a]	3.8	2.1	2.7	4.0	6.4	4.6
Switzerland	4.5	4.1	4.0	2.3	5.3	

[a]1955–68 [b]1959–69 [c]1960–69

Source: *Expenditure Trends in OECD Countries, 1960–1980*, OECD, Paris, Table 6, p. 31.

Table 2.4 brings out in another manner the unbalanced nature of growth in the developed market economies. In every country, the rate of growth of real expenditures on food was less than the rate of growth of total consumption outlays and, with few exceptions, food expenditures were the slowest-growing component of total consumption expenditures. In contrast, the relatively high rates of growth of expenditures on consumer durables reflects the well-known boom in outlays on consumer capital items taking place during this period. Thus, the postwar period saw a radical reorganization of household budgets as the share of consumer outlays on foodstuffs and, to a lesser extent, clothing and rent declined while that on durables and 'other' items rose.

Finally, additional insights into the transformation process are provided by

[2] The 'industrial' sector is defined to include manufacturing, construction, public utilities and mining.

Table 2.5. Annual average rates of growth of GNP and its major components, 1955–73

	GNP	Consumption private	Consumption public	Total fixed investment	Residential construction	Non-residential fixed investment	Non-residential construction	Machinery and equipment	Exports[a]	Imports[a]
	%	%	%	%	%	%	%	%	%	%
Canada	4.7	4.8	3.6	4.3	3.0	4.6[b]	3.6	9.2	7.1	6.3
United States	4.0	4.1	3.4	4.0	1.8	4.6	3.4	5.8	6.4	6.9
Japan[c]	10.1	8.6	5.9	14.6	14.7	14.6	n.a.	n.a.	13.2	14.3
France[d]	5.8	5.7	3.3	9.0	9.1	9.0	9.4	8.7	8.6	10.3
Germany	4.4	4.6	4.2	4.4	3.8	4.5	3.9	4.0	9.2	9.3
Italy	5.1	5.4	4.1	4.5	4.3	4.9	3.3	6.2	12.5	11.8
United Kingdom	2.9	3.0	2.2	4.9	4.6	4.9	5.3	4.8	4.1	4.7
Belgium	4.4	3.8	5.5	5.2	3.7	5.6[b]	5.8	5.5	7.9	8.1
Denmark	4.6	4.0	5.8	8.0	9.2	7.6[b]	6.7	8.3	7.2	8.6
Netherlands	4.7	5.0	2.5	6.1	6.3	6.0[b]	5.4	6.6	8.8	9.1
Norway[e]	4.4	3.9	5.7	4.3	3.7	4.3	4.2	4.4	8.1	7.4
Sweden	4.3	3.5	4.8	5.3	4.3	5.6	5.4	5.9	8.1	6.9
Switzerland[e]	4.4	4.5	4.4	6.8	6.4	6.9	6.2	7.8	7.1	8.5

[a] Goods, services and factor income
[b] Includes land improvement and plantation and orchard development
[c] Fiscal year for 1955–1969
[d] 1959–1969 [e] 1955–1969 n.a. = not available.

Source: *Expenditure Trends in OECD Countries 1960–1980*, OECD, Paris, Table 2, and *National Accounts of OECD countries, 1961–1972, 1962–1973*, Vol. I and II, op. cit.

Table 2.5. Here the rates of growth of expenditures in constant prices of the different components of GNP are given for a large group of the OECD countries. In every country, rates of growth of exports and imports exceeded the rate of growth of GNP. Growth in this sense, at least, was always 'export-led.' Except for Germany and Norway, the rate of growth of machinery and equipment investment also exceeded the rate of growth of GNP. There was a little less uniformity across countries for non-residential fixed investment, and even less for total fixed investment (which includes government sector capital formation); but in general the picture was that of a rising share of expenditures on final goods being devoted to capital formation, especially when residential construction is omitted.

In various ways the tables indicate some of the essential interactions of Svennilson's transformation during the postwar period. Rising per capita incomes (closely related to rising labor productivity) have, because of different income elasticities of demand, led to a changing composition of consumption outlays as seen in Table 2.4. In turn, it can be surmised that the rapid growth of investment outlays and the capital stock, by embodying the most advanced technology in the production of goods currently consumed as well as new goods, led to a situation where the transformation process itself was affecting productivity growth and, therefore, the growth of per capita income, etc. While there is a kind of circularity in all this, Chapters IV–VIII reformulate these ideas to bring out the essential recursive features of this growth process.

D. The Transformation of Sectoral Employment Patterns

Large as were the differences in sectoral growth rates of output, it is only by focusing on the input side of production that one can grasp how dramatic was the transformation process during the postwar period. For example, not only did the rate of growth of agricultural output lag behind the growth rates of the other two sectors, but in every market economy agricultural employment actually declined. Table 2.6 even more than Table 2.3 shows how radical was the unbalanced nature of growth for eight of these economies, this time in terms of the implied rates of growth of sectoral employment. For a long-run comparison, selected pre-World War II data are also included.

Every economy listed in Table 2.6 experienced a fall in agricultural employment and a rise in service sector employment as a share of total employment. Employment in industry as a per cent of total employment behaved in a much less uniform way. In the United Kingdom, the United States, Sweden and the Netherlands, industrial employment declined during the postwar period, while in Germany and France the per cent employed in industry tended to level off. In Italy and Japan the industrial employment share actually increased throughout the period surveyed in Table 2.6.

Table 2.6 substantiates the pronouncements of Colin Clark and others, especially their predictions as to the course of agricultural development during

Table 2.6. Percentage composition of total employment between agriculture (A), industry (In) and services (S)

	Italy		*Germany*		*France*		*UK*		*US*		*Japan*		*Netherlands*		*Sweden*	
		%		%		%		%		%		%		%		%
A	1871	62.0	1882	42.0	1866	52.0	1911	12.0	1870	50.0	1877	83.0	1909	28.0	1910	46.0
	1954	41.0	1933	29.0	1950	33.0	1951	5.0	1950	12.0	1950	49.0	1947	19.0	1950	20.0
1957		35.6		16.3		24.6		4.4		9.3		34.3		12.8		16.5
1965		25.6		10.9		17.7		3.3		6.1		23.5		8.9		11.4
1973		17.4		7.5		12.2		2.9		4.1		13.4		6.8		7.1
In	1871	24.0	1882	36.0	1866	29.0	1911	43.0	1870	25.0	1877	6.0	1909	35.0	1910	26.0
	1954	31.0	1933	41.0	1950	34.0	1951	47.0	1950	35.0	1950	21.0	1947	33.0	1950	41.0
1957		35.3		48.0		37.5		49.2		35.5		26.7		42.1		42.2
1965		41.6		50.4		39.4		48.1		33.4		32.4		40.9		43.0
1973		44.0		49.5		39.3		42.6		31.7		37.2		36.2		36.8
S	1871	14.0	1882	22.0	1866	20.0	1911	45.0	1870	25.0	1877	11.0	1909	37.0	1910	28.0
	1954	28.0	1933	30.0	1950	33.0	1951	48.0	1950	53.0	1950	30.0	1947	48.0	1950	39.0
1957		29.1		35.7		37.9		46.4		55.2		39.0		45.1		41.5
1965		32.8		38.7		42.9		48.7		60.5		44.1		50.2		45.6
1973		38.6		43.0		48.5		54.5		64.2		49.4		57.0		56.1

Sources: S. Kuznets, *Six Lectures on Growth*, Free Press, Glencoe, 1959; and *Labor Force Statistics*, OECD, Paris, various issues. Industry includes mining, manufacturing, public utilities and construction.

the process of industrialization.[3] The fact that employment in industry is still increasing by 1973 as a per cent of total employment in Italy and Japan can be to a large extent attributed to their low per capital income levels relative to the other countries in the table.[4]

The factors responsible for the decline in agricultural employment are well known. Repeated studies have indicated that the income elasticity of demand for food is substantially below one for family incomes above some subsistence level.[5] As a result, the per cent of income spent on food falls as incomes grow, a point already illustrated in Table 2.4. Unless the growth of productivity in agriculture is slower than that in other sectors, this causes employment in agriculture to decline as a share of total employment.[6] However, while the average productivity in agriculture is substantially below that of industry in most OECD countries, the rate of growth of agricultural productivity tends to be the highest of sectoral growth rates of productivity. Table 2.7 shows the wide differences between sectors in rates of growth of productivity. In every country rates of growth of output per worker in agriculture were greater than the overall rate of growth of labor productivity, and, with few exceptions, the rate of growth of labor productivity in agriculture was the highest of the three

Table 2.7. Trend rates of growth of output per employed person, 1957–73

		Annual average rates of growth		
	GDP	*Agriculture*	*Industry*	*Services*
	%	%	%	%
Canada[a]	1.8	4.3	3.5	−0.1
United States	2.2	5.6	3.0	1.4
France[b]	5.0	6.4	5.7	4.6
Germany[a]	5.2	6.8	5.5	3.6
Italy[a]	5.7	7.4	5.5	4.9
United Kingdom[c]	2.6	5.0	3.6	1.5
Austria	5.3	7.2	5.7	3.7
Belgium[d]	4.1	7.1	5.6	2.2
Denmark	3.1	3.6	4.7	1.5
Netherlands[d]	4.1	6.6	6.2	2.5
Norway[e]	3.9	2.1	3.8	3.4
Sweden	3.1	4.9	5.3	1.0

[a] 1956–73 [b] 1957–68 [c] 1957–72 [d] 1959–73 [e] 1957–69

Sources: *National Accounts of OECD Countries, 1953–1969, 1962–1973*, Vol. I and II; and *Labour Force Statistics, 1950–1960, 1957–1968, 1961–1972, 1962–1973*, op. cit.

[3] C. Clark, *The Conditions of Economic Progress*, 3rd edition, MacMillan, London, 1957.

[4] Additional factors were also at work and will be discussed in Chapter VI.

[5] See, for example, *Agriculture and Economic Growth*, OECD, Paris, 1965, Table 1.

[6] There is the possibility that the growth of demand for non-food agricultural products and exports of agricultural output could expand to offset the factors discussed in the text. This has not happened, however.

sectors. Tables 2.4 and 2.7 largely explain the exodus of labor from agriculture implicit in Table 2.6.[7] Trends in employment in the industrial and service sectors are not as clear-cut and will be discussed further in Chapters V and VIII. As with agriculture, employment trends will be seen to a large extent as the net result of an interaction between income (and price) elasticities of demand for the output of these sectors and the growth of labor productivity.

E. Unemployment

In Chapter I it was suggested that clues to the speed of the growth and transformation process could be found in the degree of demand pressures felt in the various economies along with the flexibility afforded by growth in factor supplies. Table 2.8 brings out the differences in demand pressures over time and across countries to the extent that these can be measured by unemployment rates. The depressed conditions of demand during the interwar period, to Svennilson one of the basic causes of the slow rate of growth and transformation during the interwar period, were reflected quite sharply by the relatively high rates of unemployment during this period. Unemployment rates beginning in 1974 (not shown) rose and have remained high following the most extensive and pronounced decline in economic activity in the postwar period. This is discussed further in Chapter XI.

Not only was the level of demand during the postwar period maintained at a higher level on the average relative to maximum output, but variations around this level were much smaller in the recent period compared to earlier periods.

Table 2.8. Average unemployment rates in selective OECD countries

	1920–29	*1930–38*	*1950–60*	*1961–73*
	%	%	%	%
United States	4.8	18.2	4.5	4.9
Canada	3.5[a]	13.3	4.4	5.2
France	—	—	1.3	2.2
Germany	3.9	8.8	4.1	0.6
United Kingdom	6.3	9.8	2.5	3.6[c]
Italy	—	4.8[b]	7.9	3.6
Japan	—	—	—	1.3
Sweden	3.2	5.6	1.7	1.9

[a] 1921–29 [b] 1930–34, 1937, 1938 [c] Figures are for Great Britain.

Source: A. Maddison, op. cit., Table E-1; *Monthly Labor Review*, US Department of Labor, June 1972, Table 1, and June 1975, Table 2. Figures have been adjusted for comparability across countries.

[7] In most of these economies, earnings in agriculture were substantially below those in industry and in many of the subsectors of the service sector. See *The Growth of Output, 1960–1980*, OECD, Paris, 1970, Table 8.

Recessions when they did develop were mild and short-lived, while booms were constrained by employment and capacity ceilings soon after they developed.[8] Equally important, the duration of booms in the postwar period were long compared with both the duration of recessions within the same country and the booms of earlier periods.

F. Flexibility in the Postwar Period

An important part of the growth and transformation process outlined in Chapter I, a link that had much to do with the rapidity of this process, was the flexibility accorded by the growth of factor supplies. Other things being equal, a higher rate of growth of the labor force and a higher rate of growth of the capital stock would accelerate the rate of growth and transformation. Table 2.9 indicates the rates of growth of important demographic forces during the postwar period for several countries. Of special interest is the discrepancy between the natural rate of increase of the population and the rate of growth of the population (and labor force) in Switzerland, France, Germany, Canada and the United States. These differences record the large-scale migration of workers across national boundaries, to a large extent from Mediterranean to north-west Europe and to North America during this period, a movement that

Table 2.9. Trend rates of growth of population labor force and employment, 1955–68 (average annual rates)

	Natural increase[a]	*Total population*[b]	*Population age 15–64*	*Labor force*	*Employment*
Canada	1.7	2.1	2.1	2.4	2.5
United States	1.3	1.5	1.4	1.4	1.5
Japan	1.0	1.0	2.0	1.4	1.5
France	0.7	1.1	1.0	0.4	0.3
Germany[c]	0.6	1.1	0.5	0.4	0.6
Italy[d]	0.9	0.9	0.8	−0.9	−0.8
United Kingdom	0.6	0.6	0.5	0.5	0.5
Belgium	0.5	0.6	0.2	0.3	0.4
Netherlands	1.3	1.3	1.5	1.1[e]	1.0[e]
Norway	0.8	0.8	0.7	0.4	0.4
Sweden[f]	0.6	0.8	0.5	0.5	0.4
Switzerland	0.9	1.8	1.6	1.4	1.4

[a]Resulting from the excess of births over deaths
[b]Including migration
[c]1956–68 [d]1959–68 [e]Man-years [f]1961–68
Source: *The Growth of Output 1960–1980*, OECD, Paris, 1970, Table 4.

[8]See A. Maddison, *Economic Growth in the West*, Twentieth Century Fund, New York, 1964, Chapter II, and E. Lundberg, *Instability and Economic Growth*, Yale University Press, New Haven, 1968, Chapter 2.

has been compared in its impact to the migration waves of the nineteenth and early twentieth centuries to North America. Chapter V discusses some of the implications of the flexibility accorded to an economy willing to import foreign labor.

Another demographic movement that took place during this period was equally if not more important. Table 2.6 indicated a decline in the relative share of agricultural employment in total employment. This resulted from an absolute decline in the size of the agricultural labor force in the different countries, in turn permitted by the rapid growth of labor productivity in agriculture and the low income elasticity of demand for agricultural output. Table 2.10 attempts to summarize the impact of the various demographic movements into one important measure of flexibility for the seven largest market economies by combining the influence of growth of the total labor force (from whatever cause) with the labor released from agriculture. The change in total employment during some period minus the change in agricultural employment (always negative), $\Delta E - \Delta E_a$, is used to give a measure of the increase in labor force available for industrial and other non-agricultural forms of employment. The data for each country begins with the first year

Table 2.10. Changes in employment by sector (in thousands)

		ΔE	ΔE_a	$\Delta E - \Delta E_a$	ΔE_{in}	ΔE_s	ΔE_m
Canada	(1951–66)	2055	−438	2493	613	1880	394
	(1966–73)	1606	−75	1681	297	1384	224
France	(1957–64)	549	−1036	1585	589	996	507[a]
	(1964–73)	1532	−1043	2575	585	1990	435
Germany	(1956–65)	1666	−1306	2972	1624	1348	1611[a]
	(1965–73)	−216	−922	706	−331	1037	32
Italy	(1956–63)	−451	−2162	1711	1181	530	776[a]
	(1963–73)	−1169	−2099	930	58	872	210
Japan	(1957–64)	3740	−3180	6920	3500	3420	3169[a]
	(1964–73)	5780	−4460	10,240	4550	5690	3070
UK	(1957–65)	1491	−199	1690	438	1252	−231
	(1965–73)	−686	−124	−562	−1686	1124	−1283
USA	(1957–66)	8824	−1968	10,792	2270	8522	2040[b]
	(1966–73)	11,514	−527	12,041	1744	10,297	840[b]

ΔE, ΔE_a, ΔE_{in}, ΔE_s and ΔE_m represent the change in total, agricultural, industrial, service and manufacturing employment, respectively

[a]Extrapolated using Cripps and Tarling's growth rates for wage and salary workers in manufacturing

[b]Wage and salary workers

Sources: *Labour Force Statistics. 1962–1973, 1961–1972, 1957–1968, 1950–1960*, op. cit.; *Handbook of Labor Statistics – 1975*, Bureau of Labor Statistics, Washington; and T. Cripps and R. Tarling, op. cit.

for which reliable, comparable data are available for all sectors. For each country, a peak year in economic activity is used to divide the postwar period into two parts.

It is clear from the table that, while some countries like Italy may have suffered a decrease in total employment, the decline in agricultural employment of over 4 million 'released' enough workers to enable non-agricultural employment to expand by over 2.5 million from 1956 to 1973.[9] For other countries such as the United Kindom no large exodus from agriculture took place primarily because of the very low numbers in agriculture at the beginning of the postwar period. However, the United Kingdom experienced a substantial increase of the employed labor force of approximately 1.5 million through natural increase and immigration during the first period. Finally, there were those countries like France and, especially, Japan that achieved flexibility through both relatively large increases in total employment and large decreases in agricultural employment.

Table 2.10 indicates that fairly substantial differences took place in the manner in which this 'surplus' labor was allocated. For example, over the whole period roughly one million workers were available in the United Kingdom for allocation in non-agricultural industries. All of these and over 1.2 million more were allocated to the service sector. Japan, on the other hand, with over 17 million such workers to allocate, allocated about one-half to the industrial sector.[10] Chapter VIII discusses some of the reasons for these differences.

Finally, Table 2.11 offers an alternative measure of flexibility, this time in terms of the growth of the capital stock. Taking the long view, investment ratios have a noticeable upward trend in every country except Canada and the United States. In keeping with the emphasis on the changing nature of output as an economy grows and transforms itself, high rates of investment become a measure of high rates of capital formation in new lines of production and thereby speed up the rate of transformation. In Chapter VI an argument is advanced that the investment ratio in manufacturing is an important determinant of the rate of growth of manufacturing output and ultimately total output.

[9] Strictly speaking, it is not correct to say that, for example, 2079 thousand workers left agriculture in France for non-agriculture employment; only that the size of the agricultural labor force declined by that much during the period. However, since birth rates tend to be substantially higher relative to death rates in agricultural areas and to birth and death rates in urban areas, substantial net migration from agriculture actually took place in France and other countries depicted in Table 2.10.

[10] Statements in the text are not meant to suggest that, say, Britain literally moved 1.2 million workers from industry to services; rather, this result came about largely through a failure of industry to replace workers as rapidly as they retired (or quit) while school-leavers and others moved into the service sector.

Table 2.11. Total gross domestic investment as a proportion of GNP

	Average of years cited			
	1900–13	*1914–49*	*1950–60*	*1961–72*[e]
Belgium			16.5	21.0
France			19.1	24.6
Germany		14.3[a]	24.0	26.0
Italy	15.4	13.5	20.8	20.4
Japan			24.0[d]	35.1
Netherlands			24.2	25.6
Norway	12.7	15.4[b]	26.4	26.9
Sweden	12.3	15.5	21.3	23.0
United Kingdom	7.7	7.6	15.4	18.3
Canada	25.5	16.0[c]	24.8	22.2
United States	20.6	14.7	19.1	16.8

[a]1925–37 [b]1914–38 [c]1926–49 [d]1953–60 in constant prices [e]Figures in constant prices
Source: Maddison, op. cit., Table III-I; and *National Accounts of OECD*, OECD, Paris, various issues.

G. Conclusions

One of the essential tasks of the next five chapters will be to develop a framework for analyzing economies undergoing the kind of transformation just described. Clearly this involves a framework that focuses on the unbalanced nature of growth, qualitative change and perpetual disequilibria together with a stress on the importance of demand pressures and flexibility. Chapter III contains a criticism of the mode of dynamic analysis that has been the most popular during the postwar period. As will be clear, its stress on the balanced nature of growth and instantaneous adjustments at the margin allowing markets to always clear, its inadequate treatment of change and its neglect of the demand side of the market and the market imperfections that are so much a part of the real world; all these special assumptions and others make such a framework unsuitable for handling the tasks of this study. Beginning in Chapter IV an attempt is made to develop an approach that can more readily incorporate some of the important 'stylized facts' of recent history outlined above.

Chapter III Alternative Views of the Workings of Modern Capitalism

A. Introduction

In the first two chapters, great emphasis was placed on the unbalanced nature of growth. Whether the economy was viewed in terms of inputs or outputs, differences in sectoral growth rates over time were one of the more notable features of capitalist development in the postwar period. In addition, the importance of differences in demand pressures and differences in flexibility stemming from differences in the rates of growth of capital formation and the supply of labor available to industry were singled out as possible causes of differences in growth rates and the speed of transformation.

In this chapter these notions are developed further in a manner such as to suggest how a more intensive and detailed analysis might proceed in an attempt to understand why growth rates differed in the postwar period.[1] In order to understand better the theoretical approach adopted in this study, the discussion in this chapter will contrast two alternative theoretical approaches to the study of growth: the one adapted in this study, and the more popular neoclassical analysis that has developed during the postwar period. For want of a better expression, the former will be termed 'disequilibrium analysis.' In Section B some general comments on neoclassical analysis are made. Sections C, D and E discuss macro-neoclassical models, while in Section F attention is focused on some of the micro-underpinnings of these macro-models. Sections G, H and I give the outlines of the method of analysis employed in the remaining chapters.

[1] The analysis throughout most of the study will be phrased in terms of the causes of differences in growth rates across countries in the postwar period. What is said in explanation of this phenomenon carries over almost completely to Svennilson's question; namely, why were growth rates and the speed of transformation so slow during the interwar period compared with, say, the postwar period in so many countries? However, there is one important additional cause involved in answer to Svennilson's question. Demand pressures were strong in the postwar period in every country compared to the interwar period. This is discussed further in Chapter XI.

B. The Neoclassical Analsysis of Growth

The basic neoclassical method of explaining why growth rates differ assumes that for the economy as a whole there are constant returns to scale.[2] Each of the inputs in the production process is homogeneous within itself allowing only for a competitive relationship between different units of an input group.[3] Competitive pricing prevails throughout the economy; i.e., monopoly elements are non-existent with no individual having any control over market prices. There are no problems of 'information' since the relevant information for organizing economic activities is automatically and costlessly generated as part of the workings of the economy; i.e., there is perfect knowledge of all past, present and future events. In particular, prices are known (and are all that needs to be known) and all economic actors act and react instantaneously to market prices. As a result, all trading is at equilibrium prices as prices instantaneously adjust to any momentary disequilibria, i.e. situations of excess demand or supply. What improvements there are in the growth of labor productivity result either from an increase in the capital–labor ratio or from the growth of knowledge. The latter is usually treated as some exogenous process revealing itself in the form of disembodied technical progress (i.e. manna from heaven) or is embodied in the factors of production themselves in a very simple way. From all this, but especially from the assumptions about information and knowledge, the role of the entrepreneur is simply that of a coordinator adjusting outputs, inputs and prices in response to momentary situations of disequilibria.

From these assumptions it is but a short step to deriving a Pareto-type optimal situation. In particular, resources or inputs are allocated in such a way that each homogeneous unit of an input is paid the same factor return equal to its marginal product. In other words, resources are allocated so efficiently between alternative uses that it is not possible to increase real income at any point in time by reallocating capital or labor. Differences in growth rates of aggregate output can then be attributed to differences in the rate of growth of factor inputs, technical progress or both.

There are additional assumptions employed in varying degrees that have become identified with neoclassical analysis. The government and foreign trade sectors are usually ignored. Different units of some inputs are sometimes distinguished in terms of their date of production, and when multi-sector analysis is employed the assumptions usually require that growth be balanced

[2] See T. Cripps and R. Tarling, *Growth in Advanced Capitalist Economies 1950–1970*, Cambridge University Press, 1973, Chapter 1. Applied studies often drop the constant returns assumption. See reference in fn. 12 below.

[3] In particular, each unit of a (homogeneous) factor class bears only a competitive relationship to other units of the same group. This remains true even if units of the same factor group are distinguished on the basis of their 'vintage,' i.e. when they were produced. In contrast it is possible to think of units of a certain factor group being similar but not identical and actually complementing other units in the same factor class. This allows the marginal product of existing units of a factor to rise when changes in the stock of the factor are positive.

in the sense that all sectors grow at the same rate in the long run. The assumption about malleability of factors, i.e. the ability to alter the nature of the production process so that capital and labor can be combined in whatever factor proportions desired, varies from model to model. The usual assumptions vary depending upon whether there is *ex ante* and *ex post* substitution in production, the choices being (1) both *ex ante* and *ex post* subscription; (2) *ex ante* but not *ex post* substitution; or (3) neither *ex ante* nor *ex post* substitution possibilities.[4]

But the heart of neoclassical analysis lies in the basic assumptions about returns to scale and the absence of market imperfections. The frictions, rigidities, uncertainties and mistakes of the real world are assumed away in order to obtain well defined determinant solutions to a rather narrow set of questions, e.g. the existence and stability of some long-run equilibrium.[5]

C. The Basic Neoclassical Model

In neoclassical analysis stress is placed on the lack of frictions, uncertainty or market imperfections. Rather, the world is viewed as one of pure competition, perfect foresight and instantaneous adjustments at the margin. The absence of situations of disequilibria (except for momentary ones) leads to a situation of full employment with both labor and capital markets instantaneously adjusting to changes in underlying data. Moreover, these adjustments are such that efficiency is always maximized as the allocation of factors leads to all units of a factor receiving the same factor return equal to their marginal product. Given the assumption of constant returns to scale, the distribution of income is also fully determined once the properties of the production function are known.

These and additional implications of neoclassical analysis can be shown better with help of one of the better known neoclassical models, the one-sector, one-commodity malleable capital model.[6] Write $Q = F(K, L)$ where Q, K and L represent total output, the capital stock and the labor force respectively. Assume that production is carried out under constant returns to scale, giving

$$q = Q/L = F(K/L, 1) = f(K/L) = f(k). \tag{1}$$

Assume further that the production function is continuous and twice differentiable with marginal products of capital and labor (F_K and F_L) continuous and positive and declining; i.e., $F_K > 0$, $F_L > 0$, $F_{KK} < 0$, $F_{LL} < 0$.

[4]See Hahn and Mathews, op. cit., Harcourt, op. cit. Many text books are now available also. See for example Burmeister and Dobell, op. cit.

[5]See various references in fn. 4. The next three sections may be skipped by any reader uninterested in some of the workings of the basic neoclassical model.

[6]This version of the model originated with R. Solow, 'A Contribution to the Theory of Economic Growth,' *Quarterly Journal of Economics*, February 1965, and T. Swan, 'Economic Growth and Capital Accumulation,' *Economic Record*, November 1956.

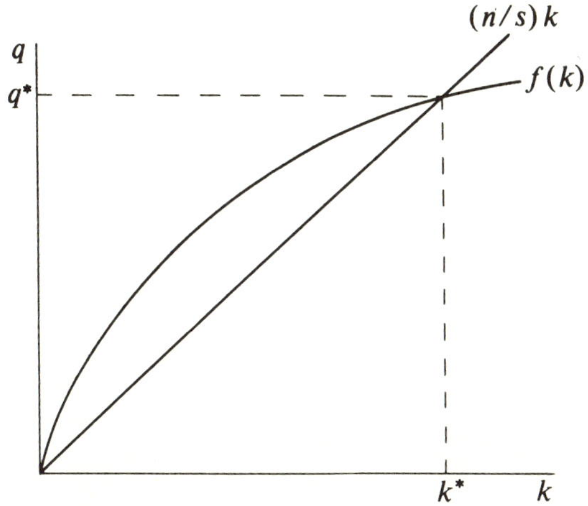

Diagram 3.1. Equilibrium in the neoclassical Model

Equation (1) is shown in Diagram 3.1 as line $f(k)$ where output per worker, q, is measured on the vertical axis and capital per worker, k, is measured on the horizontal axis. Next write

$$L = L_0 e^{nt} \qquad (2)$$

and

$$dK/dt = I = S = sQ \qquad (3)$$

where n is the (exogenous) rate of growth of the labor force and s, I and S are the savings ratio, investment and savings respectively. Finally, assume that the economy is in continuous, instantaneous competitive equilibrium with capital and labor always paid their marginal products, or

$$w_r = F_L \qquad (4)$$

and

$$r = F_K \qquad (5)$$

where w_r and r represent the real wage and the rate of profit, respectively. Given these assumptions it is possible to describe the workings of the neoclassical model as well as the impact of changes in factor supplies or flexibility.

Since $k = K/L$, then $lnk = lnK - lnL$. Differentiating with respect to time gives

$$\dot{k} = \dot{K} - \dot{L}$$

where the dot over each variable represents the geometric rate of growth of that variable; e.g., $\dot{L} = (dL/dt)/L$. Substituting the right-hand side of equation

(3) into this expression and using n instead of $\dot{L}$ gives $\dot{k} = sQ/K - n$. Finally, dividing Q and K by L gives

$$\dot{k} = sq/k - n = sf(k)/k - n.$$

Next define the equilibrium growth path of the model as $\dot{K} = \dot{Q} = \dot{L} = n$ or $\dot{k} = \dot{q} = 0$ and designate the equilibrium values of any variable by an asterisk, e.g. q^*. Since the equilibrium of the model is $\dot{k} = 0$, this is easily seen to be equivalent to $sf(k^*)/k^* = n$. Rearranging terms gives $q^* = f(k^*) = (n/s)k^*$ as the equilibrium value of output per unit of the labor force. This equilibrium is depicted in Diagram 3.1. A line through the origin representing $(n/s)k$ as a function of k is shown together with a graph of $q = f(k)$. Where these two lines intersect ($k = k^*$, $q = q^*$), $f(k) = (n/s)k$; and therefore $\dot{k} = 0$. To the left of k^*, $f(k) > (n/s)k$; and therefore $\dot{k} > 0$, causing the system to move toward k^*. In a similar manner, values of $k > k^*$ lead to a convergence toward k^*.

D. The Unimportance of Flexibility – The Theoretical Case

The $(n/s)k$ line can be described as a 'factor flexibility' line in that rotations of the line due to changes in the savings (= investment) ratio, s, and the rate of growth of the labor force, n, depict the impact on the model of changes in the degree of flexibility that arise from changes in factor supplies.

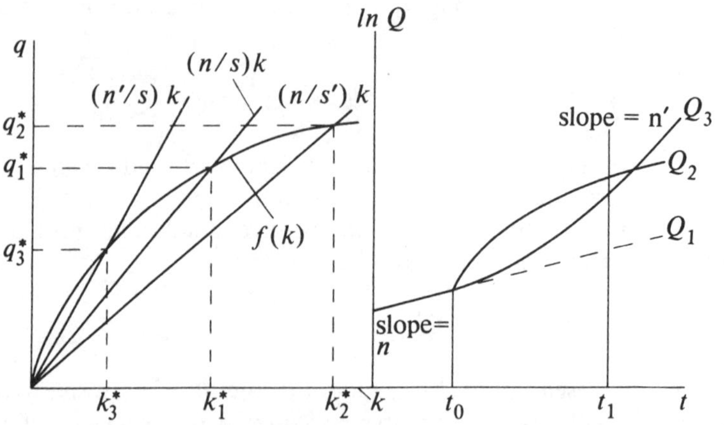

Diagram 3.2 **Diagram 3.3**

The impact of factor flexibility

Diagrams 3.2 and 3.3 illustrate the effects on growth of changes in the extent of flexibility so defined. Starting from an equilibrium $q = q^*_1$ (and $k = k^*_1$) in Diagram 3.2, allow for a once-over increase in the savings rate from s to s'. This results in a flattening of the factor flexibility line to that represented by $(n/s')k$ and a new equilibrium $q = q^*_2$ and $k = k^*_2$. However, the growth rate of the output per worker (and aggregate output) is unaffected since the long-run equilibrium ($\dot{Q}^* = \dot{K}^* = \dot{L} = n$ or $\dot{Q}^* - n = \dot{q}^* = 0$) is independent of the savings ratio.

This is illustrated in Diagram 3.3, where it is assumed that the economy was growing steadily at rate n until period t_0 at which time the savings ratio increases to s'. At that point, the economy grows more rapidly than rate n until time t_1 (as indicated by the steeper slope of the Q_2 line between t_0 and t_1). However from time t_1 onward the economy grows again at rate n but at a higher level of Q and q.

Similarly, as is well known, an increase in the rate of growth of the labor force, n, while affecting $\dot{Q}^*$, has no effect on $\dot{q}^*$. An increase in n is shown in Diagram 3.2 as a rotation of the factor flexibility line upward to that with slope $= n'/s'$ $(n' > n)$ with a new equilibrium $q = q^*_3$. The long-run equilibrium is $\dot{K}^* = \dot{Q}^* = \dot{L}^* = n'$, with $\dot{Q}^* = n' > n$ but $\dot{q}^* = \dot{Q}^* - n' = 0$ unaffected. The former result is illustrated in Diagram 3.3 by the steeper slope of line Q_3 beyond point t_1. Again it is assumed that the economy was growing steadily at rate n until t_0, at which time a once-over increase in the rate of growth of the labor force to n' takes place. At that point $\dot{Q}$ increases until a new long-run equilibrium is reached at time t_1 where $\dot{Q}^* = n'$ with $q = q^*_3 =$ constant.

The basic model can be altered in different directions. Technical progress can be introduced, say, by allowing for increases in efficiency of labor that are a simple function of time. Thus write $E = Le^{\lambda t}$, where E is labor measured in efficiency units and λ is the rate of growth of labor embodied technical progress. Since $L = L_0 e^{nt}$, $E = L_0 e^{(n+\lambda)t}$. Define the long-run equilibrium as $\dot{q}^* = \dot{E}^* = \dot{K}^* = n + \lambda$ and the results are little changed. Diagram 3.2 can still be used to depict the equilibrium as long as $[(n+\lambda)/s]k$ replaces $(n/s)k$ and q and k are redefined as $q = Q/E$ and $k = K/E$. Diagram 3.3 can also be used to depict the path of Q over time by merely adjusting the slopes of the Q lines to take account of $\lambda > 0$. As in the case where $\lambda = 0$, changes in the savings ratio and the rate of growth of the labor force, n, have no long-run effect on the rate of growth of labor productivity or per capita income which now grow at rate $\dot{q}^* = \dot{Q}^* - n = \lambda$.[7] Only changes in the exogenously given rate of growth of technical progress, λ, can affect the long-run rate of growth of labor productivity.

Other alterations have been introduced. Different savings functions have been used besides the fixed proportion savings relationship of equation (3). Different forms of the production function have also been tried, whereby, for example, the elasticity of substitution between factor inputs is allowed to take different values, technical progress is embodied in investment or affects the productivities of the inputs unequally, etc.[8] But the long-run properties

[7] Assuming that the labor force is some fixed proportion of total population.

[8] See for example C. Ferguson, 'The Simple Analytics of Neoclassical Growth Theory,' *Quarterly Review of Economics and Business*, Spring 1968.

of the model are little affected. The growth of factor supplies at the margin in the form of higher investment (= savings) ratios and more rapid rates of growth of the labor force – what was earlier referred to as additional flexibility – have no affect on the rate of growth of labor productivity and per capita incomes, $\dot{q}$. Since rising per capita incomes will be and have been seen as one of the most important factors leading to changes in the composition of output, it can also be concluded that added flexibility has no effect on the speed of transformation in neoclassical analysis.

E. The Unimportance of Flexibility – The Applied Case

In trying to answer a practical problem such as why growth rates have differed, economists have tended to distinguish between the long run and the short run. The long run has been the particular concern of the theoreticians. As just seen, in the long run the rate of growth of output per worker or labor productivity is given by $\dot{Q}^* - n = \dot{q}^* = 0$ or $\dot{q}^* = \lambda$, depending on whether technical progress is allowed. But since λ, the rate of growth of technical progress, is given exogenously, this means that differences in long-run growth rates go largely unexplained. Thus, the theoretical version of neoclassical analysis turns out to be of little use in handling an important applied problem in macrodynamics.[9]

However, most applied work has been limited to the short run in the sense that it has concerned itself with such matters as the impact of different rates of growth of the labor force and the capital stock (owing, perhaps, to a change in the savings ratio) on growth rates, say, in the postwar period compared with the interwar period.[10] Write

$$A = \frac{Q}{K^{w_1} L^{w_2}}$$

where A is a geometric index of total factor productivity and w_1 and w_2 are weights with $w_1 + w_2 = 1$. The rate of growth of total factor productivity, $\dot{A}$, is then $\dot{A} = \dot{Q} - w_1\dot{K} - w_2\dot{L}$. In trying to determine why growth rates differ, applied studies often begin with the assumption that the elasticities of output with respect to the factors, i.e. w_1 and w_2, are equal to the factor shares. In this case, the measured contributions of capital and labor to the growth of output are given by $(P/Q)\dot{K}$ and $(W/Q)\dot{L}$, respec-

[9] One economist takes exception to this. It is argued that simple neoclassical models can explain the historically high rates of growth of output in Western Europe in the postwar period in terms of a convergence from above to a lower long-run equilibrium growth path. See J. Stein, 'Economic Growth in the West,' *Economica*, February 1965.

[10] A study by Tobin makes clear the need to distinguish between the short and long run when discussing the impact of one form of possible flexibility, an increase in the savings ratio. See J. Tobin, 'Economic Growth as an Objective of Government Policy,' *American Economic Review*, May 1964.

tively, where P/Q is profits as a share of output and W/Q is wage income as a share of output. The justification for this kind of weighting procedure is based on the assumptions of constant returns to scale and competitive pricing and in this respect much of the applied work on growth resembles neoclassical analysis. Unfortunately, the contributions of these factors to the rate of growth of output so measured hardly accounts for even most of output growth. Write

$$\dot{Q} - (P/Q)\dot{K} - (W/Q)\dot{L} = \dot{A}$$

where $\dot{A}$, referred to as technical progress in theoretical studies, is the residual or unexplained part of growth. Estimates of $\dot{A}/\dot{Q}$ show the unexplained part of growth so measured to vary anywhere from one-half to two-thirds; i.e., differences in growth rates are still largely unexplained.

Various attempts have been made in applied work to overcome this deficiency, e.g. by measuring the inputs K and L in 'efficiency' units rather than natural units.[11] Unfortunately, while in principle all of growth can be 'explained' this way, such attempts do not come to grips with the basic shortcoming of this approach. Rewriting the last expression as

$$\dot{Q} = (P/Q)\dot{K} + (W/Q)\dot{L} + \dot{A},$$

it is clear that, even if $\dot{K} = \dot{0}$, the rate of growth of output, $\dot{Q}$, will not fall to zero. More important, since (P/Q) is substantially less than one, say $\frac{1}{4}$, $\dot{Q}$ or $\dot{q}$ need little be affected if $\dot{K} = 0$. This is easily demonstrated. Assume aggregate output and capital grow at approximately the same rate, i.e. $\dot{Q} \simeq \dot{K}$. Then the per cent of the growth of output attributable to the rate of growth of the capital stock is

$$(P/Q)\dot{K}/\dot{Q} \simeq (P/Q)\dot{Q}/\dot{Q} = P/Q.$$

Similarly, an increase in the investment–savings ratio, while increasing $\dot{K}$, will have little impact on $\dot{Q}$. In one of the more comprehensive attempts to apply this 'sources of growth' approach it was found that, even if net investment was zero throughout much of the postwar period, i.e. $\dot{K} = 0$, growth rates were little affected.[12]

Finally, write

$$\dot{q} = \dot{Q} - \dot{L} = (P/Q)\dot{K} - [1 - (W/Q)]\dot{L} + A.$$

[11] One study argues that all growth can be explained by correct measurements of the two inputs, capital and labor, leaving nothing to be 'explained' by technical progress. See D. Jorgenson and S. Griliches, 'The Explanation of Productivity Change,' *The Review of Economic Studies*, July 1967.

[12] For example, according to Denison's estimates, if net investment during the period 1950–62 had been zero the rate of growth of output would have fallen from 3.36 to 2.93 per cent in the United States and from 4.70 to 4.06 per cent in the countries of north-west Europe. See J. Cornwall, 'Postwar Growth in Western Europe: A Re-evaluation,' *Review of Economics and Statistics*, August 1968. The original Denison estimates are found in E. Denison, *Why Growth Rates Differ: Postwar Experience in Nine Countries*, The Brookings Institution, Washington, DC, 1967.

Since $0 < (P/Q) < 1$, higher rates of growth of the capital stock increase the rate of growth of labor productivity. But since P/Q historically has been found to be approximately $\frac{1}{4}$ ($W/Q = \frac{3}{4}$), the benefits to growth of cutting consumption in order to increase $\dot{K}$ are small indeed. The impact of higher rates of growth of the labor force on $\dot{Q} - \dot{L}$ are obviously even more discouraging since $1 - (W/Q)$ enters with a negative sign.

Summing up Sections D and E, it should be stressed that neoclassical analysis and the kind of applied work outlined above evolved during a period in history when many of the developed capitalist countries were trying not only to move resources into new lines of production but also to rebuild their economies from the ravages of war. Yet a clear implication of most if not all neoclassical theorizing was that growth in factor supplies at the margin had little impact on the rate at which this transformation was allowed to proceed. This was true for much of the applied work carried out during this period to the extent that the importance of capital formation was played down.[13] Section F discusses some of the important but largely implicit assumptions needed to justify the conclusion that growth in factor supplies have little effect on per capita incomes and productivity.

F. Neoclassical Analysis and the Reallocation of Resources

The discussion in Section D was essentially an exercise in comparative dynamics. What was studied was the impact of changes in certain key parameters on the long-run growth path together with the process by which the economy proceeds from one 'steady-state' growth path to another.[14] Additional features of neoclassical analysis can be better illustrated within the context of a different model, different at least in terms of the questions it was developed to answer. Thus, while the model just outlined stresses the process through time of output in a simple one-commodity world, there has developed another version of the neoclassical model that is best described as an intertemporal version of modern general equilibrium theory.[15] This was not discussed in the previous section since this form of the model is admittedly most unsuited for studying processes through time of capitalist economies.[16] However, the allocative features of the general equilibrium models are of interest here since this element of neoclassical analysis is identical with what was described earlier as one of its essential features – the efficient allocation of resources across firms and industries and over time.

Instead of dealing with aggregate output, investment and the capital stock,

[13] Denison's study, op. cit., allowed for economies of scale and a reallocation of labor to affect the rate of growth of output per worker. However the estimates of the contribution of capital were derived essentially as described in the text. See Denison, op. cit.

[14] See especially Harcourt, op. cit., for various references.

[15] G. Harcourt, 'The Cambridge Controversies: Old Ways and New Horizons – Or Dead End?' *Oxford Economic Papers*, March 1976.

[16] See F. Hahn, 'The Winter of Our Discontent,' *Economica*, August 1973.

the economy in this section is seen in its disaggregative neoclassical form in order to study its allocation features and the effects of a reallocation of resources. As indicated earlier, underlying the neoclassical mode of analysis is a framework that explicitly or implicitly assumes the existence of some kind of Pareto optimum. Resources are allocated in such a way across firms and industries as to equalize marginal products and factor returns at any point in time and, therefore, over time. The competitive 'micro-underpinnings' of the neoclassical approach generate this allocative result as a property of its general solution. A reallocation of factors within any short period cannot by assumption increase output in that period or any other, nor can such reallocations over time affect the growth rate.[17]

The allocative efficiency results flowing from the neoclassical model have far-reaching implications for the explanation of why growth rates differ.[18] However, these conclusions are derived from assumptions that are widely known to be unrealistic. Moreover, all too often additional assumptions that are necessary parts of the analysis are not made explicit. These assumptions deal with the mobility and malleability of factors of production and the balanced nature of the growth process and are part of the conditions that must be fulfilled if an intertemporal Pareto optimum is to be realized.

First, take the case where the stock of capital and labor is given with no possibilities of augmenting these stocks. Suppose in the interests of realism it is assumed that growth is unbalanced because of intersectoral differences in income and price elasticities. Then, by allowing the composition of output to change over time, it is necessary that this existing stock of capital and labor be reallocated continuously in order to satisfy these changing demands.[19] Now in order for this to take place, very strong assumptions must be made about the mobility and malleability of resources. Since economic activities take place over space as well as over time, a changing composition of output requires a reallocation of resources as well as industries over space. Capital and labor must be willing to respond very quickly to the 'signals' generated by the system to induce the reallocation in response to the changing composition of output and ultimately demand.[20]

But with a changing composition of output, the fixed stock of capital and labor must also be highly malleable in the sense that, even if all production took place on the head of a pin, it must be technically feasible to transfer units of capital and labor to the production of different goods. This applies whether or not capital goods initially employed in the ith industry have fixed *ex post*

[17] The instantaneous short-run equilibrium in a two-sector neoclassical growth model where marginal products are equalized across the two sectors or industries is shown graphically in Hahn and Mathews's survey article. See Hahn and Mathews, op. cit., p. 813.

[18] See, for example, W. Henrichsmeyer, 'Economic Growth and Agriculture: A Two-Sector Analysis,' *German Economic Review*, No. 4 1972.

[19] Unless by some accident growth rates of sectoral productivities differ in such a way as to just offset differences in income (and price) elasticities and lead to balanced growth in sectoral inputs.

[20] This must occur rapidly enough so that further changes in the composition of demand do not lead to an ever-greater divergence of relative demands and the capacities to satisfy them.

manning requirements in that industry. From the point of view of the *j*th industry, capital goods must be 'jelly' in order that they can always be reallocated to the *j*th industry up to a point where marginal products are equalized, should demand conditions warrant it. Malleability in this inter-industry sense must be retained if the Pareto optimum is to be realized. This applies to units of both capital and labor. It must be possible to quickly (and costlessly) retrain units of labor who are also willing to move to produce different goods so that marginal products are equalized.

However, the analysis to this point has assumed a fixed stock of capital and labor and it is here that we see the importance of augmenting the capital stock and the labor force as a source of flexibility. Thus, if the composition of output and the derived allocation of inter-industry capital and labor are not changing too rapidly, positive savings and growth of the labor force may allow sufficient flexibility so that it is not necessary to assume the existence of the kind of malleability and mobility of the existing stock of capital and labor just discussed.

Further, the more rapid is the increase in the labor force and capital stock at the margin, the more rapid will be the increments to the stock of both factors that need not be remolded and retrained for new lines of production but whose design and training can be structured so as to incorporate the technologies and skills for which they are intended. Thus the rate of increase of capital and labor should be an important determinant of the speed of transformation and growth, provided inter-industry malleability and mobility of factors are not perfect. The greater these imperfections and frictions, the more important becomes the flexibility given by growth of factor supplies. Or to put the matter somewhat differently, the more rapid are the rates of growth of factors of production, e.g., the higher are s and n, the more rapidly can the reallocation of resources proceed for the same given degree of immobility and non-malleability of factors.[21]

What has just been argued is that the conclusion of neoclassical analysis that additions to the stock of factor inputs are not important in determining why growth rates of output per worker differ is based on very strong assumptions. Either the analysis must allow for *ex post*, free substitution of factors between industries and therefore production processes, or it must fall back on a balanced-growth assumption whereby all expanding, equally productive sectors continually require new capital and labor.[22] Either assumption is very questionable. But other assumptions of neoclassical analysis are equally unrealistic, and these strengthen the argument that (1) the rate at which factor supplies are augmented may be an important influence on

[21] Johansen was one of the first to stress in detail the importance of investment for flexibility. See L. Johansen, 'Substitution vs. Fixed Production Coefficients in the Theory of Economic Growth,' *Econometrica*, May 1959.

[22] In this latter case, the assumption of malleability is not needed. See Burmeister and Dobell, op. cit., pp. 148–9.

growth rates, and (2) there may be no tendency towards equalization of factor returns and productivities. As will be stressed beginning in the next chapter, a modern capitalist system does not function in such a way that the allocation of factors and the distribution of output is accomplished on the basis of perfect and complete information that is generated automatically by the workings of the system. In particular, changes in relative prices (factor and product) are not the main instruments that (automatically) reorganize production and demand in a capitalist system. To a large extent this arises because the institutional structures of these economies are not designed to allow the economic participants to induce and respond to changes in price 'signals' in order to organize production and demand. For example, certain institutional features discussed in Chapter IV give rise to monopoly power and monopoly earnings that lead to a lack of mobility and malleability of factors.

G. Disequilibrium Analysis – an Alternative Framework

It has long been agreed that the assumptions underlying neoclassical analysis, such as the absence of monopoly elements, uncertainty, rigidities and various other market imperfections, are questionable. In spite of this, the neoclassical analysis of growth has had wide appeal among economists in the postwar period. In part, its appeal stemmed from a desire for theoretical rigor and to escape any charge of what has come to be called '*ad hoc* theorizing.' This was accomplished by specifying very simple profit and utility functions for the economic actors that allowed determinant, specific consequences to be deduced about the results of the behavior of these same actors. But whatever the cause, it has been suggested above (and will be argued below) that this framework of analysis has not been a useful one for studying an important macrodynamic problem. This in turn suggests that a new strategy for pursuing this problem should be developed. For example, each of the various assumptions of neoclassical analysis, such as the assumptions about mobility and malleability, could be relaxed one at a time to see if the various amended models could give us a workable framework for explaining why growth rates differ. This, of course, means that the investigator can no longer necessarily claim that the behavior of, say, workers or entrepreneurs flows from a simple, well defined utility or profit function that has been maximized, but some semblance of simplicity and theoretical rigor can still be maintained. However, try as one might to explain what has transpired under market capitalism in the postwar period within some amended neoclassical framework, the position adopted here and argued throughout future chapters is that such an effort will not be successful. What is required is a more radical form of surgery. The end result is an approach referred to earlier as disequilibrium analysis.

H. A Checklist of Required Changes

A convenient summary of what this radical restructuring of methods of analysis entails is facilitated by simply listing and contrasting the assumptions to be employed here with those of neoclassical analysis. Later chapters will elaborate on these points in some detail.

(1) Instead of assuming constant returns to scale, the analysis will allow for the possibility of increasing returns at the firm, industry and economy levels. In an applied study utilizing the approach discussed briefly in Section E, it has been found that $\dot{A}$, the 'unexplained' part of growth, is positively correlated with $\dot{Q}$, the growth rate itself.[23] Since the size of $\dot{A}$ is often determined by a process that assumes constant returns to scale, i.e., $w_1 + w_2 = 1$, one possible source of unexplained growth overlooked in neoclassical and other models could be the existence of increasing returns to scale.

(2) Instead of adopting the competitive model, this study will allow for monopoly elements in both factor and goods markets such that groups and individuals will be allowed to have control over market prices. As indicated in Chapter II, the postwar period was one of rapid and pronounced shifts in the distribution of labor both within countries and between countries. Much of our attention will be directed towards explaining this changing structure of employment. Unfortunately, neoclassical analysis with its assumption that firms are always 'price-takers' and never 'price-makers' in both goods and factors markets is especially ill-suited for analyzing and explaining these events. For example, the ability of workers to earn monopoly rents in certain jobs together with an ability and willingness of firms to pay such wage premiums will have much to do with the direction and extent of inter-industry labor mobility. Furthermore, and related to this, the analysis need not be constrained by the need to assume that factors are always paid their marginal products.

(3) Rather than assume perfect foresight or certainty on the part of the economic actors, uncertainty of a type that cannot be reduced to certainty equivalents will be introduced. In particular, instead of assuming that prices are known and reflect all information that one needs to know (for instituting trading, say), a lack of information about prices and even misinformation is permitted. It is especially desirable to allow for the likelihood that much more information than prices needs to and is desired to be known. For example, it will be argued that changes in relative wages do not lead to changes in the industrial or occupational allocation of labor in any determinant, simple way because information about relative wages is not well known; and even if known with absolute certainty, changes in relative wages are neither the primary signal used by firms to induce mobility nor the type of information most sought after by workers contemplating a change in jobs. An implication

[23]See G. Vaciago, 'Alternative Theories of Growth and the Italian Case,' *Banca Nazionale del Lavoro Quarterly Review*, June 1970. As already pointed out in fn. 13, one comprehensive study of postwar developments does allow for economies of scale.

of this is that prices do not necessarily adjust instantaneously to clear markets and, thus, most 'trading' is done at disequilibrium prices allowing excess demand and supplies in most markets.

(4) Neoclassical analysis leads to a situation where resources are allocated efficiently between alternative uses. Once monopoly elements are introduced along with uncertainty and the consequent rigidities and market imperfections, it is only a matter of accident if some sort of Pareto optimum results. A possible interpretation of the facts, facts consistent with a world of market imperfections, is that the process of growth and transformation in most, if not all, of the countries studied is to a large extent the result of increased efficiency in use of resources. In a world where factor productivities and returns are not equalized across industries, a shift in resources to high productivity and rapidly growing industries can have a major impact on the rate of growth of total output, particularly when economies of scale and 'linkages' are allowed. This sort of reallocation was a reoccuring feature of most economies studied and will be discussed beginning in Chapter IV. Furthermore, it will be argued that, while this reallocation was a strong and continuous process throughout the postwar period, there is little evidence indicating that a point of maximum efficiency was eventually reached in any of the countries studied. On the contrary, even a cursory look at any of the countries under review suggests that differences in efficiency wages or rates of return on capital across firms or industries were never eliminated. Elements of 'dualism' with parts of the economy relatively backward, paying low wages and employing capital with a low rate of return, were found to be a reoccuring feature in the OECD countries whatever the level of modernism of the advanced sectors.

(5) Neoclassical analysis assumes that technical progress, which accounts for a large part of the growth of labor productivity, either falls like manna from heaven or is embodied in capital or labor in a rather rigid way. This study argues that differences in the rate of technical progress, while often embodied in the factors of production, are very much the outgrowth of endogenous events. But besides the extent to which new capital goods and labor embody the latest technology, the amount of learning by doing and research and development expenditures, the kind of industrial relations system adopted by a firm, industry or economy and the ability and desire to borrow foreign technology will also play an important role in determining the rate of growth of labor productivity in a country.

(6) When discussing possibilities of substitution in production, the tendency of most studies has been to take a polar position. Either there are, say, no *ex post* substitution possibilities in production, or there are unlimited possibilities. In contrast, in this study a much less tidy environment is assumed in which some capital goods, *ex post* as well as *ex ante*, can be combined with varying amounts of labor while others cannot. For example, by redesigning the production layout, existing business plant can be combined with varying amounts of labor. Existing equipment may not be so malleable. A similar

approach can be taken with labor. Because of differences in training, union agreements, work rules and the existence of 'internal' labor markets, it is possible that some kinds of labor can only be used in a limited number of production processes and, therefore, only with certain amounts and kinds of capital. With other laborers, especially new entrants to the labor force (as with investment projects *ex ante*), greater substitution possibilities may be possible. In general, the less malleable is a factor, the greater is the rate of economic obsolescence since the less can existing units of some factor be used in new lines of production or in new processes within existing lines of production.

The importance of spatial mobility of factors is relevant here. As just suggested, existing capital in the form of physical plant may have considerable malleability compared with existing equipment in that, by merely changing the physical layout of the production process within a plant, it may be possible to work a given plant with varying degrees of labor. However, if labor is immobile then the feasible set of production processes will be limited by more than would be allowed through technical substitution possibilities. Naturally, there is a certain amount of symmetry here. If labor is malleable, in the sense that it can be retrained in order to work with different production processes that have different capital intensities, but capital is immobile, then production possibilities are similarly restricted. In general, equipment is likely to be more mobile than plant. As suggested in the discussion of flexibility and equalization of factor productivities above, the lack of factor malleability and mobility have important consequences not covered at all well by neoclassical analysis. *A priori*, no particular factor can be considered either fixed or variable. Most units of all factors are to some extent quasi-fixed.

(7) Instead of assuming that units of any factor of production are homogeneous and therefore competitive with one another, this study emphasizes the need to consider another type of relationship between units of the same 'factor;' that of complementarity arising out of the heterogeneity of the units considered under such broad headings as 'labor' or 'capital.' What is involved here is the notion of interdependence or interrelatedness of units of the labor force or the capital stock, forcing us to speak of the structure of a country's capital or its labor force and the linkages between elements of these structures. As will be shown, the migration of labor from one sector of an economy to another or from one country to another can be interpreted as the result of a kind of complementarity between industrial workers who have been promoted to skilled jobs and unskilled, often former agricultural, workers whose industrial employment has made promotion of the former group possible. Parallel examples are suggested when the capital stock is broken down into that which could be considered social overhead capital and that part dependent upon a previous development of this infrastructure.[24] It will

[24] See, for example, M. Gort and R. Boddy, 'Vintage Effects and the Time Path of Investment in Production Relations,' in M. Brown (ed.), *The Theory and Empirical Analysis of Production*, National Bureau of Economic Research, New York, 1967.

also be suggested that interrelatedness, especially of units of the capital stock, may be an impediment to growth for the 'early starters' in the growth process; e.g. the United States and the United Kingdom. In addition, interdependence of factor units that are complementary introduces a kind of lumpiness or indivisibility in production. This alone adds importance to growth of factor supplies at the margin.

(8) The government and foreign sectors need not be ignored and will be considered in this study. It will be argued that the behavior of these sectors can greatly influence the extent to which economies overcome various constraints and imperfections.

(9) Multi-sector models of balanced growth assume that no one sector is more important than any other in determining the overall rate of growth. In the analysis to follow, it will be argued that the manufacturing sector plays a critical role as the 'engine of growth' for the whole economy. The more rapidly the manufacturing sector grows, the more rapidly will aggregate output grow, other things being equal. This key role of manufacturing in growth has always been recognized in studies of developing, semi-industrialized economies. Manufacturing will continue to play a key role in the growth process of developed, industrialized economies in this study.

(10) Last but not least, it is necessary to incorporate into the analysis several basic ideas stressed by Svennilson and Schumpeter but neglected by neoclassical analysis. Growth is unbalanced and involves qualitative change and transformation including the continuous introduction and development of new technologies. It also requires strong and sustained demand pressures and flexibility. These important (and almost obvious) factors cannot be neglected if an investigator hopes to understand differences in economic performances.

I. A Restatement

Tying together most of the proposed changes discussed up to this point, it follows that, in explaining why growth rates differ, emphasis must be given to the degree of flexibility of an economy as measured by the rate of growth of factor supplies. As pointed out in the first part of this chapter, neoclassical analysis de-emphasized the impact of the rate of growth of the labor force and the capital stock on the rates of growth of output per worker and per capita income. In a world where growth is balanced and resources, once allocated to some sector, make an important contribution to production over their physical lifetime; where a large part of growth in labor productivity is due to an exogenously determined rate of growth of technical progress; where there is no problem of specificity of factors of production owing to spatial immobility or non-malleability; in short, in a world of no market imperfections and inflexibilities, the rate of growth of output per worker might well be little dependent upon the growth of factor supplies. But in a world of market imperfections, rigidities and uncertainties, with existing factor supplies specific in varying degrees to production plans of the past at a time when the economy is transforming itself further, flexibility becomes an important condition enabling rapid growth and transformation. Higher rate of growth of capital and labor are a means of overcoming the market imperfections and rigidities of the real world because they facilitate the reallocations of resources into new lines of production and allow firms to take advantage of new technologies and the possibilities of increasing returns to scale. This relationship between growth of factor supplies, especially those available to the industrial and manufacturing sectors and the growth of output per worker or per capita, will not be seen as a simple, positive relationship such that more of the former always leads to so much more of the latter. But there will be seen to be periods when the rapid expansion of output of certain key sectors is quite dependent upon the rapid infusion of large amounts of capital and labor.

Finally, while the flexibility accorded by a growing stock of capital and labor is necessary for a rapid growth of productivity and a rapid transformation of the economy, flexibility is only a permissive factor.[25] The greater the degree of flexibility in this sense, the more rapidly can resources be redirected into new lines of production and the more easily can bottlenecks be overcome. But behind it all there must be an entrepreneurial class that is growth-oriented. Neoclassical analysis treats the entrepreneur as a mere coordinator, adjusting prices and outputs to the signals thrown up by the 'invisible hand.' This view is consistent with a world of certainty and pure competition, where change is almost totally unrelated to the actions of the economic actors in the economy. But the quality of entrepreneurship cannot be overlooked in a world of friction, uncertainty, innovation and transformation. The frictions and rigidities of real life becomes the obstacles to growth and transformation that must be overcome if there is to be growth and transformation. The extent and rapidity with which these obstacles are overcome is very much a function of the commitment to growth made by the leaders of industrial enterprises.

This checklist of changes that must be incorporated into any framework that attempts to explain growth and transformation would be considered reasonable by most economists. To some extent, what has just been said seems to be belaboring the obvious. However, as suggested above, the method of analysis adopted here has been frequently subject to the charge of '*ad hoc* theorizing,' i.e. constructing behavioral relationships between variables that cannot be said to flow from some basic profit or utility function at the micro-level. In contrast, neoclassical analysis does come with its microeconomic underpinnings. However, the domain of 'rational' behavior as developed in neoclassical analysis has never been extended to include the kinds of frictions and problems just outlined. To say this is but another way of describing the

[25] The notion that this kind of flexibility was only a necessary condition for rapid growth is found in C. Kindleberger, *Europe's Postwar Growth: The Role of Labor Supply*, Harvard University Press, Cambridge, 1967.

main criticism brought against the neoclassical form of analysis. And the fact that the present study will not explicitly derive the micro-underpinnings of the model does not in any way imply that such an extension is not possible. If the arguments to follow are at all convincing, then the analysis should be suggestive of means to extend micro-theory in ways that takes accounts of the constraints on the form of rational behavior introduced by the numerous types of frictions and imperfections accounted for here.

Chapter IV marks the first stages in the development of a model that incorporates the many required changes just described. It attempts to outline the manner in which labor resources are allocated in developed capitalist economies and thereby gives an indication of the constraints within which entrepreneurs and labor operated in the growth and transformation process during the postwar period.

Chapter IV **The Dual Structure of Modern Capitalism**

A. Introduction

In Chapter III it was suggested that, rather than study the effects of altering the different assumptions of neoclassical analysis one at a time, an understanding of why rates of growth differ requires a more radical alteration of the method of analysis. The main task of this chapter will be to lay the groundwork for a very different kind of theoretical framework.

In a search for an alternative method of analysis it seems reasonable to look first for an established theoretical framework which, because of its emphasis, thrust and orientation, can serve as a useful point of departure. To anticipate the conclusions of this chapter, what has come to be known as the ('classical') model of the dual economy has been found to be a highly appropriate starting point.

The usefulness of extending the dual model to developed economies is suggested by a number of its characteristics: (1) the stress on the lack of equalization of factor returns and productivities as a source of growth; (2) the downgrading of changes in relative factor prices as an allocative mechanism; (3) stress on the unbalanced nature of growth; (4) the critical role assigned to the industrial and manufacturing sectors; (5) the importance of flexibility; and (6) the importance, implicitly at least, of entrepreneurship.

Chapter IV has two aims: to formulate a general model of the dual economy, and to determine to what extent developed market economies conformed to the workings of this dual model in the postwar period. Section B discusses the essential features of dual models that have been developed to explain growth in both developed and developing economies. A common set of features or criteria is then formulated leading to a more general model of the dual economy. Sections C through E attempt to show that the conditions necessary for the existence of 'surplus labor,' one of the essential features of a dual economy, were met in most if not all the developed market economies during the postwar period. This involves a brief discussion of inter-industry mobility and wage structures in Sections C and D and a rather extended study of the basic mechanism allocating labor in market economies in Section E. Section F gives details of sectoral rates of growth of output and employment of various countries in the postwar period indicating further the applicability of the model of the dual economy.

B. The Essential Features of a Dual Economy

It has been recognized for some time that important insights into the growth and development processes of developing economies can be gained by explicitly emphasizing structural differences between key sectors of such economies. To this end, models of the dual economy have been developed whereby the economy is bisected into two sectors according to such criteria as differences in technologies, productivity, demographic patterns, 'technical dynamism,' consumer behavior, etc.[1] For the most part, models of the dual economy have been developed to gain insights into the transformation of underdeveloped economies as they emerge from a state of backwardness to that of modernity.[2] However, more recently it has been argued that real insights can be gained into the nature of the growth and transformation process of countries with incomes well above the subsistence level by stressing the presence in these economies of certain dualistic elements heretofore associated only with underdeveloped economies.[3] These elements, it is said, are important factors not only in allowing underdeveloped economies to develop rapidly but equally in explaining rapid growth in modern economies. Writers analyzing more developed economies differ in their emphasis from those concerned with less developed economies. However, the similarities of the models suggest that models of growth and development stressing dualism may have wider application than originally thought and might be very useful for present purposes.

Two reasons are most often cited in support of the usefulness of bisecting developed (as well as developing) economies in order to understand the growth process. First, only in this way is it possible to highlight the presence in one sector of 'surplus labor' (variously defined). Second, this approach lends itself to illuminating the importance of the 'technical dynamism' in the other sector. For example, according to Kindleberger, as long as the industrial sector of an economy is faced with a very elastic supply of labor 'super-growth' is permitted, while those economies unable to tap some source of

[1] See A, C. Kelley, J. G. Williamson and R. J. Cheetham, *Dualistic Economic Development, Theory and History*, University of Chicago, 1972, pp. 8–9.

[2] W. A. Lewis, 'Economic Development with Unlimited Supplies of Labor,' *The Manchester School*, May 1954, and G. Ranis and J. C. H. Fei, *Development of the Labor Surplus Economy: Theory and Policy*, Irwin Press, Homewood, Illinois, 1964.

[3] See for example N. Kaldor, *Strategic Factors in Economic Development*, Cornell University, Ithaca, 1967; C. P. Kindleberger, *Europe's Postwar Growth: The Role of Labor Supply*, Harvard University, Cambridge, 1967; V. Lutz, 'Foreign Workers and Domestic Wage Levels, with an Illustration from the Swiss Case,' *Banca Nazionale del Lavoro Quarterly Review*, March 1963; R. Minami, *The Turning Point in Economic Development: Japan's Experience*, Tokyo, 1973; Vaciago, op. cit., and Henrichsmeyer, op. cit.

surplus labor are faced with an additional burden in attaining rapid growth and development.[4]

The model of the dual economy as first developed by Lewis and later by Ranis and Fei envisaged a 'capitalist' and a 'subsistence' sector characterized by markedly different techniques of production. The subsistence sector (hereafter referred to as the agricultural sector) was a capital-poor, low-wage and low-productivity sector while the capitalist sector (hereafter known as the industrial or manufacturing sector) was a high-wage, high-productivity, capital-intensive sector with production guided by the profit motive. For reasons that varied depending on the model-builder, the demand for labor in industry was not sufficient to employ all labor that would prefer non-agricultural employment.[5] But whatever the reason, at any point in time the agricultural sector served as a residual employer, employing what was not demanded by the industrial sector. Over time the agricultural work force served as a pool of labor that the industrial sector could draw upon; a pool, moreover, that was constantly being replenished by the rapid rates of growth of population in the rural sectors.[6] Given sufficient demand in the industrial sector, the model envisaged a net transfer of labor out of agriculture to industry such that the rate of growth of employment in the latter exceeded the overall rate of growth of the employed labor force and, naturally, that in agriculture. At the same time, industrial output grew rapidly relative to total and agricultural output.

Since the industrial sector was the high-wage sector, and since development was assumed to consist essentially of a movement of labor to the high-wage sectors, relative wages in such an economy acted as 'signals' for labor movements in the right direction. This would have a lot to do with the willingness of agricultural labor to undertake 'complex mobility' patterns, i.e. mobility involving a change in industry, occupation and/or residence as well as a change in employer. In addition, the rapid growth of the population in the agricultural sector meant that a large per cent of the workers attracted to industry would likely consist of new entrants to the labor force involved only in geographic mobility and with relatively few economic ties to the agricultural sector. Finally, since the industrial sector was the high-productivity sector, any transfer of labor from agriculture to industry would raise the overall average and rate of growth of productivity and, therefore, output.

Most of these features of an underdeveloped dual economy were emphasized by later writers, who stressed the importance of dualism in certain developed capitalist economies. However, one important difference between the two groups of model-builders concerned the nature of the behavior of

[4] Kindleberger, op. cit:, pp. 1–5'

[5] See for example S. Marglin, in I. Adelman and E. Throbecke (eds.), *The Theory and Design of Economic Development*, John Hopkins, Baltimore, 1966, for a view somewhat different than that cited in fn. 2, above.

[6] With Kindleberger and others this pool of labor could also be located in some other (low-wage) country.

inter-industry productivity and wage differences as labor shifted from agriculture to industry. In the models developed for analyzing the underdeveloped economies, little regard was given to the possibility that the production function in agriculture might be constantly shifting over time because of 'technical progress' which would lead to steady increases in the rate of growth of labor productivity in agriculture. Instead, these models of dualism concentrated on the case where the agricultural wage was assumed to be fixed at the subsistence level; a kind of average product of labor which exceeded the marginal product of labor in agriculture. In the extreme case, the marginal product of labor was zero or negative, allowing a transfer of labor out of agriculture without a decline in total output, i.e. the 'disguised unemployment' case. And as long as the marginal product of labor remained below the subsistence wage of labor in agriculture, a net transfer of labor out of agriculture was possible without a change in relative wages between the two sectors.

However, sooner or later in this (special) version of the dual model, the movement of labor out of the agricultural sector would lead to a rise in the marginal product of labor until it equaled the subsistence wage. At this point the appropriateness of the model supposedly ceased as marginal products and wages across industries would be equalized; i.e., there would no longer exist surplus labor, and neoclassical analysis would take over.[7]

However, much of this discussion of the origin of surplus labor and of the appropriateness of the 'classical' (as opposed to the neoclassical) model of the dual economy was considered to have missed the essential points by writers dealing with the importance of dualism in advanced economies. The neglect of steady growth in labor productivity owing to shifts in the production function and the assumption of a fixed agricultural wage in dual models was viewed by these economists as merely a metaphor, reflecting the importance of wage differentials between sectors in the dual model.[8] Furthermore, there was no presumption that rising agricultural wages necessarily led to the elimination of wage differentials through inter-industry (or inter-country) mobility of labor as required by the neoclassical framework. On the contrary, these models of the dual economy often stressed the persistence of wage differentials in the face of rising agricultural wages, as industrial wages also rose as a natural outcome of the industrialization process.[9]

What was considered essential for the persistence of a relatively rigid wage structure was: (1) the existence of a high-wage sector in which employment was determined by the demand for labor in that sector and the existence of a low-wage residual employment sector; and (2) rates of growth of agricultural productivity and the 'residual' labor force which, summed together, exceeded

[7] See D. Jorgenson, in Adelman and Throbecke, op. cit.

[8] Besides, Marglin, op. cit., and Minami, op. cit., see A. Sen, 'Peasants and Dualism with or without Surplus Labor,' *Journal of Political Economy*, October 1966.

[9] See especially Vaciago, op. cit.

the rate of growth of demand for the output of the low-wage agriculture sector.[10] Given these conditions, an increase in the demand for labor in the high-wage sector could give rise to an increase in the supply available without any change in wage differentials between the two sectors, i.e. the response expected when job vacancies develop in the industrial sector of an underdeveloped dual economy.

In his discussion of the relevance of dualism in explaining development in advanced capitalist economies, Kaldor emphasized the presence or absence of surplus labor (in agriculture) whose presence is indicated if a more rapid increase in the demand for labor in the high-productivity, high-wage sector will give rise to a more rapid increase in supply without a change in wage differentials.[11] For the purposes of this study, it can be concluded that, since an increase in the demand for labor in the industrial sector of an underdeveloped economy generates a similar response by labor, Kaldor's definition of surplus labor is analytically more useful in analyzing the nature of dualism and will be used hereafter. However, surplus laborers will be defined so as to include all laborers, agricultural and otherwise, who so respond to new job openings. In any case, disguised unemployment, a fixed wage or a wage greater than the marginal product of labor need not be considered an essential feature of the low-wage sector in a dual structure or a necessary condition for the existence of surplus labor. These are special features of an underdeveloped dual economy. It would appear that the presence of three conditions are necessary for the existence of surplus labor in Kaldor's sense:

(1) a labor force with substantial numbers willing to undertake complex mobility patterns,

(2) a rather rigid inter-industry wage structure that persists in spite of the fact that members of the labor force are willing (and able) to undertake complex mobility strategies; this has partly to do with the growth of productivity and

[10] The use of some identities and a little algebra helps bring out what is involved here. Let r_{s1}, $\dot{\rho}_1$, n_1 and r_{D1} stand for the rate of growth of maximum output or supply, labor productivity, the labor force and the demand for output respectively in sector 1. For convenience assume that there are only two sectors and that sector 1, agriculture in this case, is the low-wage sector. Furthermore, assume that sector 1 is a 'dump sector' for labor in the sense that the size of its labor force depends upon the demand for labor in the high-wage industrial sector. Then by definition $r_{s1} = \dot{\rho}_1 + n_1$, *and* $r_{s1} - r_{D1} = \dot{\rho}_1 + n_1 - r_{D1}$ or $r_{s1} - r_{D1} = \dot{\rho}_1 + 1/u_1(n - u_2 n_2), - r_{D1}$ where n and n_2 are the rates of growth of the total labor force and that employed in the industrial sector respectively, and the u's are weights measuring the relative importance of the two sectors. If we then define $r_{s1} - r_{D1}$ as the rate of growth of surplus labor, we see that surplus labor will exist and grow as long as the rate of growth of productivity in agriculture plus what is roughly the difference between the rate of growth of the labor force and the rate of growth of labor employed in the high-wage, high-productivity sector is greater than the rate of growth of demand for agricultural output. See *Agriculture and Economic Growth*, op. cit., Chapter II, for the relevance of defining surplus labor in this manner.

[11] N. Kaldor, 'Productivity and Growth: A Reply,' *Economica*, November 1968, p. 386. We have altered somewhat Kaldor's definition of surplus labor, which unfortunately is consistent with the long-run behavior of relative wages in a neoclassical world. While capturing the spirit of Kaldor's meaning, the text definition is more helpful in pointing up the differences between the neoclassical world and that envisaged by people like Kaldor.

the elasticities of demand for the output of the low wage sector, but it is also a matter of

(3) the existence of an allocative mechanism in labor markets that does not reflect some sort of equalization of net benefits for workers.

If, in addition to the presence of these three conditions, the demand for industrial output and the derived demand for labor by industry is strong enough so that the rate of growth of output and employment in industry exceeds that in the whole economy, then it will be said that such an economy conforms to the workings of a dual economy.

For most of the remainder of the chapter some important characteristics of modern-day capitalism are analyzed in order to discern if the conditions necessary for the existence of surplus labor were indeed widespread during the postwar period. The presence or absence of each of these features will be discussed one at a time. There will be a slight change in focus, however, as attention will be centered on the manufacturing rather than the industrial sector, where the latter is defined to include mining, construction and utilities as well as manufacturing. This change is in keeping with the emphasis on the manufacturing sector as the 'engine of growth,' a view that will be developed in Chapter VII.

C. Inter-Industry Mobility

The first task is to determine whether in developed market economies there existed a substantial number of workers willing to undertake complex mobility patterns. The expression 'substantial numbers' can be made more precise by recalling that, in the early discussions of the dual economy, it was always assumed that there was a general willingness of labor to move out of agriculture to industry. This willingness, in turn, could be traced to higher wages and various superior non-pecuniary benefits received in industry or manufacturing. All that was required was sufficient demand since the demand for labor created its own supply. The outlines of the dual model were then revealed if this demand was such that the rate of growth of employment in industry was greater than the overall rate of growth of employment and, naturally, the rate of growth of employment in agriculture. Similarly, then, the question comes down to whether or not in the postwar period there was enough willingness on the part of the labor forces of the various market economies to generate a greater rate of growth of employment in manufacturing or industry than in the whole economy should this demand for labor be strong enough.

As seen in Table 4.1 below, the wage incentives for a movement from agricultural to non-agricultural jobs were certainly in evidence for most of the market economies cited. Except for Belgium, the Netherlands and the United Kingdom, incomes in agriculture were approximately one-half those in the rest of the economy. To this can be added the (real or imaginary) greater appeal of urban living to workers in agriculture. Belgium, the Netherlands and the United Kingdom were also economies with a small proportion of their labor forces engaged in agriculture from the beginning of the postwar period. These considerations suggest that it might be useful to distinguish between two kinds of postwar economies: those with a large proportion of their labor forces engaged in agriculture and with sizeable differences in wages and incomes between the agriculture and non-agricultural sectors, and those few economies with only a small proportion of their labor forces in agriculture and with only moderate differences in wages and incomes between these sectors.

Now, given the assumptions of how labor markets work in the dual economy, a matter to be discussed presently, the actual performances of most economies of the first type indicated that, when the demand for manufacturing (and industrial) workers was strong, employment patterns were such as to conform to the workings of the dual economy. In other words, economies with relatively large agricultural labor forces had little difficulty in expanding employment in manufacturing relative to total employment if they so desired. The willingness of agricultural labor to be mobile in the dual model sense was always there. This was partly a matter of productivity and demand interacting to cause an absolute decline in the demand for agricultural labor, and partly a matter of a lack of 'seniority benefits' for agricultural workers. Naturally, this willingness could also be traced to differences in wages and other job benefits.

However, there were other countries that had small agricultural labor forces at the beginning of the period (less than 10 per cent for Britain and Belgium and only 13 per cent for the Netherlands) and similar income levels between agriculture and the rest of the economy. The interesting but difficult question to answer was whether the labor forces of economies of the second type contained enough mobile workers to allow employment growth in manufacturing to exceed overall employment growth should the demand be there. If the answer is in the affirmative, this would indicate a possibly wider application of dual models.

The change in employment in some sector of the economy from one period to the next can be broken down into two parts: (1) the 'net flow' between this sector and all other, i.e. the difference between total inflows of previously employed workers from other sectors and total outflows from the sector in question to other sectors; and (2) 'net entrants,' which is a catch-all representing all other flows and includes young persons just entering the labor force, immigrants, the previously unemployed, etc., and losses because of retirement, unemployment, emigration, etc. The question at issue is whether or not inter-industry net flows between non-agricultural sectors were and are widespread enough to be even considered as a substitute for a large agricultural labor force as a means to expanding labor in manufacturing.[12]

Orders of magnitude are difficult to come by. What data are available will

[12] In Chapter V, a natural increase in the population and labor force and the importation of foreign labor, i.e. increases in net entrants, are considered as substitutes.

be considered in Chapter V. In concluding the discussion for the moment, consider the following. A rather prevalent view among labor economists, especially in America, is that under modern capitalism there has developed a network of highly structured closed internal labor markets that greatly decreases the incentive to change employers (let alone occupations or industries). For example, some of these markets tend to be 'closed' in the sense that ports of entry (for new workers) tend to be limited to the lowest-paying, lowest-skilled jobs while the better jobs are filled by promotion from within on the basis of some mixture of ability and seniority.[13] The importance of internal labor markets for inter-industry mobility has been considered in a recent comprehensive survey that dealt with inter-industry mobility or net flows in the non-agricultural sectors of the OECD economies.[14] While the authors suggest that inter-industry mobility is negatively related to the prevalence of closed internal labor markets, they state that such barriers to inter-industry mobility are greatly lessened during periods of high employment such as have prevailed in Western Europe.[15] Moreover, the authors' conclusion, while somewhat impressionistic, is quite definite:

> [The studies indicate] that much of the movement taking place is across industrial and occupational lines, *even when these are drawn very broadly*, implying that the changes in job category are quite radical. [p. 158 emphasis in original]

and

> even without the increased absorption of unemployed, new entrants, etc., the scale of movements is such as to permit significant changes in the industrial structure of the labor force. [p. 72]

Their explanation of such movements is based on the existence of large numbers of young workers with limited skills which are easily transferred to other industries and occupations but who are adverse to changing their place of residence. As a result, a substantial amount of intra-market shifts will have to involve changes in occupation and/or industry if such workers hope to improve their incomes and status.

These findings are supported by a recent case study of the United Kingdom by MacKay and associates as well as an earlier exhaustive study of several OECD countries.[16] In the former study the authors conclude, after studying recruitment policies of firms in the engineering industry, that '... the walls between industries, may in some cases be a statistical artifact rather than a serious obstacle to inter-industrial movement' (p. 394).

[13] P. B. Doeringer and M. J. Piore, *Internal Labor Markets and Manpower Analysis*, D. C. Heath, Lexington, Mass., 1971, Chapters 1–4. See Chapter V, section B for a fuller discussion.

[14] L. C. Hunter and G. I. Reid, *Urban Worker Mobility*, OECD, Paris, 1968.

[15] ibid., p. 65.

[16] D. I. MacKay, D. Boddy, J. Brack, J. A. Kiack and N. Jones, *Labour Markets Under Different Employment Conditions*, George Allen and Unwin, London, 1971; and *Wages and Labour Mobility*, OECD, Paris, 1965.

Finally, citing findings of the OECD study that gross inter-industry mobility rates in different countries have been ten to forty times as great as changes in net employment, Hunter and Reid conclude that the volume of mobility has been just 'about right' to effectively reallocate labor during the postwar period.[17]

This section considered the question of whether or not inter-industry net flows of labor between non-agricultural sectors could serve as a substitute for agricultural labor. Could, for example, a higher rate of growth of demand for labor by manufacturers so speed up inter-industry flows that the rate of growth of employment in manufacturing exceeded the overall growth of employment? An affirmative answer to this question would indicate a possibly wider applicability of the dual model. Unfortunately, the studies just discussed lead only to the conclusion that the demand by the manufacturing sectors of the different market economies was never so strong during the postwar period up to the late 1960s that a pronounced and prolonged labor supply 'ceiling' was encountered. This important distinction will be discussed further in Chapter V.

D. The Inter-Industry Wage Structure

Whether the model of the dual economy was applied to underdeveloped economies or to those more advanced, an important element supposedly allowing for a rapid expansion of labour into the manufacturing (or industrial) sector was the presence of persistent wage differentials generating an inter-industry wage structure with the right signals. Similarly, a pronounced narrowing of the differentials signaled the exhaustion of surplus labor and thus an end to the possibility of rapid expansion of employment in manufacturing.[18]

Table 4.1 presents evidence of the relevance of the dual model for the twelve OECD economies. In every country employment in agriculture declined, by amounts ranging from approximately 10 per cent (Denmark) to 38 per cent (Italy).[19] However, only in Belgium and Canada was this accompanied by any appreciable increase in income in agriculture relative to average income in the rest of the economy. On the other hand, relative income in agriculture in Denmark declined appreciably. In those other economies where relative wages in agriculture rose moderately, such as France, Germany and the United States, the relative wage was still so low by the end of the period that

[17] Hunter and Reid, op. cit., p. 162.

[18] Minami defined the end of the year of surplus labor in Japan as the point in time when the agriculture–manufacturing wage differential narrowed sharply. See Minami, op. cit., p. 77.

[19] Similar results were found for Japan where employment in agriculture declined from a little over 16 million in 1954 to 9½ million in 1969 while wages in agriculture as a proportion of wages in manufacturing changed from 28 to 27 per cent. See Minami, op. cit., Tables A-2 and A-7. The letter E, with the appropriate additional lettering, is used in the text to indicate employment in contrast to labor supply, indicated by the letter L.

Table 4.1. Income in agriculture as a percentage of average income in rest of the economy per employed person (q_a), and employment in agriculture (E_a) (in thousands)

	1953–55[a]	*1959–61*	*1965–67*		*1953–55*[a]	*1959–61*	*1965–67*
Austria				Italy			
q_a	41%	42%	39%	q_a	50%	46%	49%
E_a	920	798	662	E_a	7453	6540	4656
Belgium				Netherlands			
q_a	86%	100%	110%	q_a	86%	90%	91%
E_a	337	299	218	E_a	521	465	376
Canada				Norway			
q_a	49%	47%	69%	q_a	45%	43%	40%
E_a	971	796	668	E_a	330	300	242
Denmark				Sweden			
q_a	70%	62%	57%	q_a	52%	49%	54%
E_a	338	365	315	E_a	553	524	387
France				UK			
q_a	n.a.	39%	47%	q_a	104%	95%	106%
E_a	4639	4191	3341	E_a	1045	1002	818
Germany				USA			
q_a	40%	47%	45%	q_a	54%	53%	60%
E_a	4182	3630	2768	E_a	6283	5408	4061

[a] 1956 or 1957 value

Source: *Economic Survey of Europe, 1969, Part I*, United Nations, New York, 1970, Table 3.20; and *Labour Force Statistics*, OECD, Paris, various issues.

the changes can be ignored. What stands out for all other countries were movements of labor out of agriculture, usually on a very large scale, together with a lack of any pronounced narrowing of wage differentials, except in the two cases mentioned.

This stability of the wage structure in developed economies has been revealed in other ways. Less aggregative studies of inter-industry wage structures dealing primarily with manufacturing industries have been undertaken, but the findings are of some relevance here and in the next section. Papola and Bharadwaj, and Mitchell, in their comprehensive studies covering much of the postwar period, found a great deal of stability in this inter-industry wage structure across countries and over time.[20] For example, rankings of manufacturing industries by average earnings showed a very similar structure across countries and a great deal of stability over time within the individual developed economies in spite of redistributions of labor among these industries. As revealed in these and other studies, rankings tend to be such that high-wage sectors are the expanding ones; i.e., even within manufacturing the signals are right.[21]

Turner and Jackson's study of eighteen market economies also attempted to measure the stability of the wage structure in manufacturing.[22] A coefficient of inter-industry wage stability was computed by determining the proportion of manufacturing industries in any country in 1965 whose average earnings had the same rank in relation to average earnings in manufacturing as they had had in 1956. The sample was subdivided into three groups according to the degree of centralization of wage negotiations in a country. The lowest value of the coefficient for any subgroup was 87 per cent and the highest 95 per cent. Moreover, in nearly one half of the individual countries, 95 per cent of the manufacturing industries had the same rankings at the beginning and end of the period.

E. The Allocative Mechanism

The discussions in Sections C and D indicated that a common feature of developed capitalist economies has been the existence of fairly widespread inter-industry mobility along with a rather rigid inter-industry wage structure. There remains the task of determining whether patterns of employment across industries reflect the workings of a neoclassical allocative mechanism. In

[20] See T. A. Papola and V. P. Bharadwaj, 'Dynamics of Industrial Wage Structure: An Inter-country Analysis,' *Economic Journal*, March 1970, and D. Mitchell, 'Some Aspects of Labour Mobility and Recent Policy in Britain,' *British Journal of Industrial Relations*, November 1969. Table 5.7 below is also relevant.

[21] Besides Papola and Bharadwaj, op. cit., see *Wages and Labour Mobility*, op. cit., Chapter II. Professor Kindleberger has pointed that, while in general there has been a high degree of stability of rankings as stressed in the test, coal mining went from one of the lowest-paying industries before World War II to one of the highest afterwards.

[22] H. A. Turner and D. A. S. Jackson, 'On the Stability of Wage Differences and Productivity Based Wage Policies: An International Analysis,' *British Journal of Industrial Relations*, No. 1 1969.

particular, do workers react so efficiently to changes in relative wages (and other conditions) that the differences in wages across industries more or less reflect a balancing of net benefits with workers unable to improve themselves by moving to another job with a different 'bundle' of present and future earnings, non-pecuniary benefits, etc? An affirmative answer to this question would raise serious doubts as to the existence of surplus labor and the relevance of models of the dual economy. Since there is evidence that wages and non-pecuniary aspects of a job are positively correlated, the two terms, wages and net benefits, will be used interchangeably throughout the analysis.[23]

1. The competitive hypothesis

Neoclassical theorists have argued that the dualistic structure of an economy ends once the marginal product of labor has risen above the subsistence wage in agriculture.[24] From this point on wage differentials would narrow as the market mechanism, unhampered by frictions and imperfections, would induce labor (and capital) to reallocate until factor returns were equalized across industries. One implication of the neoclassical view of the labor market is the absence of a residual labor force, at least of any appreciable size. Pools of surplus labor wanting to move, but somehow unable to, cannot exist because the neoclassical theory of labor mobility assumes that, if there are jobs with higher returns or net benefits, workers will move to these job areas and bid down money and real wages inducing firms to take them on.[25]

In Section D it was suggested that wage differentials have been substantial in the postwar period. Incomes (and wages and earnings) in agriculture relative to those in the rest of the economy changed little in most countries and rankings within manufacturing were little changed in spite of large-scale movements between industries. Furthermore, Table 5-7 below indicates that within manufacturing, there has been an increase in the absolute dispersion of the wage structures and a narrowing of the relative dispersion in only one economy in the postwar period. This was often accompanied by shifts of labor to the high wage sectors. To this a neoclassical theorist could

[23]See Mackay (*et. al.,*) op. cit., p. 96, and *Wages and Labour Mobility*, op. cit., pp. 52–3. In his discussion of the neoclassical mechanism or 'competitive hypothesis' M. Reder states that: 'By the "competitive hypothesis", I mean the hypothesis that prices and quantities behave as though they were in long-run equilibrium under conditions of pure competition. When we speak of the short-run competitive hypothesis we mean the same hypothesis except for the modifications introduced by the substitution of Marshallian short-run equilibrium for long run.' See M. Reder, 'Wage Differentials: Theory and Measurement,' *Aspects of Labor Economics*, National Bureau of Economic Research, New York, 1962, p. 279, fn. 45. In a more recent study the neoclassical label is used by M. Wachter to include every view of labor markets except the 'dual' theory of the labor market and 'the competitive model that rules out institutional barriers and industrial and demographic segmentation and in which human capital considerations are dominant....' (M. Wachter 'Primary and Secondary Labor Markets: A Critique of the Dual Approach,' *Brookings Papers on Economic Activity*, No. 3 1974, p. 642.) Such a definition of the neoclassical model, unfortunately, blurs some of the more important distinctions in the theories of just how labor markets work. Moreover, as pointed out in the text, this definition of the neoclassical model is not the one that has been generally adopted.

[24]See Jorgenson, in Adelman and Throbecke, op. cit.

[25]See Reder, op. cit., p. 294.

respond that the lack of any narrowing of inter-industry wage structures is consistent with a neoclassical allocative mechanism that results in the equalization of efficiency wages. True, wages are not equalized but when account is taken of differences between the relative efficiencies or human capital endowments of workers, the data on wages over time can be seen as tracing out an intertemporal equilibrium.

Two comments are in order at this point. First, in neoclassical analysis human capital endowments are treated as endogenous variables. Differences in money wages because of differences in efficiency are supposed to induce efforts by workers to invest in human capital (which is usually assumed to mean that they add to the length of their formal education), which in turn leads to a shift in the supply curve of labor in the high wage industries and a tendency toward equalization of wages.[26] Second, assume for the moment that differences in money wages are due solely to differences in efficiency but that these latter differences arise from firm-specific training. Since the latter is only available after vacancies have opened up and been filled, a situation of equalization of efficiency wages is quite consistent with the widespread existence of surplus labor. And the latter phenomenon is certainly something not readily associated with a neoclassical allocative mechanism.

2. *The 'wage competition' model and its critics*

There are additional difficulties with the neoclassical model and these have to do with the assumptions about the function and behavior of prices (i.e., wages) in labor markets in neoclassical analysis. This can be seen more clearly if a kind of 'fall-back' neoclassical position is formulated. This reinterpretation of the neoclassical theory of labor markets, which has been adopted by some neoclassical labor economists, argues (sometimes only implicitly) that in a world of constant change and transformation there will be a continuous shifting of the distribution of demand and output and the sectoral derived demand for labor. Because of this the intertemporal behavior of the wage structure cannot be expected to trace out a pattern of convergence to some kind of long-run equality of wages across industries. However in spite of this, wages can be considered market prices which reflect the interplay of short-run shifts in demand and supply curves. Flexible wages, in this view may never lead to an equalization of inter-industry wages, but they do act as market clearing devices eliminating excess demand and supply situations in the different markets. This amended, less demanding version of the neoclassical, competitive model will be referred to as the 'wage competition' model or theory of labor markets.

The wage competition model necessarily implies that changes in relative

[26] 'The degree of inequality in earnings is difficult to reconcile with the neoclassical model of a competitive economy, particularly when the models assume that acquired human capital is endogenous.' G. Cain, 'The Challenge of Segmented Labor Market Theories to Orthodox Theory: A Survey,' *Journal of Economic Literature*, December 1976.

wages will be associated with change in relative employment between industries.[27] Such a position is also consistent with some tendencies toward the equalization of wages. For example, assuming fixed demand curves for labor in different markets, wage differentials would tend to induce shifts in supply curves in a direction that, other things being equal, would act to reduce wage differentials. Nevertheless, such tendencies are not inevitable. Using the same example, if demand curves for labor in the high wage industries are shifting more rapidly to the right than supply curves, greater dispersion in the inter-industry wage structure is likely. However, the wage competition version of the neoclassical model by way of contrast brings out more clearly the distinctive features of an alternative allocative mechanism, one that does much to explain why there has been no tendency for the wage differentials to narrow.

Thus, there are those economists who stress the importance of market imperfections (e.g., lack of information, discrimination, wage premiums, immobility, etc.) and take issue even with the fall-back position arguing that: (1) changes in relative wages do not necessarily lead to variations in relative employment in the same (or even opposite) direction and (2) changes in relative employment do not necessarily induce changes in wage differentials. Industry wage levels according to this view are not market prices and typically do not change in order to clear markets. Wages tend to be rigid with wage offers by workers largely irrelevant in determining employment.[28] As a result inter-industry mobility can be widespread and pronounced without significant changes in the wage structure and the wage structure can reveal wide dispersion across industries without there being any tendency for these differentials to be eliminated through movements of labor. The close tie in neoclassical analysis (either version) between changes in relative wages and employment is broken. Naturally, there would be little tendency for wages to equalize in this view. The expression 'job competition' or 'job vacancy' theory of labor markets has been used to describe this position and will be adopted here. Additional characteristics of this viewpoint will be developed shortly.[29]

[27] L. Ulman, 'Labor Mobility and the Industrial Wage Structure,' *Quarterly Journal of Economics*, February 1965, p. 76, fn. 2. It should be stressed that it is blue collar workers that are the center of attention in the text.

[28] See *Wages and Labour Mobility*, op. cit. The modern version of this position is given in L. Thurow, *Generating Inequality: Mechanisms of Distribution in the U.S. Economy*, Basic Books, New York, 1975.

[29] Cain, in his survey, states that the job competition model is the closest to the neoclassical wage competition model of all the various challenges to the latter. In addition to wage rigidity and the unimportance of wage offers by workers in determining employment, Cain adds two other elements in his description of the job competition view: first, the number and type of job vacancies are technologically determined; second, employers 'use screening devices to hire workers based on their trainability and adaptability.' See Cain, op. cit., pp. 1221–2. These two additional elements are certainly consistent with the position adopted in the text, especially the latter. It should be recalled, however, that the main determinant of job and employment patterns stressed in the text is the demand for labor in the high-wage high-technology sectors.

3. An evaluation

Different approaches have been followed by economists trying to determine whether a job competition or wage competition model best describes the allocative features of a real life labor market. For example, numerous examples of statistical testing of the theories have been undertaken, although there are difficulties involved here in interpreting the results.[30] An OECD study of the relationship between changes in relative wages and employment provides the most extensive statistical testing of this issue to date. For a wide range of developed economies it was found that there existed relatively large shifts in industry employment along with relatively small changes in relative wages. As a result, no significant correlation was found between variations in wages and employment. The study concluded that the reallocation of labor in these economies had been and could be carried out within the existing wage structure with one possible exception: industries low on the wage scale, wishing to expand employment and not being in a position to easily intercept workers, might be forced to raise wages in order to expand employment. In general, this study and others support the job competition or job vacancy explanation of inter-industry labor movements.[31]

Empirical studies of wage structures during different phases of the cycle are also relevant, and here again the evidence lends support to the job competition theory. Thus, it has been found that during the boom phase of the cycle employment expands most rapidly in the high wage industries. According to the wage competition hypothesis, this should lead to a widening of wage differentials since firms in the high wage industries are required to raise relative wages to attract workers. In fact, wage differentials have tended to narrow during the boom (and widen during the slump). This is consistent with the findings of the OECD study just mentioned where during an expansion high wage industries need only to open vacancies in order to fill jobs while firms in low paying industries may be forced to raise wages in order to keep or expand employment.[32]

Furthermore, these findings are supported by case studies as well as theoretical considerations which indicate why the behavior of wages are not such as to clear markets and, at least, induce a tendency towards equalization. Thus, the competitive model hypothesizes a spectacle whereby workers, when they become aware of an increase in relative wages elsewhere, move to the job sites and induce management to hire them at a lower money (and real) wage

[30] See R. Perlman, *Labor Theory*, John Wiley & Sons Inc., New York, 1969, Chapter V.

[31] See *Wages and Labour Mobility*, op. cit. It should be noted that in evaluating the two alternative explanations of allocation in labor markets, it is not necessary to try and explain what determines existing wage differentials.

[32] See A. Okun 'Upward Mobility in a High Pressure Economy,' *Brookings Papers on Economic Activity*, No. 1, 1973, p. 209 and; M. Wachter, 'Cyclical Variations in the Inter-industry Wage Structure,' *American Economic Review*, March 1970.

than that currently earned in those jobs.[33] This competitive model of mobility and wage changes has been updated somewhat by search theorists. The search theory of unemployment maintains that unemployment is largely, if not entirely, voluntary and is the result of unemployed workers searching for information about current wage offers. The rate of search unemployment may vary around some 'natural' rate of unemployment (e.g. that which exists when prices are stable), owing to faulty information and expectations in the short-run, but in the long-run the natural rate of unemployment will be realized. For example, assume an initial situation where unemployment is at the natural rate (somehow defined) and there is a decrease in the rate of growth of demand that is sustained. This allegedly causes both prices and wages to fall but prices by more than wages; i.e. the real wage rises. The unemployed who are searching for information about current money wages will begin to sample money wage rates that are lower than those they had previously experienced. Since they can and will be fooled in the short-run into thinking that real wages are also lower (they do not realize that prices have fallen by more than the money wage), there will be an increase in the amount of unemployment as unemployed workers prolong the duration of their search. Additionally, some of the employed are assumed to quit their jobs in order to search for jobs with higher money and real wages.[34] However, unemployed workers will eventually realize that real wages have actually risen and offer their labor services at lower (acceptance) wages. This new offer by labor is then accepted by management and the actual money wage will fall into line with the lower acceptance wage.

Search theorists have presented their arguments in a forceful manner, but the sophistication of their mode of analysis runs up against the plain facts of the matter. In real-life labor markets the general situation is one in which either employers set wages (and care little whether job applicants are willing to work for less) or employers and union leaders work out an agreement. In neither situation is the sort of haggling described by search theorists important in wage setting.[35] The issue therefore comes down to whether or not management considers utilizing changes in wages as an instrument for eliminating excess demand and supply situations in those cases where it has

[33] Compare this view with: '... in general the buyer and not the seller in labor markets quotes the starting wage. The employer usually has little interest in discovering applicants willing to work at less than the prevailing rate; if he is covered by a union contract, he has none at all.' A. Rees, 'Information Networks in Labor Markets,' *American Economic Review*, May 1966, p. 561. There are any number of other reasons why activity on the supply side of labor markets does not work to equalize wages.

[34] In models where the demand for and supply of labor are both functions of the real wage, the initial increase in the real wage is alleged to induce management to lay off workers.

[35] To use the terminology of Chapter V, the search theorists' explanation of wage bargaining is relevant only for certain submarkets of the 'unstructured' labor market or the 'secondary labor market.' For a helpful discussion of the issues involved and a critique of the search theory approach to labor markets, see the discussants' remarks on the session devoted to 'Wage-Price Dynamics, Inflation and Unemployment,' in the *American Economic Review*, May 1969, pp. 161–8.

some choice in the matter. With few exceptions, the evidence indicates that management does not use changes in wages as an instrument for adjusting labor supply.[36]

The reasons advanced and the types of evidence are of several kinds. First, there exists a widespread feeling that wage increases will not work as an inducement to expand labor because of the existence of 'coercive comparisons', i.e. the view that firms competing in the same labor market will always match wage increases in order to restore the initial 'local' market wage differentials.[37] Second, at the firm level fairly elaborate internal wage structures develop so that on grounds of equity any change in the wages of one group of workers will require adjustments all through the firm in order to restore the original intra-firm structure; i.e., the marginal cost of an additional worker would be much higher than the supply price of labor.[38] Third, in many cases, anti-pirating schemes are worked out whereby competition for labor in the local labor market through wage inducements is ruled out.[39]

In addition, and in many ways the most important factor, in most developed capitalist systems short-run adjustments in the labor markets can be achieved without recourse to changes in relative wages. In those cases where the demand for labor by the high-wage industries is strong, inter-industry and inter-firm reallocations can be achieved without changes in these structures by merely altering the number of job vacancies; i.e., the 'signals are right.' Conversely, when such demands are weak, employment may expand or decline less rapidly in the low-wage sectors without any change in the wage structure, provided the demand for labor there is not large relative to the available supply of labor not absorbed by the high-wage sectors. For example, during the depression of the 1930s there was a net migration in America from urban to rural areas as one-time agricultural workers returned to agriculture and often to their previous jobs. This often resulted in a larger number of family members sharing the work in a manner very similar to what takes place today in developing economies. More recently it has been argued that the service or tertiary sector also serves as a 'sponge,' absorbing workers who are unable to find employment in the high-wage industrial sector.[40] Certain

[36] During periods of low national unemployment all firms may be forced to raise wages to retain their work forces. This, however, is not the same as a firm trying to increase its labor force, relative to other firms, by increasing wages, relative to other firms.

[37] Mitchell's study of inter-industry 'linkages' of wage changes suggests that coercive comparisons extend far beyond local markets. See Mitchell, op. cit.

[38] See Doeringer and Piore op. cit., p. 97 and; MacKay *et al.*, op. cit., p. 130.

[39] See M. Reder, 'The Theory of Occupational Wage Differentials,' *American Economic Review*, December 1955.

[40] See Kaldor, *Strategic Factors*, op. cit., as well as 'The Slowing Down of the Economy during Recent Years,' in *Staff Report on Employment, Growth and the Price Levels*, Joint Economic Committee, 86th Congress, 1st Session U.S. Government Printing Office, Washington, D.C., 1960; also R. Sleeper, 'SET and the Shake-out: A Note on the Productivity Effect of the Selective Employment Tax,' *Oxford Economic Papers*, July 1972, and; 'Manpower Redeployment and the Selective Employment Tax', *Bulletin of the Oxford University Institute of Economics and Statistics*, November 1970.

subsectors of the service sector such as retail trade are structured in such a way that additional employment is made possible by the larger work force sharing the total transactions and thus reducing the number of transactions per worker.

Taken together, these considerations lead to the conclusion that changes in wages are one of the most constrained instruments for adjusting shortages (and excesses) of labor. At the same time, changes in job vacancies have been found to be one of the most unconstrained instruments of labor force adjustment.[41] Obviously in the real world there may be attempts to alter relative wages in order to eliminate excess demand or supply, especially among firms employing non-union workers and especially when it is a matter of increasing the going wage. But the discussion among economists as to the relevance of the dual model compared to the neoclassical model has been conducted in 'either/or' terms. Therefore, if one is forced to choose between one labor market adjustment mechanism or the other, the evidence clearly points to the operation of a job-vacancy mechanism in the developed capitalist economies just as in Lewis's underdeveloped dual economy.[42] In other words, opening up (or eliminating) job vacancies with a given wage structure has allowed inter-industry movement of the labor force without significant changes in wage differentials because the signals were often right and because there is no reason to believe that a large part of the labor force employed in low-wage industries, e.g. agriculture or certain service subsectors, is anything more than a kind of surplus labor.

F. Output and Employment Patterns

By Kaldor's definition, surplus labor exists if an increase in demand for labor in the high-wage sectors give rise to an increase in the supply of labor forthcoming without a change in wage differentials. The discussion so far has sought to establish that, for a large number of developed capitalist economies, there is evidence that the three conditions necessary for the existence of surplus labor do in fact exist. The quantitative significance of surplus labor is another matter, as is the likelihood of the demand for this labor being sufficient to draw these workers out of the low-wage sectors. These issues will be discussed in Chapter V.

This chapter concludes with an investigation of the extent to which

[41] See Doeringer and Piore, op. cit., Chapter 5.

[42] Let p_1 and p_2, and w_1 and w_2, represent the probability of finding employment and actual wages in industries 1 and 2, respectively. It has been argued that search theorists take account of changes in relative wages and job vacancies by dealing with expected wages, w^e, where the latter are defined as $w_1{}^e = p_1 w_1$ and $w_2{}^e = p_2 w_2$. However, this 'generalization' of the two labor allocative mechanisms discussed in the text is more apparent than real. Since changes in relative wages (i.e. w_1/w_2) are limited, most of the changes in relative expected wages would be accounted for by changes in vacancies or probabilities of finding jobs. In this case, labor is responding to changes in vacancies even if this is termed a response to a change in relative expected wages.

movements of output and employment in the OECD countries in the postwar period also conformed to the dual model framework whereby development was characterized by a relatively rapid rate of growth of manufacturing output and a movement of labor from low-wage to high-wage sectors. However, the analysis must be extended since the original dual models were limited to only two sectors. In the two-sector case either the signals were right (i.e. labor moved from agriculture to industry or manufacturing), or the economy remained underdeveloped. Economists such as Colin Clark have for some time been stressing that the process of growth and transformation cannot be properly understood without adding at least a third sector, the tertiary or service sector.[43] This extension must be incorporated and refined. And in spite of the awkwardness of the term, the expression 'dual model' will be retained even though the discussion explicitly deals with models and economies of more than two sectors.

In the earlier discussion, after indicating the conditions necessary for the existence of surplus labor, the additional criteria adopted for determining the applicability of the dual model was that the process of development must involve a more rapid rate of growth of output and employment in industry than agriculture. Alternatively, this criterion can be formulated as a more rapid rate of growth of output and employment in industry than the rate of growth of total output and employment, respectively. Once more than two sectors are allowed for, different criteria are necessary and this will involve a certain amount of arbitrariness. However, recall that surplus labor was defined earlier in terms of the response of labor in the low-wage sector to an increase in demand for labor by the high-wage sector. Furthermore, since wages and labor productivity were always positively correlated, an increase in demand for labor by the high-wage sector always led to an increase in the level and overall rate of growth rate of productivity and output even if sector productivities were fixed. The dual economy framework allowed for this source of growth to be isolated and stressed. This suggests that, if the model is extended to allow for more than two sectors, any criterion adopted to determine the applicability of the dual model should be formulated in such a way as to also isolate and stress the reallocation of labor (and capital) as a possible source of output and productivity growth.

Table 4.2 gives a more detailed breakdown of sector productivities and earnings for various OECD countries in 1963. Typically, the high-productivity (and -wage) sectors are manufacturing, public utilities and mining, together with transportation and communication, while agriculture and certain subsectors of the tertiary sector tend to be the low-productivity, low-wage sectors, e.g. trade and miscellaneous services.[44] This suggests that one of the criteria for the applicability of the extended model of the dual economy be formulated in these terms: if the relative growth of employment in

[43] See Clark, op. cit.

[44] Current factor cost per person and value added per person are the same.

Table 4.2. Output at current factor cost per person, and wage and salary bill per wage and salary-earner, by sector, 1963 (percentages; manufacturing = 100)

Country	Agriculture[a]	Mining	Manufac-turing	Public utilities	Con-struction	Transport and com-munications	Trade	Miscellaneous services including ownership of dwellings	Miscellaneous services excluding ownership of dwellings	Public services	Total economy
A. Output per person employed											
	%	%	%	%	%	%	%	%	%	%	%
Austria	41.4	198.2	100	310.2	129.6	99.6	83.7	70.9	63.8	111.7	87.8
Belgium	120.2	100.5	100	271.9	93.1	117.6	100.0	143.3	95.1	108.4	111.4
France	48.1	165.2	100	280.1	84.2	105.1	123.5	83.0	57.4	103.7	92.0
Netherlands	89.5	124.0	100	260.4	67.4	121.7	92.2	93.8	69.1	99.7	97.1
Norway	39.1	145.1	100	284.2	92.9	148.3	103.2	101.0	72.0	84.2	93.0
Germany	50.0	125.0	100	300.0	100.0	116.7	100.0	100.0	75.0	133.3	100.0
Italy	56.8	100.6	100	414.9	73.9	141.5	88.1	167.7	110.8	142.6	98.8
Sweden	49.0	195.4	100	303.0	102.1	100.1	81.2	143.4	98.0	83.4	93.7
United Kingdom	102.1	104.5	100	201.9	95.8	127.1	89.6	138.7	107.3	77.1	103.9
Canada	58.7	356.9	100	259.1	75.8	101.0	61.3	93.7[c]	93.0	114.9	92.2
US	50.0	200.0	100	259.1	70.0	120.0	80.0	90.0	60.0	90.0	90.0
Japan	37.5	200.0	100	–	–	–	–	–	–	–	83.8
B. Wage and salary bill per wage and salary-earner											
Belgium	69.7	107.5	100	184.0	81.3	130.7	106.7		100.7	–	–
France	43.4	115.5[b]	100	135.4[c]	79.8	132.8	102.1		87.4	131.4	102.6
Germany	72.1	118.7	100	125.1	101.7	105.1	83.3		85.2	128.8	99.1
Italy	39.4	94.6	100	263.7	64.2	170.1	88.5		108.9	170.7	101.9
Netherlands	101.1	137.1	100	131.2	85.8	119.5	83.2		79.8	123.1	100.3
Norway	86.9	110.1	100	129.5	118.3	124.0	89.8		78.4	115.9	102.7
Sweden	94.4	98.1	100	106.8	124.0	112.5	108.1		87.5	165.0	104.3
United Kingdom	87.9	119.5	100	130.8	117.8	131.7	91.3		129.1	113.0	109.1
US	27.9	105.1	100	115.7	99.1	111.1	81.6		74.3	79.4	86.5

[a]Includes forestry and fishing [b]Including public services [c]Not fully comparable with the other sectors

Source: United Nations, *Economic Survey of Europe, 1969, Part I*, p. 125.

manufacturing and the other high productivity sectors exceeded (a) the overall rate of growth of employment, or (b) the rate of growth of employment in the tertiary sector (or certain subsectors within it), then one could say that the economy conformed to the workings of the extended dual model. If, on the other hand, the relative growth rates were reversed, then such an economy would not have satisfied one condition necessary for the application of the dual model. More important, it would be expected that such an economy would have a relatively slow rate of growth of output and productivity.

However, in Chapter VII it is argued that the development of the manufacturing sector is important not so much because levels of productivity are relatively high there, but because rapid growth of output of the manufacturing sector tends to generate rapid growth of productivity not only in manufacturing but throughout the economy. In other words, it is not as much shifts in employment that generate productivity growth for the economy (although such shifts may be a necessary condition for the latter), as it is shifts in output. Therefore, the following criteria (in addition to the existence of surplus labor) for the applicability of the extended model of the dual economy will be adopted: if in some country in the postwar period, the rate of growth of manufacturing output and employment was greater than the overall rate of growth of output and employment, it will be said this country's development showed characteristics of growth of a dual economy. Other things being equal, it would be expected that such an economy would experience rapid rates of growth relative to an economy where manufacturing output and employment grew less rapidly than total output and employment.

In Table 4.3, rates of growth of employment in manufacturing, industry and the entire economy are shown for periods covering roughly the early 1950s to the late 1960s or early 1970s and the early 1950s to 1973, the latter a year of relative prosperity for most of the countries. The twelve countries chosen were those for which accurate data were available for most of the postwar period.[45] Employment patterns fall into two distinct groups with Norway a possible borderline case. In one group are the economies that conform to the workings of the dual economy: Austria, Denmark, France, Germany, Italy, Japan and Norway up until 1970. In Austria employment overall actually declined while manufacturing and industrial employment rose. In the other six countries, rates of growth of manufacturing employment ranged from slightly less than double to almost triple the overall growth rate of employment. Belgium, Canada, the Netherlands, the United Kingdom and the United States comprise the other group with rates of growth of employment in manufacturing (and industry) less than or approximately equal to the overall rate of growth of employment. The table also indicates a tendency for rates of growth of employment in manufacturing to decline relative to the overall growth of

[45] Extended employment data for Sweden and Switzerland are not available. Hence, less attention is given to these two countries throughout the study than would be the case had such data been available.

Table 4.3. Average annual rates of growth of total ($\dot{E}$), manufacturing ($\dot{E}_m$) and industrial ($\dot{E}_{in}$) employment

	$\dot{E}$	$\dot{E}_m$	$\dot{E}_{in}$		$\dot{E}$	$\dot{E}_m$	$\dot{E}_{in}$
Austria				Italy			
1951–70	−0.40[a]	0.80	0.05[a]	1951–70	0.64	2.21	1.26[b]
1951–73	−0.55[a]	0.73	−0.24[a]	1951–73	0.50	1.93	0.99[b]
Belgium				Japan			
1951–70	0.52	0.49	−0.11[a]	1953–69	1.56	4.62	3.70[a]
1951–73	0.53	0.41	−0.18[a]	1953–73	1.46	4.02	3.39[a]
Canada				Netherlands			
1951–69	2.36	2.20	1.78[a]	1951–70	1.19	1.19	0.76[b]
1951–73	2.45	2.13	1.85[a]	1951–73	1.01	0.70	−0.05[b]
Denmark				Norway			
1957–69	1.33	2.27	1.84	1951–70	0.38	0.89	0.76[b]
1957–73	1.30	n.a.	0.95	1951–73	0.79	0.65	0.64[b]
France				UK			
1951–69	0.50	1.01	0.81[a]	1951–69	0.38	0.39	−0.04[a]
1951–73	0.51	1.06	0.96[a]	1951–73	0.25	−0.25	−0.70[a]
Germany				USA			
1951–70	1.18	2.84	0.88[b]	1951–69	1.44	1.16	1.20[a]
1951–73	1.01	2.38	0.62[b]	1951–73	1.53	0.97	1.02[a]

a = from 1957 b = from 1956

Sources: *Labour Force Statistics, 1956–1967, 1962–1973*, OECD, Paris; Cripps and Tarling, op. cit.; and *Economic Report of the President*, US Government Printing Office, Washington DC various issues.

employment for the longer period, indicating less conformity with the dual model for the period beginning in the 1970s. An explanation of these different patterns of labor allocation will be offered in the Chapters V and VIII; for, even if the reallocation of labor from low- to high-productivity sectors is not an important source of growth of overall productivity, an explanation of these markedly different employment patterns is of interest in its own right.

Table 4.4 approaches the issue of the applicability of the dual model from the point of view of the output criterion. Rates of growth of total and manufacturing output are shown for the countries treated in Table 4.3. In every case output of the manufacturing sector exceeded that of total output. In addition, rapid rates of growth of total output were positively correlated with rates of growth of manufacturing output in such a way that the size of difference between the rate of growth of manufacturing output and total output was positively correlated with the rate of growth of manufacturing output. The discussion of the manufacturing sector as a leading sector or 'engine of growth' will be taken up further in Chapter VII. For the time being it is enough to note that, in terms of the output criterion, all countries in the

Table 4.4. Annual average rates of growth of aggregate output ($\dot{Q}$) and manufacturing output ($\dot{Q}_m$), 1951–73

	$\dot{Q}$	$\dot{Q}_m$		$\dot{Q}$	$\dot{Q}_m$
	%	%		%	%
Austria	5.0	5.5	Italy	5.1	7.1
Belgium	3.9	4.9	Japan[c]	9.5	13.6
Canada	4.6	4.9	Netherlands	5.0	6.1
Denmark[a]	4.2	4.8	Norway	4.2	4.3
France	5.0	5.5[b]	UK	2.7	3.4
Germany	5.7	7.4	USA	3.7	3.9

[a] 1954–73 [b] 1953–69 [c] 1953–73
Sources: Cripps and Tarling, op. cit.; and *National Accounts of the OECD, 1962–1973*, op. cit.

sample conformed to the workings of the dual model. Chapter VIII will consider why a similarity in employment patterns did not arise in these circumstances.[46]

G. Summary

As the title of this chapter suggests, modern-day capitalism contains many of the essential features ascribed to economies at an early stage of industrialization. Thus, development theory has often stressed these features of a less-developed economy which have been thought to be largely responsible for a radical change in the pace of their rate of growth. These features made up the essential elements of a dual economy. They included a labor force willing and able to move from low-wage and low-productivity industries to high-wage and high-productivity industries when vacancies opened up in the latter sectors. And all this was to occur within the framework of a relatively rigid inter-industry wage structure. This was permitted because the structure of the dual economy was such that much of the labor force in the low-wage–low-productivity sector was clearly a residual labor force, eagerly waiting for the opening up of employment opportunities in the high-wage sector. When they did open up, this pool of surplus labor readily moved across industry lines and in so doing accelerated the pace of development. And only by stressing this dual structure of employment conditions, earnings and productivities could it be said that one of the chief sources of growth had been effectively isolated and stressed.

Various attempts have been made in more recent years to draw out the similarities between the workings of countries in the early stages of industrialization (according to the model of the dual economy) and more

[46] Table 2.3 above gives related data on growth rates of industrial output.

modern economies of the postwar period. A further analysis and to some extent a synthesis of these writings reveals that the features that justify the application of dual models to underdeveloped economies are the same features that justify applying a dual model of growth to economies well advanced in their development and transformation process. What has been argued above is that something qualitatively different in the workings of an economy does not necessarily occur when the marginal product of labor in agriculture rises above the subsistence wage; when productivity growth in agriculture is accelerated because it too has become modernized; or, when per capita incomes have risen so high that consumers reorganize their budgets away from necessities such as foodstuffs and proportionately increase their outlays on 'luxuries.' In Chapters VI and VII it will be argued that by continuing to emphasize the dual structure of modern capitalism real insights into its performance are permitted, so much so that important influences on the growth performance of different economies can be isolated.

Moreover, it is important to point out again that many of the departures from the neoclassical approach suggested as essential in Chapter III for explaining why growth performances differ are contained in or easily incorporated within the framework of a model of the dual economy. For example, the shift of labor from agriculture to manufacturing and the rapid expansion of capital and output in manufacturing point up the unbalanced nature of growth. Dual models also stress, implicitly at least, the importance of entrepreneurship in directing resources and production into new lines. And even in the most simple version of the model, the rate of growth of demand plays an important role in determining the rate of growth of productivity, as job openings in the high-wage–high-productivity sector lead to an increase in the rate of growth of overall labor productivity even if sectoral rates of growth of productivity are zero.

Finally, while emphasis throughout this chapter has been on labor and its movements, the role of capital formation was an important one in models of the dual economy. Rapid growth and transformation consisted of flows of both new capital and labor into the manufacturing sector. This neglect of the role of capital formation in this chapter is largely rectified in Chapter VI, when the emphasis shifts to the factors pulling labor into manufacturing. There the importance of capital formation is rightly stressed.

Beginning with Chapter V, important extensions of the model are undertaken. These include a generalization of the model to include additional sectors besides agriculture and industry, as well as additional sources of surplus labor. The latter extension includes a treatment of the importation of foreign labor. In addition, it will be necessary to discuss additional sources of productivity growth. The simple models of the dual economy just outlined emphasize the importance of shifts in labor from low- to high–average-productivity sectors as a source of productivity growth. However, the possibility of productivity growth owing to dynamic economies of scale, 'linkage effects' and the 'interrelatedness' of factor units must also be taken into account. Finally there exists a large number of extensions of the model that 'fall out' when the model is expanded to include a foreign sector. The impact of surplus labor on real and money wages has important implications for investment, productivity costs and international competitiveness. The notions of 'virtuous and vicious circles' will be useful in analyzing the working of an open dual model. Consideration of a foreign sector leads to a further stress of the importance of aggregate demand, and thereby serves to complement the emphasis on the supply side of the market inherent in the dual model.

Chapter V The Supply of Labor to Manufacturing

A. Introduction

The model of Chapter IV stressed the importance of demand pressures in reallocating labor as revealed in the opening and closing of job vacancies. This was contrasted with the neoclassical view whereby changes in relative wages in response to excess demand and supply situations induced a movement of labor between firms and industries until net benefits were again equalized. The former view of how labor is allocated relies on the existence of surplus labor in the Kaldor sense, i.e., on the existence of workers who stand ready to respond to an increase in demand for labor in the high-wage industries without requiring a change in relative wages. An argument was advanced that surplus labor existed in various developed market economies in the postwar period and could be tapped should demand increase in the high-wage, high-productivity sectors. However, the analysis was limited in that, except for the brief discussion in Section C, the only possible source of surplus labor singled out was the agricultural sector. Nothing was said as to the possible impact of an increase in the number of net entrants to the labor force on employment patterns. Yet an increase in the size of the labor force, either because of an earlier increase in the size of the indigenous population or immigration, might possibly serve as a substitute for a large agricultural labor force if and when efforts are made to expand manufacturing employment. The same possibility arises with respect to those employed in the service sector. Indeed, as will soon be apparent, several countries did in fact draw heavily upon these new entrants to the labor force and those already employed in the service sector in their efforts to expand employment in manufacturing. This too was accomplished within a relatively fixed wage structure. These possibilities will be allowed for in the discussion to follow.

The primary task of this chapter is to determine whether differences in employment patterns in the postwar period were primarily the result of demand or supply forces. In particular, the analysis seeks to determine whether some countries were unable to expand employment in the manufacturing sector as rapidly as desired. It does this largely by examining the means by which an increase in aggregate demand for labor works its way through the economy. Section B sets out in summary form the notion of a 'mature economy,' i.e. one lacking in surplus labor. Section C serves largely as an introduction to much of the rest of the chapter; in it various types of promotional schemes are sketched, each viewing labor's response to increased demand as essentially a 'bumping-up' process or an upgrading of the labor force. In Section D this analysis is pursued with greater detail. Of special interest is whether the 'secondary labor force' and workers in the service sector can compensate for a small agricultural labor force in the sense that they can serve as substitute sources of surplus labor for manufacturing. Section E continues the discussion of the service sector. Section F extends the dual model of Chapter IV by treating the importation of foreign labor as another source of surplus labor. Section G tackles the question of whether Britain (and, by implication, any other country with a small agricultural labor force) suffered from labor shortages during the postwar period. Section H contains a summary.

B. The Mature Economy

While it might be expected that in every country there will always be workers in low-wage, low-productivity sectors whose transfer to other sectors is possible without changes in relative wages, there may be barriers to a substantial and rapid reallocation between industries in some countries. Thus, we may envisage a situation whereby the initial demand for labor by the high-wage industries is met by a transfer out of low-wage sectors, but where this demand is so strong that adjustments must be made in the wage structure signaling the end of surplus labor and, therefore, dualism. For example, if the income elasticity of demand for agricultural products were high, the price elasticity of demand low and productivity growth low, a rapid and sustained expansion of demand for labor by manufacturing would very likely involve rising prices and wages in agriculture as the latter sector, seeking to retain labor, would be forced to raise relative wages. Sooner or later, wage differentials between agriculture and manufacturing would narrow to such a point that job openings in manufacturing would no longer attract labor from agriculture. Furthermore, since a transfer of labor from agriculture to manufacturing could no longer be achieved, this source of productivity growth would now effectively be ruled out.

In actual fact, as pointed out in Chapter II, productivity growth in agriculture has been very rapid and the income elasticity of demand very low in most all of the economies studied. As a result, rapid and sustained demands for labor by manufacturing have resulted in substantial movements of labor out of agriculture in most countries without any marked change in relative wages as seen in Table 4.1. However, if initially there is little labor employed in agriculture, then a situation may arise that precludes a rapid transfer of labor into, say, manufacturing.

It has been contended that Britain and perhaps other economies were faced with this kind of shortage of surplus labor in agriculture even at the beginning of the postwar period.[1] In this situation it is implicitly assumed that the job-vacancy mechanism can no longer reallocate labor in Britain because of this shortage associated with an industrial wage structure characterized by a small dispersion around its mean.[2] To attract more labor into manufacturing in such a situation, this view argues, other sources of surplus labor have to be found or relative wages have to be changed. In terms of the differences between countries seen at the end of Chapter IV, this view suggests that the employment patterns in certain OECD countries were not primarily the result of an elastic supply of labor responding passively to the relative strengths of labor demand in the high-wage, high-productivity sectors. Rather, in some countries at least, employment patterns were greatly influenced by a lack of surplus labor that could be reallocated to these sectors where demand pressures were relatively strong.

According to this view, a country like Britain has suffered from a kind of premature 'maturity' whereby returns to labor across sectors have become equalized at a comparatively low level of per capita income as the size of the agricultural work force declined. Leaving aside for the moment the truth of the assumption that returns have been equalized, it does remain true that Britain was one of the few OECD countries that had both a small proportion of the labor force in agriculture from the very beginning of the postwar period (less than 10 per cent) and a low rate of growth of population and the labor force (less than 1 per cent). In addition, Britain placed full employment very high on its list of economic goals to be achieved, thus strengthening the case for those who believe Britain suffered from labor shortages. The issue is seen more clearly with the help of Table 5.1.

Table 5.1 gives a useful measure of the flexibility available for those economies for which relatively long-term postwar data are available. It takes account of the decline in employment in agriculture but in addition recognizes that additions to the labor force (i.e. the net entrants) can also serve as a source of surplus labor in Kaldor's sense. Like Table 2.10 earlier, it combines the growth of the labor force with the amount of labor released from agriculture and therefore available to both industry and the service sector. A low rate of growth of this combined figure allows for the possibility that an economy, faced with various institutional rigidities that diminish the spatial and industrial mobility of labor, may be 'frozen' into

[1] Kaldor, op. cit. Kaldor has subsequently altered his position about the absence of surplus labor in Britain. See N. Kaldor, 'Economic Growth and the Verdoorn Law: A Comment on Mr Rowthorn's Article,' *Economic Journal*, December 1975. The text uses the expression 'high-wage, high-productivity sectors' more or less interchangeably with the 'manufacturing sector.' As seen from Table 4.2, this is not quite accurate. For example, productivity and wages are very high in public utilities. At this stage of the analysis no harm is done by a failure to be more precise.

[2] Emphasis in the text is on blue-collar workers.

Table 5.1. Annual average rates of growth of supply of labor available to the non-agricultural sector

	%		%
Japan (1953–73)	3.48	Italy (1951–73)	1.74
Canada (1950–73)	3.29	France (1954–73)	1.70
Germany (1951–73)	3.08	Netherlands (1950–73)	1.25
Denmark (1956–73)	2.06	Belgium (1950–73)	0.97
USA (1950–73)	1.90	Austria (1951–73)	0.69
Norway (1950–73)	1.76	United Kingdom (1950–73)	0.51

The rate of growth of supply of labor available to the non-agricultural sector (r) is given by;

$$r = \frac{1}{T} ln \left(1 + \frac{\Delta E - \Delta E_a}{E - E_a} \right)$$

where T is the number of years in the interval and E, ΔE, E_a and ΔE_a are total civilian employment in the first year, the change in total civilian employment, agricultural employment in the first year and the change in agricultural employment, respectively.

Source: *Labour Force Statistics, 1956–1966, 1962–1973*, op. cit., extrapolated where necessary using growth rates compiled by Cripps and Tarling, op. cit.

some inter-industry distribution of labor.[3] Thus, to center on the United Kingdom, it is clear from Table 5.1 that the growth of labor available for redistributing among the various non-agricultural sectors was relatively small compared with the other developed OECD countries cited.

However, before conceding the point that Britain and others suffered from labor shortages in this extended sense, it must be recognized that various other influences were at work here and must be disentangled. First, there may have existed sources of surplus labor other than the agricultural sector and additions to the labor force that could have been tapped had the demand by the high-wage sector been strong. Second, both demand and supply forces were at work during this period. Thus, it has been argued that there is little evidence that a shortage of labor was responsible for the slow rate of growth of manufacturing employment in the United Kingdom. Rather, the latter should be attributed to a lack of strong demand for labor by manufacturers.[4]

Most of the remainder of the chapter will outline the various kinds of responses by labor to an increase in aggregate demand. As suggested, this framework is helpful in determining just where pools of surplus labor might exist and have existed in the postwar period. However, additional points of interest develop when the supply response to an increased demand at the firm and industry level is also studied. In analyzing these responses, it is

[3] See Table 2.9 for related data.

[4] See J. Wolfe, 'Productivity and Growth in Manufacturing Industry: Some Reflections on Professor Kaldor's Inaugural Lecture,' *Economica*, May 1968.

necessary to work within the context of a more complex industrial structure than that envisaged in Chapter IV. Thus, it is appropriate to consider the nature of job and wage structures within an individual firm as well as allowing for a finer breakdown of the non-agricultural sector as in the discussion of the industrial wage structure. This allows for a more thorough analysis of the response of labor to changing demand conditions.

C. Labor's Response to Increased Demand: Part One

1. The supply response as a 'bumping-up' process

The model of Chapter IV (and indeed most models of the dual economy) envisages an increase in demand for labor in manufacturing leading to a particular type of response on the supply side as workers are induced to move out of agriculture and fill jobs in the high-wage sectors. However, analysts of developing countries have found that the actual reallocation of labor in such a situation is somewhat more complicated than this. For example, while an opening up of vacancies in the high-wage sectors leads to an expansion of employment, these jobs need not be filled by agricultural workers newly arrived from rural areas. Instead, previously employed, underemployed and unemployed members of the urban labor force, many of whom may have migrated from rural areas during some earlier period, are more likely to be the workers moving into the expanding sectors, with their ranks in turn filled by newly arrived workers from agriculture.[5] A similar sort of pattern has been observed in more developed economies with large agricultural sectors. This view of the supply response to higher demand as an upgrading of labor or a 'bumping-up' process serves to shed light on the possible existence of surplus labor, on the importance of demand pressures for exploiting the various sources of surplus labor and determining the flows of labor throughout the economy, and on the kinds of institutional frictions found in labor markets which slow down the speed of any reallocation of labor. The response of labor will be studied first in terms of upgrading the labor force according to several promotional schemes suggested by labor economists. In so doing distinctions between external and internal labor markets, the 'primary' and 'secondary' labor *force* and the 'primary' and 'secondary' labor *markets* will be highlighted since they provide a useful starting point in understanding this bumping-up process.

2. Internal vs. external markets

As suggested in Chapter IV, the internal–external labor market distinction has been found helpful in understanding labor mobility. As before, there

[5] See M. P. Todaro, 'A Model of Labor Migration and Urban Unemployment in Less Developed Countries,' *American Economic Review*, March 1969, and Vaciago, op. cit.

is the neoclassical, unstructured market with 'no attachment except the wage between the worker and the employer. No worker has any claim on any job and no employer has any hold on any man.'[6] This is in contrast with an internal, closed and highly structured labor market where pricing, promotion and allocation decisions tend to be governed by a set of administrative rules and procedures with economic variables having only an indirect influence.[7]

Consider the case in which the internal labor market is identified with an administrative unit such as a manufacturing plant. Here a distinction is made both by workers and management between the 'ins' (those currently employed in the plant) and the 'outs' (those in some outside 'external' market). However, there do exist connections between the two markets, the most notable being the ports of entry into the internal market. These comprise the various job classifications into which workers from the outside can be hired. The more numerous are the ports of entry, the more 'open' is the internal market and the more the market resembles the neoclassical competitive market. For example, a modern manufacturing plant is likely to fill semiskilled and skilled jobs from within by promoting workers with some work history at the plant. Ports of entry are limited to the low-skilled, low-paying jobs. In contrast, there are the unstructured labor markets for casual labor where vacancies in all job classifications are filled directly from outside, i.e. the external market of neoclassical theory.

Internal labor markets develop where there are labor skills specific to the firm. This skill-specificity leads to employers' undertaking investment in human capital, usually in the form of on-the-job training. As a result of this investment, employers have a strong incentive to reduce turnover and stabilize employment in order to capture the benefits (and recoup the costs) of their investments. This is accomplished to a large extent by promotion from within, good fringe benefits and wage premiums allowing workers to earn more than they could in the external market; i.e., monopoly rents are earned.

This has several important ramifications. First, labor becomes something of a 'quasi-fixed factor' in the sense that reductions in demand for output do not lead to proportionate declines in employment as employers, fearful that any layoffs may permanently result in losses of skilled workers, retain workers in the face of rising average costs and declining productivity.[8] In addition, with promotion from within along fairly well defined 'promotional ladders,' growth of demand, production and employment will result in a 'bumping-up' process where workers with seniority and accumulated skills will be upgraded to more highly skilled, better-paying jobs and vacancies

[6] See C. Kerr, 'The Balkanization of Labor Markets,' in E. W. Bakke *et al.*, *Labour Mobility and Economic Opportunity*, MIT Press, Cambridge, Mass., 1954.

[7] See Doeringer and Piore, op. cit., Chapters 2–4.

[8] See W. Oi, 'Labor as a Quasi-Fixed Factor,' *Journal of Political Economy*, December 1962.

in the lower-skilled, lower-paying jobs will be filled from the external market. Relatively closed internal labor markets are a common feature of the high-wage, high-productivity subsectors of manufacturing and the non-manufacturing parts of industry.[9] Only the lower-skilled, low-paying jobs in this group are likely to be filled by some sort of surplus labor (or new entrants to the labor force).

In the discussion of inter-industry mobility in Chapter IV, the importance of closed, highly structured internal markets was mentioned as a force that would reduce such mobility. This is primarily the result of the monopoly rents or wage premiums earned and seniority and retirement benefits accumulated by workers in an internal market, rewards that cannot be transferred to new jobs. Although it was suggested earlier that internal markets tend to be more open in terms of the number of ports of entry in a full-employment economy, the analysis did suggest that, if large and sustained increases in labor are desired by, say, a manufacturing plant, it may be difficult to satisfy this requirement by inducing a 'net flow' of labor from other non-agricultural industries. Rather, it may be necessary to fill vacancies through 'net entrants' to the non-agricultural labor force, e.g. former agricultural workers, immigrants, school-leavers and re-entrants to the labor force. These possibilities will be discussed presently.

3. Primary vs. secondary workers and jobs

The distinction between external and internal labor markets is based primarily on the different manner in which pricing and allocation decisions are carried out. Labor economists have also found it useful to distinguish between different types of workers, one of the most common distinctions being a contrast between workers in the 'primary labor force' and those in the 'secondary labor force.' The latter term applies to males over sixty-five or under twenty-five years of age and women of all ages; the former to males between the ages of twenty-five and sixty-five. Members of the secondary labor force are alleged to have a low attachment to their jobs, high turnover rates, a lack of interest in advancement in their work and a willingness to undertake unpleasant jobs. They also represent the 'discouraged workers,' i.e. those potential wage-earners who withdraw from the labor force when job vacancies are few but who re-enter when job opportunities increase. As such they qualify as a source of surplus labor and have been treated as such in manpower programs.

More recently, advocates of what has come to be known as 'dual labor market theory' have stressed the need to distinguish between different kinds of jobs as well as different kinds of workers and have used the expressions 'primary labor market' and 'secondary labor market' to denote the different

[9] A. Alexander, 'Income, Experience and Internal Labor Markets,' *Quarterly Journal of Economics*, February 1974.

job markets.[10] According to these writers, jobs in the primary labor market have the following characteristics: high wages, good working conditions and a desirability on the part of management to stabilize employment. Workers in these jobs tend to be well disciplined and have a low quit rate. In contrast, jobs in the secondary labor market have low wages, few fringe benefits, poor working conditions and offer little chance of advancement. Workers in these jobs exhibit high quit rates, absenteeism, insubordination and a low attachment to their jobs. Members of the secondary labor *force* and workers in secondary labor *markets* have much in common. However, an important difference is that dual labor market theorists stress the high frequency of unemployment of adult males between the ages of twenty-five and sixty-five (and female heads of households) in the secondary labor market.[11]

There is also a good deal of overlapping of the primary–secondary labor market categories with the internal–external labor market categories. The primary sector of the labor market can be thought of as consisting of a group of internal labor markets that are relatively closed, at least according to number of ports of entry. In contrast, the secondary labor market illustrates three kinds of employment situations: (1) employment in completely unstructured markets which resemble the external or competitive markets of economy theory, e.g. domestic work and dishwashing; (2) jobs in 'secondary' internal labor markets where there is some internal structure and rules for advancement and pay raise, but many ports of entry and poor working conditions, e.g. menial jobs in hospitals; and (3) jobs that have no promotion prospects or rights but that are attached to internal labor markets where the remaining jobs have all the characteristics of jobs in the primary sector of the labor markets.[12]

D. Labor's Response to Increased Demand: Part Two

1. The response of the secondary labor force

The analysis of the previous section is valuable for three reasons. First, the discussion of highly structured internal labor markets with their relatively well-defined system of rules for promotion illustrates a kind of bumping-up process or upgrading of employed workers at the firm level when demand and production pick up. Second, the distinction between internal and external labor markets points up many of the institutional factors that constrain movements of the labor force. For example, wage premiums earned

[10] See Doeringer and Piore, op. cit., Chapter 8.

[11] Advocates of the 'dual labor market' would certainly feel an affinity towards those advocating the use of 'dual models of the economy' (such as in Chapter IV). However, dual labor market theorists tend to stress the various barriers to the mobility of labor from secondary to primary labor markets. Models of the dual economy, if anything, downplay these barriers, arguing that, provided the demand for labor is strong in the high wage sectors, labor flows freely.

[12] See Doeringer and Piore, op. cit., pp.164–9. As will be seen later, foreign workers are a very good example of the kind of workers found in the third kind of employment situation.

in the high-wage sectors plus the relatively generous non-monetary benefits conferred in these sectors indicate that benefits are not equalized across industries in modern capitalist economies. This greatly reduces, if not eliminates, the likelihood that an increase in relative wages paid by industries further down in the inter-industry wage scale will attract labor out of the high-wage industries. In addition, the restriction of ports of entry into the high-wage industries to the lower-paying jobs reduces flows in the other direction, whether relative wages are increased in the high-wage industries (along with the creation of new vacancies) or not. High-paid workers in industries with a low to medium average level of wages will not desire to move to the higher-paying industries in such a situation. Rather, expansion of employment in firms and industries with relatively closed, highly structured, internal labor markets will be very much dependent upon the existence of low-wage workers somewhere else. These institutional factors must certainly work to slow the rate of transfer of labor as compared with the frictionless, highly competitive neoclassical world.

Third, the distinctions between primary and secondary jobs on the one hand and primary and secondary labor markets on the other are also useful preliminary steps in analyzing the main problem tackled in this chapter: the overall and sectoral response of labor supply to increases in aggregate demand. Indeed, a large body of literature has been developed with a view to determining to what extent an increase in aggregate demand can lead to 'discouraged workers' re-entering the labor force.[13] More recently economists have examined this response to demand in more detail, combining it with a study of the upgrading of labor from the secondary to the primary labor force and from secondary to primary labor markets. This response requires additional study.

The distinction between the primary and secondary labor force has been important in studies highlighting a kind of hidden unemployment that is usually neglected in recorded unemployment data. An offshoot of these studies is an increased awareness by economists that a great deal of flexibility exists in any modern economy that is often overlooked by theorists who think in terms of *the* labor force (or *the* capital stock) existing at any point in time. In particular, these studies have stressed the flexibility arising from changes in the labor force participation rates of a population in response to demand conditions that allows a redistribution of labor within an existing inter-industry wage structure.

One of the earliest studies was that by Okun.[14] Write:

$$(Q - Y)/Y = 3.2[(L - E)/L - 0.04]$$

where Q, Y, L and E represent 'full-employment' GNP and actual GNP

[13] See Okun, op. cit., pp. 210–11 and footnotes.

[14] A. Okun, 'Potential GNP: Its Measurement and Significance,' *Proceedings of the Business and Economic Statistics Section* (American Statistical Society), 1962.

(both measured in real terms) and 'the' labor force and employment respectively. When $(L-E)/L=0.04$, i.e. when the unemployment rate is 4 per cent, the figure in the bracket becomes zero, thus defining a full-employment GNP as that GNP prevailing when 96 per cent of the labor force is employed. Noteworthy in Okun's study is that the number before the expression in brackets is substantially greater than one. This means that a reduction in the unemployment rate from, say, 5 per cent to 4 per cent generates a 3.2 per cent decline in the gap between full employment and actual GNP. Alternatively, if unemployment is currently at 5 per cent, aggregate demand would have to be increased by enough to increase real GNP by 3.2 per cent to achieve full employment.

The explanation of these (short-run) increasing returns to labor alone is to be found in three sources: (1) a lengthening of the work week of those already employed; (2) increased productivity of those already employed; (3) additional jobs for people who were not counted among the unemployed when unemployment rates exceeded 4 per cent. When the additional vacancies created by the increase in demand necessary to reduce unemployment by 1 per cent open up, these discouraged workers enter the labor force and take jobs.

The impact of the first influence needs no further comment. The increased productivity of those employed when demand (and production) picks up is easily explained in terms of firms being reluctant to lay off workers who embody human capital in the form of firm-specific training paid for by management but not yet recouped. This group of workers become underemployed during slack periods as their retention adds little to output during slumps.

The third source of increasing returns illustrates the flexibility of labor mentioned earlier. In his early study Okun argued that, for every ten people recorded as unemployed in excess of 4 per cent unemployment, there might exist three people not actively seeking work who would take jobs if additional vacancies opened up. These were the hidden unemployed.[15]

A more recent study expanded on these sources of increasing returns to labor in such a way as to illustrate both the flexibility just mentioned and also a bumping-up process. The latter process, in turn, indicated another example of a reallocation of labor as a source of (short-term) growth.[16] The problem as before was to isolate and quantify the different kinds of responses on the supply side that result from reduction of the unemployment rate from 5 to 4 per cent, activity expanding either as a result of discretionary action or because of greater demand pressures generated as part

[15] The analysis was implicitly limited to participation rates when unemployment varied between the extremes of the sample period, say 4 to 7 per cent. Too little is known about participation rates at unemployment rates above, say 7 per cent. It can be argued that at historically high unemployment rates participation rates again rise as wives increasingly join the labor force.

[16] Okun, 'Upward Mobility,' op. cit.

of the natural course of a boom. Three sources of additional labor input were again found that helped to explain the increase in output of over 3 per cent that accompanies a reduction in unemployment of only 1 per cent. Jobs for the previously recorded unemployed were found to increase the labor input by a little over 1 per cent (a 1/95 increase in labor input, holding participation rates, etc., constant); a lengthening of the work week of the previously employed added 0.4 per cent to the labor input; and an increase in labor force participation added 0.65 per cent to the labor input for a total increase in labor input of 2.1 per cent. In other words, about two-thirds of the increase in output resulting from a decrease in the unemployment rate of 1 per cent was accounted for by an increase in labor input of a little over 2 per cent. The remaining 1 per cent increase in output was attributed to an increase in productivity, but in addition to the better utilization of previously employed workers a good part of the increase in productivity was attributed to sectoral shifts in the distribution of labor.

To illustrate this write:

$$\log \frac{N_{it}}{P_t} = a_0 + a_1 T + a_2 \log \frac{A_t}{P_t} + a_3 \log \frac{N_{it-1}}{P_t}$$

where N_{it}, N_{it-1}, P_t, A_t and T represent actual employment in the ith industry in the current period and in the previous period, total potential employment in the whole economy excluding federal government employment, total actual employment in the whole economy excluding federal government employment and a time trend respectively. The parameter estimate of a_2 gives the elasticity of ith industry employment with respect to economy-wide employment. For example, it was found that $a_2 = 2.65$ for durable manufacturing, indicating that a 1 per cent reduction of unemployment from 5 to 4 per cent (and therefore a 1 per cent increase in A/P) led to a 2.65 per cent increase in employment in durable goods manufacturing relative to total employment. On the other hand, a_2 was estimated as 0.68 for wholesale trade and -0.965 for agriculture, indicating that employment increases less than proportionately in wholesale trade and actually declines in agriculture when total unemployment declines.

Typically, industries with elasticities greater than one were found to be the high-wage, high-productivity sectors, e.g. durable and non-durable manufacturing, construction, mining and transportation. But in addition, the high-elasticity sectors were those that tended to employ a relatively high percentage of male workers over twenty-five years of age, i.e. members of the primary labor force. However, studies have indicated that the bulk of the expansion of employment was taken up by members of what was earlier referred to as the secondary labor force, i.e. women and teenagers.

Thus, an increase in aggregate demand that succeeds in lowering the unemployment rate from 5 to 4 per cent results in (1) additional *employment* going disproportionately to women and teenagers, and (2) additional *jobs* being created disproportionately in industries typically employing adult males. The apparent inconsistency is easily reconciled by the finding of an across-the-board upgrading of the labor force that shifts the distribution of the (enlarged) labor force toward the high-wage, high-productivity sectors. As a result of this bumping-up process, there is an increase of average labor productivity even if levels of productivity within each industry are fixed.

2. Net flows and net entrants in response to demand

The response of labor supply to demand pressures just discussed is essentially short-run. The reduction of unemployment from 5 to 4 per cent in the United States (in 1970) was equivalent to a decrease in recorded unemployment of approximately 1.2 million workers coupled with an increase in employment of about 0.6 million hitherto-disguised unemployed. In the process labor shifted from low- to high-wage and -productivity sectors, thereby causing productivity to grow more rapidly. This took place within the context of a fairly rigid inter-industry wage structure. But while this supply response resembles a short-run version of the workings of a dual economy, it is different in two important respects from the simple dual model response. First, as already mentioned it is short-run in the sense that it involves a 'one-shot' increase in labor available to the economy. Second, the 0.6 million previously disguised unemployed workers now available to the economy cannot be treated as net additions to the high-wage, high-productivity sectors. Using Okun's calculations again, approximately twenty-five per cent of the new jobs opened by lowering the unemployment rate one per cent were in the low-wage, low-productivity services.[17]

Okun's study does not allow a determination of how much of the expanded employment in the high-wage sectors was composed of flows between sectors of the economy by those previously employed and how much was due to new entrants to the labor force. Such a breakdown would facilitate a better understanding of the elasticity of labor supply to manufacturing. Fortunately, rather detailed information of a slightly different kind than Okun's is available for the United Kingdom that does allow a breakdown of sectoral employment changes into net flows and net entrants and over a somewhat longer period, i.e. from one boom to the next. Two studies by Sleeper utilizing these data allow a more thorough analysis of labor's response to increased demand and the resulting bumping-up process.[18]

Table 5.2 breaks down the British economy into seven sectors, and indicates net flows between industries as well as changes in employment. The column 'Net Entrants' is calculated as a residual. The grand total of net entrants, which must equal the total employment change, includes Okun's response of the secondary labor force to increases in aggregate demand as well as the response of other groups such as school-leavers. Both agriculture

[17] ibid., Table 3.
[18] See Sleeper, op. cit.

Table 5.2. Labor movements (in thousands) in the United Kingdom, June 1959–June 1966

Net gains	*Net flows* (1)	*Net entrants* ((3) – (1)) (2)	*Employment change* (3)
Manufacturing	265.1	289.5	554.6
Construction	140.8	160.9	301.7
Other services	527.1	287.3	814.4
Utilities, Transportation and Communication	48.7	–81.8	–33.1
Total	981.7	655.9	1637.6
Net losses			
Agriculture, Forestry and Fishing	–195.1	19.3	–175.8
Mining and Quarrying	–139.5	–115.1	–254.6
Distribution and miscellaneous services	–647.1	1163.4	516.3
Total	–981.7	1067.6	85.9
Grand Total		1723.5	1723.5

Source: Tables 1 and 2 in R. D. Sleeper, 'Manpower Redeployment and the Selective Employment Tax,' *Bulletin of The Oxford University Institute of Economics and Statistics*, 1970. Other services includes Professional and Scientific Services, Public Administration and Insurance, Banking and Finance.

and distribution and miscellaneous services were net suppliers of labor to the three industries in the top half of the table. However, this service subsector, unlike agriculture, experienced a net increase in employment during the period.

Table 5.2 is particularly revealing since the data cover a period from the middle stages of a boom to the final stages of the succeeding boom, ending just before the imposition of the Selective Employment Tax.[19] The data suggest that the distribution and miscellaneous service sector acts as a funnel through which members of the labor force passed on their way to other industries. This is borne out by annual figures which indicate that net outflows increase during boom periods compared with periods of stagnation (although always remaining positive). The direction of these outflows is especially interesting and is illustrated in Table 5.3. Columns (1) and (2) indicate, respectively, the net flows of distribution and miscellaneous services into manufacturing. Column (3) shows the total net flows into manu-

[19] The Selective Employment Tax was selective in the sense that it fell on firms in the service sector but not in manufacturing. The period covered in Tables 5.2 and 5.3 came before the imposition of this tax, and therefore labor movements would not be distorted by this fiscal measure.

Table 5.3. Net flows (in thousands) to manufacturing from individual service industries in the United Kingdom

	Distribution (1)	*Miscellaneous services* (2)	*Net flows from all industries into manufacturing* (3)
1959–60	55.9	25.8	134.2
1960–61	55.2	3.7	60.5
1961–62	20.3	−11.0	−51.4
1962–63	20.3	−14.7	−50.1
1963–64	51.6	9.3	82.8
1964–65	53.8	7.6	53.0
1965–66	44.0	1.1	36.1
Total	301.1	21.8	265.1

Source: Sleeper, op. cit., Table 7.

facturing from all sectors, two of which are distribution and miscellaneous services. The difference between column (3) and the sum of columns (1) and (2) is net flows from all sectors other than distribution and miscellaneous services into manufacturing. From one boom to the next the net outflows from distribution alone were greater than the total net flows from all sectors into manufacturing. Table 5.3 also indicates that during the two booms, roughly 1959–61 and 1964–66, net flows from both service subsectors increased.

E. The Service Sector as an Alternative Source of Surplus Labor

1. Relative income elasticities and productivity growth

Tables 5.2 and 5.3 suggest that certain subsectors within the service sector served as a source of surplus labor supplying labor to manufacturing when demand picked up in the latter in a manner analogous to the behavior of the agricultural sector in other countries. This is supported for the United Kingdom by Department of Employment and Productivity data, which indicate that wages of manual workers in distribution and miscellaneous services remained between 75 and 80 per cent of wages of manual workers in manufacturing throughout the postwar period.[20] Thus, while employment in agriculture was less than one million and declining in the United Kingdom, employment in distribution was large and rising during the period from the late 1950s until 1966. These two low-wage groups accounted for over 20 per cent of the labor force by 1966 with the distribution sector alone accounting for about 12.5 per cent of the employed labor force in Britain.

[20] *Department of Employment Gazette*, various issues.

Sleeper's analysis suggests that, in the United Kingdom and other developed economies, pools of surplus labor may exist outside of agriculture which have been and can be tapped by industry and manufacturing. In such cases, labor markets in economies without large agricultural labor forces or large increases in the labor force may perform their allocative function in much the same way as they do in those economies with surplus labor in agriculture: demand picks up, vacancies rise in the high-wage sectors, and labor moves out of the low-paying jobs with no change in wage differentials.

However, there are likely to be limits to the amount of labor that can be drawn out of the service sector of the economy, suggesting that, if the demands by the high-wage sectors are sustained and very strong, the allocative features of economies with small agricultural sectors and low rates of growth of the labor force might change drastically. These limits are suggested by the necessary ancillary role played by many service workers (as already suggested in Sections D and E above) and by the behavior of productivity in the service sector, on the one hand, and the income elasticity of demand for services, on the other.

Income elasticities of demand for services tend to be relatively high, especially compared with agricultural products. The difficulties in accurately determining income elasticities of demand in the service sector are formidable, and this applies not only to the government subsector. However, a comprehensive study has indicated that, in the United States at least, estimates of income elasticities of demand are not overly sensitive to alternative assumptions about the behavior of 'prices' of services.[21] Thus, whether it is assumed that prices of services rise at the same rate as wages paid in service employment (the zero productivity growth assumption) or that they rise at the same rate as the prices of consumer goods, the estimated income elasticities are not significantly different, being of the order of magnitude of one. The net result in the United States, a country with relatively high per capita income, is that the outputs of the non-agricultural goods and the service sectors have tended to bear a more or less fixed relationship with one another.[22] This results most likely from an income elasticity of demand for services slightly greater than that for non-agricultural output, coupled with a relative rise in the price of services resulting in some substitution of goods for services.[23]

Table 2.7 gave sectoral rates of growth of productivity for several

[21] See V. Fuchs, *The Growing Importance of the Service Industries* (Occasional Paper No. 96), National Bureau of Economic Research, New York, 1965.

[22] ibid. The same result was found for Australia: see J. Dowie, 'The Service Ensemble,' in C. Forster (ed.), *Australian Economic Development in the Twentieth Century*, George Allen and Unwin, London, 1970.

[23] In his study, Haig found that the relative rise in the price of services served to reduce the difference between the rate of growth of employment in services and manufacturing by 0.7 per cent. See B. Haig, 'An Analysis of Changes in Distribution of Employment between the Manufacturing and Service Industries 1960–70,' *Review of Economic and Statistics*, February 1975.

of the OECD countries. Unlike agriculture, where the rates of growth of labor productivity were above the average for both the economy and industry, rates of growth of productivity in services were definitely below average. Taking the service sector as a whole, then, the general picture is one of low rates of growth of labor productivity together with relatively high income (or growth) elasticities of demand. This is to be contrasted with the rapid rates of growth of productivity in agriculture and low income (and growth) elasticities of demand for agricultural output.

2. Induced productivity growth in the service sector

However, rates of growth of productivity in services detailed in Table 2.7 varied considerably from one country to another. Partly this difference could be due to induced productivity growth in countries where demand for surplus labor was strong and sustained. This raises the question of whether or not sustained and strong demands for labor in some country might induce such a rapid increase in productivity in the service sector that a great deal of labor could be released from that sector. Unfortunately, no definite answer can be given to this question but recent research at least indicates many of the underlying issues.

In Chapter IV, it was pointed out that many models of the dual economy stress the existence of disguised unemployment in agriculture in countries about to begin their industrialization process. This allows an increase in total output in the agricultural sector even as labor is drawn out of agriculture, i.e. an increase in labor productivity without any reorganization of agriculture production. However, during the process of industrialization, including that experienced by many OECD countries in the postwar period, a dramatic reorganization of agriculture accompanied the movement of labor out of agriculture.[24] This included the consolidation of holdings into larger units, an increase in the capital intensity of production and widespread introduction of fertilizers, hybrid seeds, etc. Again, an important result was an increase in labor productivity, in this case accompanied by a reorganization of production.

Similar sources of productivity growth are supposedly available in the service sector. Thus, it has been suggested that something akin to disguised unemployment exists in the service sector. This arises from the existence in the distribution subsector of the service sector of opportunities to engage in 'work-sharing,' i.e. the establishment of competing units which merely divide a given volume of business.[25] The general notion here is that at any point in time there exists a certain volume of transactions that must be performed depending, say, on the level of aggregate economic activity. How-

[24] See *Agriculture in Economic Growth* op. cit.

[25] Kaldor, *Strategic Factors*, op. cit., pp. 37–44. The examples of this study tend to be limited to self-employed shopkeepers, but the argument is easily generalized to those working in large business units, often on commission.

ever, it is alleged that this same level of aggregate transactions could just as efficiently be performed by a smaller amount of labor since much of the existing labor force is underemployed, waiting for customers between transactions and the like. Thus removing part of this labor force will not lead to a decrease in the total amount of transactions performed but only to an increase in the amount of transactions performed per worker or manhour. Further, the amount of service supplied per transactions need not fall either, since 'idle capacity' existed before the transfer.

The possibility of this type of response by the service sector when the demand for labor increases elsewhere has been given some support by the first report of Reddaway *et al.* on the distributive sector in Britain.[26] Reddaway found that, following the imposition of the Selective Employment Tax in 1966 and up through 1968 (basically, a tax on workers employed outside of manufacturing), productivity increased substantially in the distributive sector. However, there is evidence that this kind of measured growth in productivity in the private subsectors of the service sector arises either from a decline in the amount of service performed per unit of factor input or from an induced reorganization of the distributive sector. For example, Schwartzman, in his study of retailing in the United States, found that productivity growth in that sector was largely due to (1) an increase in the size of the average transaction per man hour in constant dollars and (2) a decline in the quantity of service supplies with each transaction.[27] The former he attributed to a growth in incomes (and not the elimination of idle capacity), while the latter was allegedly induced by the rising relative price of services.

Both of these responses act to release labor from services should demand rise elsewhere, but the released labor is conditional upon some reorganization of (service) production and not on the existence of idle capacity or zero marginal productivities of those employed. The same can be said for Fuch's study of beauty parlors in the United States, which indicated relatively high rates of growth of productivity resulting from an increase in the size of the transactions performed without a decline in the quantity of services performed per transaction. In this case, technical improvements were important. In contrast, productivity growth in a declining sector, haircutting for men, was very small.[28] More recently it has been suggested that, in the public subsectors of the service sector at least, 'idle capacity' has become more widespread with the expansion of employment, especially at the local government level.[29] Thus, given a commitment to full employment and a rate of

[26] W. B. Reddaway *et al.*, *Effect of the Selective Employment Tax First Report: The Distributive Trades*, Her Majesty's Stationery Office, London, 1970.

[27] See D. Schwartzman, 'The Growth of Sales Per Man-Hour in Retail Trade, 1929–1963,' in V. Fuchs (ed.), *Production and Productivity in the Service Industries*, National Bureau of the Economic Research, New York, 1969.

[28] V. Fuchs, *The Service Economy*, National Bureau of Economic Research, New York, 1968, Chapter 5.

[29] R. Bacon and W. Eltis, *Britain's Economic Problem: Too Few Producers*, Macmillan, London, 1976.

growth of productivity that exceeds the rate of growth of output in those sectors producing a marketable output (e.g. manufacturing), rapid expansion of employment in the public sector becomes a distinct possibility. While it is only suggested that the quality of services has not expanded at the same rate as employment, the possibility of substantial disguised unemployment in the public sectors cannot be ruled out.[30]

3. Summary

Unfortunately, a review of the different studies of productivity growth in the service sector allows little more than an understanding of the results pointed out in Table 2.7; i.e., productivity growth in the service sector was not zero. There is no obvious way of knowing if differences across countries in the rate of growth of productivity in this sector can in any way be attributed to differences in the strength of demand for surplus labor in the service sector. What is suggested is that, without a reorganization in the production of a particular service, workers currently employed in that service subsector are imperfect substitutes for workers in agriculture. Thus, the behavior of the market economies during the postwar period suggests that the service sector may act as a funnel through which labor often stops before finding employment in the high-wage manufacturing and industrial sectors. However, there are basic differences based on consumer demand as well as productivity patterns that do not allow equal numbers in the service and agricultural sectors to be treated as equal numbers for potential employment in manufacturing.

This was clearly seen in studies summarized in Section D above. Whether discussing the response of the labor force to an increase in demand that pushes the economy closer to full employment or dealing with the behavior of an economy from one boom to the next, an increase in employment in manufacturing and industry was accompanied by a sizeable expansion in employment in the service industry, the alleged source of surplus labor. In contrast, agricultural employment declined absolutely in every developed market economy throughout the period. To be sure, Table 11.1 indicates that, in the three fastest growing economies (in terms of growth of total and manufacturing output), there was a tendency to 'economize' on the use of labor in the service sector. Thus, in the fastest growing economy, Japan, the rate of growth of employment in manufacturing exceeded the growth of employment in 'commerce' (which includes banking services and finance as well as retail and wholesale trade) and also in 'other services' (which includes public employment). In Germany and Italy, the growth of manufacturing employment exceeded that in other services but not growth of employment in the commerce sector. However, these three examples were countries with large agricultural labor forces and relatively rapid rates of growth of supply of labor available for non-agricultural employment. As

[30]ibid., p. 16.

a result, the economizing need not have reflected any sizeable reorganization of these service subsectors. The test case of whether demand pressures could have, in fact, induced such a radical reorganization of the service sector as to allow employment in manufacturing to expand relative to total employment was Britain. Unfortunately, as Section G makes clear, demand pressures were never strong or sustained enough in Britain to test the hypothesis.

F. Surplus Labor Abroad

1. An extension of the dual model

So far the analysis indicates that economies with a slow rate of growth of the indigenous labor force and a small agricultural labor force may be limited in any attempt to rapidly and extensively expand employment in manufacturing and industry. However, what has been missing in the analysis so far is the possibility of expanding the labor force in the high-wage, high-productivity sectors by importing labor.

Table 2.9 indicated quite clearly how important a role migration played in the postwar growth of population of several of the OECD coun-

Table 5.4. Trends of immigration (+) and emigration (−) in European countries, 1950–72 (net migration in thousands)

Country	*Annual average 1950–54*	*Annual average 1955–59*	*Annual average 1960–64*	*Annual average 1965–69*	*Annual average 1970–72*
Belgium	+3.2	+10.6	+19.2	+12.2	+14.0
France	+27.8	+156.0	+316.0	+115.4	+145.0
Germany (FR)	+221.4	+297.2	+312.6	+229.8	+445.7
Luxembourg	+0.9	+0.6	+2.1	+0.9	+3.1
Netherlands	−20.6	−3.2	+6.4	+10.6	+28.0
Sweden	+9.2	+9.8	+14.0	+25.6	+13.3
Switzerland	+22.8	+32.0	+56.4	+17.0	+8.7
United Kingdom[c]	−33.6	−1.3[a]	+27.0	−72.2	−53.0
Greece	−13.8	−25.0	−44.2	−23.8	−11.0
Ireland	−34.8	−44.4	−22.2	−15.2	−2.3
Italy	−100.8	−127.4	−113.2	−123.8	−1.7
Portugal	−64.2	−68.0	−60.2	−130.2	−106.0
Spain	−51.8	−104.0	−80.6	−42.2	−14.6
Turkey	n.a.	n.a.	+26.9[b]	n.a.	n.a.
Yugoslavia	n.a.	n.a.	+34.0[b]	n.a.	n.a.

[a] 1956–59 [b] From *Migrants in Europe* [c] The accuracy of the UK data has been questioned.

Sources: 1950–54: Arnold Rose, *Migrants in Europe*, University of Minnesota Press, Minneapolis, 1969, Tables 2 and 3; 1955–72: *Labour Force Statistics, 1960–1971, 1961–1972*, OECD, Paris.

Table 5.5. Net immigration as a percentage of population increase

	1950–54	*1955–59*	*1960–64*	*1965–69*	*1970–72*	*1950–72*
	%	%	%	%	%	%
Belgium	7	18	34	27	47	25
France	9	32	48	30	31	33
Germany	−48	25	49	63	83	47
Luxembourg	40	77	65	60	84	66
Netherlands	−16	−2	4	7	19	3
Sweden	19	21	31	44	34	30
Switzerland	39	49	52	24	18	39

Source: Table 5.4 and *Monthly Bulletin of Statistics*, United Nations, New York, various issues.

tries. Given the characteristics of the migrants, foreign migration can be assumed to have played an even bigger role in influencing the rate of growth of the labor force. Table 5.4 indicates the orders of magnitude involved. The top half of the table shows the annual average flow of immigrants for various periods into several of the developed market economies while the bottom half gives figures for emigration from some of the chief supplying countries. The importance of immigration in population growth is shown in Table 5.5, where the percentage of population increase attributed to immigration is shown for the same countries. The United Kingdom is omitted because of the questionable nature of the data in Table 5.4 for that country.

The employment of migrant workers extended across a wide range of industries, although differences in concentration were found. For example, Castles and Kosack found that in France male migrants were employed heavily in four industries – building and public works, engineering, agriculture and commerce – while female migrant workers tended to be concentrated in domestic service, personal services and commerce. In Switzerland the building and engineering industries were important sources of employment (as in France), as were hotels and catering, but agriculture was less important. In Germany male immigrants tended to be concentrated in the same industries as in Switzerland and France while women were used much more heavily in manufacturing than in the other two countries. Only in the United Kingdom was there found to be a lack of extreme concentration of immigrant employment.[31]

During the early part of the postwar period, migrants were overwhelmingly young, male, unaccompanied by dependents, from rural back-

[31] S. Castles and G. Kosack, *Immigrant Workers and Class Structure in Western Europe*, Oxford University Press, London, 1973, Chapter III.

grounds and embodying little in the way of skills.[32] As time went on, the characteristics of the immigrants altered. As more and more workers migrated to the more developed economies, the percentage of males migrating declined while the proportion of married migrants rose, which meant that participation rates of all immigrants fell. Skill levels, already low, tended to decline over time while the share of migrants coming from agricultural areas rose.[33]

One can reasonably assume that much if not most of this migration was the response of workers in countries with low-wage levels to job openings in more affluent countries. Indeed, the similarity of the expansion of foreign labor in the receiving countries during the postwar period to the movement of labor out of agriculture was so striking that Kindleberger viewed his study as a formulation of a more general version of the Lewis model of the dual economy.[34] To put it somewhat differently, Kindleberger and others have found it useful to view the large-scale foreign migration into many of the OECD countries in the postwar period as a long-run counterpart to studies such as those of Okun and Sleeper. While the latter attempt to draw out the response of labor supply to increase in aggregate demand in the short run by focusing on increased participation rates and induced flows between sectors, the former focuses on an induced, sustained flow of new entrants to the non-agricultural labor force just as in the dual model of Chapter IV.

It was the desire of a large number of OECD economies to expand industrial and manufacturing production at a sustained rate greater than that allowed by the combined rate of growth of the indigenous labor force and productivity that led to a large-scale and sustained international migration in the postwar period. Viewed in terms of 'push' and 'pull' forces, the prevalence of overpopulation, low wages and poor working conditions in the countries of emigration worked together with such factors as high wages, ample job opportunities and shortages of indigenous labor in the countries of immigration to provide all the incentives necessary to realize the widespread foreign migration of the postwar period. While many of the push factors were present in earlier times (such as the conditions in nineteenth- and twentieth-century Europe that lead to mass migration to the New World), what was different in the postwar period was the active encouragement and active recruitment of foreign workers by government and private businesses. A notable exception in this move was Britain, where recruitment of foreign labor was never important after the early 1950s.[35]

[32] ibid., pp. 45–56.

[33] See, for example, S. Paine, *Exporting Workers, the Turkish Case*, Cambridge University Press, 1974, Table 8.

[34] Kindleberger, op. cit.

[35] See Paine, op. cit., p. 10 and Castles and Kosack, op. cit., p. 30.

2. Upgrading the indigenous labor force

The situation in many countries has been well described by Böhning.[36] Starting with a situation of relatively full employment, an increase in aggregate demand leads initially to the kinds of movements, adjustments and reallocations described in Sections C and D. However, if demand pressures persist and intensify, the upgrading of labor will be accompanied increasingly by shortages of labor in particular sectors of the economy. These sectors need not be the same in every country but the nature of the jobs is very similar; they are low-paying 'socially undesirable' jobs or, to use the earlier terminology, jobs in the secondary labor market. However, Böhning stresses the fact that, although these labor shortages may occur in particular industries or occupations, they really signify a general shortage of labor to which there are four possible policy responses. First, a country may either undertake a program that would radically alter the relative wage structure of the economy, allowing workers in socially undesirable jobs to be paid higher relative wages.[37] Second, it could relax its full-employment goal. Third, it could fill the socially undesirable jobs with foreign workers hired on a temporary basis. Finally, it could encourage permanent settlement by foreign workers and their families.

For various reasons, the third option is usually chosen.[38] Once this happens a 'self-feeding' process of migration from certain labor-surplus countries to countries of labor shortages sets in which has two aspects. First, the arrival of foreign workers facilitates and accelerates the bumping-up of indigenous labor from whatever undesirable jobs they previously had to the more desirable jobs in the economy. Thus, the country of immigration becomes even more dependent on foreign sources of labor. Secondly, a chain reaction is set off which leads to the migratory process itself following conceptually distinct phases.

While the initial cause of the decision to import foreign workers may have been specific shortages in specific sectors of the economy, continued expansion of aggregate demand (in excess of what can be satisfied by the existing labor force) leads to the expansion of foreign employment in all sectors. But a very definite social job structure develops and intensifies throughout the process as local workers are continuously upgraded to the more desirable jobs. This process has very definite affinities with the earlier discussions of upgrading labor. However, while, for example, Okun's analysis suggests that the upgrading of labor in response to demand pressures is from sectors of low income elasticity to high, the process that took place in OECD coun-

[36] W. Böhning, *The Migration of Workers in the United Kingdom and the European Community*, Oxford University Press, London, 1972 and W. Böhning and D. Maillat, *The Effects of the Employment of Foreign Workers*, OECD, Paris, 1974.

[37] This policy response is the one usually advocated by dual labor market theorists.

[38] These choices are relevant for countries experiencing strong demands for labor. As a result Britain did not chose any of the four options.

tries is better described in terms of expansion of jobs in the three kinds of employment situations found in secondary labor markets.[39] This is seen most clearly in the creation of secondary dead-end jobs which are attached to internal labor markets where the remaining jobs – those held by local labor – have the characteristics of jobs in primary labor markets.[40] The fact that such secondary jobs attached to primary labor markets are created and expanded in number is attributed by Böhning to (1) the complementarity of jobs whereby different grades of labor and jobs must be used simultaneously if output is to be obtained, and (2) the ability of employers, especially in manufacturing, to redesign the production system in such a way that skilled jobs are subdivided into a limited number of simple tasks that require little training and ability.

Because of these two factors, a policy of sustained importation of foreign labor tends to have a scaling effect when the economy is broken down by industry. Foreign workers will be employed in high-paying as well as low-paying industries. However, when jobs are broken down according to socio-economic status, i.e. wage-earner vs. salary-earner or skilled vs. unskilled, the process of importing foreign labor results in a heavy concentration of foreigners in low-paying, unsatisfactory jobs. In this respect foreigners resemble the workers in secondary labor markets described earlier. Since the jobs were originally thought to be temporary, and since there are language or other cultural barriers to advancement, jobs of foreigners are essentially dead-end jobs. They are also low-paying jobs in comparison to those going to local workers (but not necessarily compared with workers who remained in the country of emigration); they need little human capital, and foreign workers taking these jobs often use fewer skills than in the work they did previously in the home country. However, the foreign workers differ in several respects from the workers in the secondary labor markets of the dual labor market theorists. The former are better disciplined, with fewer teenagers in their number, and their turnover is to a large extent determined by their employers' decision to renew or not to renew their contracts.[41] But most important of all, they provide a means for rapidly expanding employment in manufacturing in many countries when demand for labor is strong and sustained.

G. Did Labor Supply Adjust to Demand?

1. Did British manufacturers encounter labor shortages?

The data just cited indicate what an important role imported labor played in

[39] See p. 74.

[40] Böhning and Maillat, op. cit., argue that if shortages of labor persist long enough eventually even some of the more desirous jobs will be filled by migrants.

[41] In addition, it has been argued that employment of migrant workers gives employers a flexibility that they would not have if they were forced to employ local workers. See G. Schmid, 'Foreign Workers and Labor Market Flexibility,' *Journal of Common Market Studies*, March 1971.

the growth of the labor force and population in most of the OECD countries. One exception to this appeared to be Britain. In general, the migration data for the United Kingdom are bad and it is, therefore, difficult to make comparisons over an extended period of time. However, census data for the years 1961 and 1966, which are more reliable, do allow a comparison between the United Kingdom and other countries for a limited period of time. For example, during this period total employment of foreign workers in the United Kingdom increased by 0.394 million. During this same period the number of employed foreign workers in Germany, a country with a labor force similar in size to Britain's, increased by 0.707 million.[42] Since immigration (especially of workers) from the new Commonwealth countries was severely curtailed after 1962, it could be argued that a large part of the difference in employment patterns between Germany and Britain could be traced to restrictions on the latter's ability to import labor. These restrictions would be given added force by the strong feelings against importing foreign labor within the British labor movement.[43] In addition, immigration from Ireland, which was not restricted, declined as the Irish economy boomed during the 1960s. All of this further strengthens the case of those who believed that Britain suffered from labor shortages in the sense that a strong demand for labor by manufacturing could not be satisfied.

However, it was mentioned earlier that an argument has been made that the British economy (and possibly other economies experiencing a slow rate of growth of employment in manufacturing) did not expand its labor force in manufacturing rapidly because the demand for labor by manufacturers was just not there.[44] Essentially, what is involved here is an identification problem, since the employment data do not allow the investigator to determine whether the small growth of employment in manufacturing in Britain was due to a shortage of labor supply, a lack of strong demand for labor or both. One obvious solution to this problem would be the construction and estimation of the parameters of a simultaneous equation model. This approach had to be ruled out, if for no other reason than the lack of data for estimating such a model. The 'solution' here is to tackle the problem indirectly.

Table 5.6 shows changes in total employment and sector employment in five of the large OECD economies between peaks in economic activity in each of these countries. The periods have been chosen to coincide as closely as possible to the first half of the 1960s to facilitate comparison with data cited earlier for inter-industry labor and migration flows. It is of interest to note that $(\Delta E - \Delta E_a)$, which was used earlier to measure the flow of labor available to the non-agricultural sectors of the economy, is fairly

[42] The German data are taken from Böhning, op. cit., p. 134, while the British data are taken from K. Jones and A. Smith, *The Economic Impact of Commonwealth Immigration*, Cambridge University Press, 1970, Appendix Tables 2.1 and 2.2.

[43] See Castles and Kosack, op. cit., Chapter IV.

[44] See reference in fn. 4, this chapter.

similar for three of the five economies – Italy, France and the United Kingdom. What differs dramatically is the use made of this labor in the United Kingdom and the other two as well as in Germany and Japan. And even if Italy and Japan are treated as special cases because of low per capita incomes, the difference between the United Kingdom and France and Germany is still quite striking. The United Kingdom had more labor to allocate to industry and manufacturing than Germany and only slightly less than France, yet the propensity to employ labor in these high-wage, high-productivity sectors was substantially lower than in France and Germany as revealed in columns (6) and (7).[45] For example, for every 100 workers available to the non-agricultural sectors of the economy, 33, 28 and 20 were allocated to manufacturing in Germany, France and the United Kingdom, respectively. In other words, even if it is assumed that the small increase in imported labor into the United Kingdom relative to Germany during this period was due to legal or political restrictions in the former, it still remains true that Britain chose to employ these and other additions to the labor force much more predominantly in the low-wage, low-productivity service sector.

Table 5.2 showed over a slightly longer period than that covered by Table 5.6, that while 0.647 million workers left distribution and miscellaneous services, over a million entered this sector in Britain, allowing employment to increase by over 0.5 million. Of the 0.647 million who left,

Table 5.6. Changes in employment and sector flows between cyclical peaks (in thousands)

	ΔE (1)	ΔE_a (2)	$\Delta E - \Delta E_a$ (3)	ΔE_{in} (4)	ΔE_m (5)	(4) ÷ (3) (6)	(5) ÷ (3) (7)
						%	%
Italy (1959–63)	−508	−1556	1048	817	553	78	53
Germany (1960–65)	180	−573	753	339	247	45	33
France (1960–64)	727	−533	1260	595	353	47	28
UK (1960–65)	1070	−159	1229	293	251	24	20
Japan (1961–64)	1570	−1540	3110	1460	1180	47	38

ΔE, ΔE_a, ΔE_{in} and ΔE_m represent the change in total civilian employment, agricultural employment, employment in industry (i.e. manufacturing, mining, construction and public utilities) and employment in manufacturing, respectively.

Cyclical peaks were those used by Cripps and Tarling, op. cit.

Source: *Labour Force Statistics, 1956–66, 1957–68* and *1961–72.*

[45] None of these differences can be attributed to differences in the sex or age composition of the respective populations. Britain had a slightly small percentage of its population in the 20–64 age bracket than Germany but a higher percentage than France. Moreover, the sex composition of the German population (in 1965) indicated a much higher percentage of women than did that of Britain or France. See *Economic Survey of Europe, 1968*, United Nations, New York, 1969, Tables 20 and 21.

Table 5.3 indicated that 0.322 and 0.196 million moved into manufacturing employment during the periods 1959–60 to 1965–66 and 1960–61 to 1964–65, respectively. The fact that so many more workers entered these service sub-sectors than left for manufacturing cannot be attributed to higher relative earnings in the former. As already stressed, Department of Employment and Productivity data indicate that wages of manual workers in distribution and miscellaneous services remained between 75 and 80 per cent of wages of manual workers in manufacturing throughout the postwar period.[46] Again, this suggests that the demand for labor in manufacturing was just not there.

There are two other studies worth citing in this regard. Mention has already been made of Bacon and Eltis's finding of a rapid expansion of public employment in Britain, an expansion that was far more rapid than that experienced in other comparable economies.[47] The authors attribute this difference to lack of demand for labor in manufacturing and other sectors producing marketable output. There is also Wolfe's study of employment and vacancy patterns in Britain from the early 1960s to the mid-1960s. Wolfe found that vacancy–unemployment patterns were not significantly different between the high-paying sectors of manufacturing and the low-wage sectors of the service group. Unemployment fell and vacancies rose as a percentage of employment for both groups during this period, but not in any noticeably different way.[48] This suggests that, while demand for labor in manufacturing rose during this boom, this measure of the 'state of the labor market' did not indicate undue shortages of labor for manufacturers.

None of this is conclusive, to be sure, but in the absence of a more direct means of getting at the answer, the conclusions seem fairly straightforward. From the early part of the postwar period until the 1970s Britain differed from most of the other developed economies in two important ways. First, the percentages and absolute numbers of the total labor force engaged in agriculture were small. Second, Britain did not import foreign workers on a large scale. Having said all this, the conclusion that Britain suffered from some sort of labor supply constraint which led to a small increase in employment in manufacturing and industry is not warranted. The rate of growth of the labor force, the labor force available for non-agricultural employment and the labor force in manufacturing were all small by comparison with most other countries, taking the postwar period as a whole. But the slowness of the rate of growth of employment in manufacturing (and very likely the other two) must be attributed to a lack of a strong demand for labor by the high-wage sectors.

[46] *Department of Employment and Productivity Gazette*, various issues.

[47] Bacon and Eltis, op. cit.

[48] Wolfe, op. cit. During this same period, Department of Employment and Productivity data on basic weekly wages for manual workers in manufacturing and the distributive trades show no trend in the wage differential between these two sectors between years of cyclical peaks in economic activity.

2. A cross-section–time series comparison of wage differentials

Additional insights into the issue of labor shortages, not only for Britain but for various other market economies, can be obtained by an analysis of the industrial wage structures of the different economies over time. Section D of Chapter IV stressed that, when industries within a country are ranked by average levels of earnings, there was a great deal of stability in the inter-industry wage structure in this sense in spite of widespread reallocations of labor across industries. But it was pointed out in Section E of Chapter IV that studies have shown that, in periods of tight and tightening labor markets, industries on the lower end of the wage distribution have to raise wages relative to other industries to increase employment or merely maintain existing levels. The result has been that the dispersion of wages has been found to narrow rather than widen during periods of strong demand for labor.[49]

In general, the narrowing of both the relative and absolute dispersion of wages in response to strong demand pressures is the result of smaller percentage increases in wages in the high-wage industries.[50] Strong sustained demand pressures lead to a rapid expansion of employment in the high-wage sectors as employers in the latter merely advertise additional vacancies and increase employment without raising relative wages. Employers in the low-wage industries respond by raising relative wages in order to retain workers or slow down their rate of departure. As a result, investigators have found it useful to use movements in some measure of the dispersion of industrial wages around the mean as a measure of the tightness or ease of labor markets.[51]

Table 5.7 gives mean earnings and the absolute and relative dispersions of earnings in manufacturing for eight market economies. The years selected for each country are cyclical peak years in order to remove as much as possible any cyclical influence on measures of wage differentials.[52] As is apparent, absolute differentials widened from one peak to the next in every country. This is true for Austria and the United Kingdom, two countries with a low rate on increase of labor available for non-agricultural employment as indicated in Table 5.1 above. Unfortunately, the data for Belgium are not helpful in this regard since the coverage changes in 1970. Using

[49] Okun, 'Upward Mobility,' op. cit.

[50] See Papola and Bharadwaj, op. cit.

[51] See Böhning and Maillat, op. cit., pp. 159–60; Minami, op. cit., p. 77; M. Reder, 'The Theory of Occupational Wage Differentials,' *American Economic Review*, December 1955; and M. Wachter, 'Cyclical Variations in the Inter-Industry Wage Structure,' *American Economic Review*, March 1970.

[52] See Cripps and Tarling, op. cit. The Netherlands was excluded because the industries covered in the ILO compilations changed during the period reviewed. Italy was excluded because the number of industries in manufacturing covered changed during the period so as to bias the measures of dispersion upward. The data used in Table 5.7 are average earnings per worker and their dispersion. The standard deviation and the coefficient of variation are used as the measures of absolute and relative dispersions, respectively. The data in Table 5.7 refer to earnings that include bonuses, overtime, etc. as well as standard wages. Nevertheless, the terms earnings and wages are used interchangeable in the text.

Table 5.7. Mean earnings and absolute and relative dispersions of wage structures in the OECD countries at cyclical peaks

	Mean earnings	*Absolute dispersion*	*Relative disperson*		*Mean earnings*	*Absolute dispersion*	*Relative dispersion*
France				Japan			
1957	2.00	0.288	0.144	1957	18 888	5347	0.283
1960	2.65	0.460	0.174	1961	24 778	7992	0.323
1964	3.49	0.571	0.164	1964	33 340	7745	0.232
1969	5.33	0.969	0.182	1969	60 171	15 725	0.261
1973	8.44	1.215	0.143	1973	115 207	22 924	0.199
Germany[a]				United Kingdom[b]			
1956	2.05	0.232	0.113	1955	22.76	1.59	0.070
1961	3.08	0.287	0.093	1960	30.32	2.55	0.084
1965	4.35	0.347	0.080	1965	41.87	3.31	0.079
1970	5.88	0.797	0.135	1969	54.32	4.31	0.079
1973	8.00	1.083	0.135	1973	90.06	8.08	0.090
Austria				United States			
1957	1751	0.229	0.131	1956	1.92	0.321	0.167
1966	3406	0.538	0.158	1966	2.67	0.475	0.178
1970	4555	0.808	0.177	1969	3.14	0.521	0.166
1973	6453	1.180	0.183	1973	4.01	0.723	0.180
Belgium[c]				Canada			
1957	215.8	20.83	0.097	1956	1.57	0.203	0.129
1964	243.4	23.82	0.098	1966	2.19	0.380	0.174
1970	65.9	12.25	0.186	1969	2.83	0.540	0.190
1973	98.7	19.13	0.194	1973	3.91	0.771	0.197

Mean earnings and absolute dispersions are in local currency units and relative dispersions in percentage terms.
[a]Data for males only [b]All data for male, full time, adult, manual workers
[c]Data for 1957 and 1964 are for males only
Data for 1970 and 1973 includes male and female workers
Source: *Yearbook of Labour Statistics*, ILO, Geneva, various issues.

movements in the absolute dispersion of wages as an indicator of labor market pressures gives no evidence that from one boom to the next any of these countries suffered from shortages.[53]

The behavior of relative wage differentials is more mixed. The relative dispersion of wages widens for Austria, Canada, Germany, the United Kingdom and the United States, if the initial peak is compared with the final peak year. The relative dispersion narrows for Japan while no noticeable trend is apparent for France. However, before it is concluded that this is

[53]Table 4.1 indicated that in only two countries was there a substantial narrowing of the differential earnings in agriculture and the rest of the economy.

evidence of labor shortages in Japan, it should be recalled that there is evidence that the process of industrialization itself (i.e. rising per capita incomes) has been found to result in the narrowing of relative wage differentials.[54] All in all, then, when using changes in the dispersions (absolute and relative) of wages to indicate changes in labor market pressures, the evidence reveals no pronounced shortages of labor.

H. Conclusions

The primary task of this chapter has been to determine whether differences in employment patterns in the postwar period were primarily the result of demand or supply forces. Obviously, to the extent that such patterns are the result of a passive response of labor supply to demand pressures from the manufacturing sector, to that extent is the relevance of the dual model enhanced. A large ratio of agricultural employment to total employment has usually been accepted as sufficient evidence that the supply of labor to manufacturing was highly elastic. The same can be said in those situations where foreign labor was imported on a large scale and growth of the indigenous population and labor force were rapid. The use of figures for the rate of growth of the supply of labor available for non-agricultural employment as seen in Table 5.1 above was designed to capture these views.

However, data in Table 5.1 suggested that three and possibly four countries for which comparable data are available (the United Kingdom, Austria, Belgium and the Netherlands) might have suffered from shortages of labor. And, indeed, Table 4.3 indicated that in only one of these four countries (Austria) did employment in manufacturing expand more rapidly than total employment. Section G above presented varied sorts of evidence to indicate that, in Austria and the United Kingdom, at least, employment patterns were not strongly influenced by the operation of supply constraints. The case of the Netherlands and Belgium was not clear, because of data problems. However, in Section C of Chapter IV various case studies were cited supporting the view that, whatever labor shortages there were in the postwar period, at the economy level they were neither pronounced nor prolonged. Some regression results in Chapter VIII point to a similar conclusion.

The analysis henceforth will assume with good reason that for all practical purposes employment patterns were demand-determined in the various market economies in the postwar period. It is undoubtedly true that the supply of labor available for manufacturing was more elastic in some countries than others. But the evidence, however limited, consistently suggested that, when entrepreneurs in the manufacturing sectors of the different economies wanted labor, they found it one way or another. If not enough was available in the agricultural sector, then additional amounts were found

[54] See Papola and Bharadwaj, op. cit.

by allocating a high proportion of, say, school-leavers or members of the secondary labor force to manufacturing and economizing on what was allocated to the different service subsectors. And if this wasn't sufficient, vacancies were advertised abroad, initially in those countries adjacent to the hiring countries. And if there was not enough labor available in, say, Italy, German and Swiss firms went looking in Greece or Turkey.

What took place in the postwar period up to the early 1970s was a situation in which the developed capitalist economies were uninhibited in their growth and transformation process by any serious or prolonged supply of labor constraint. The patterns of employment shown in Table 4.3 were the result. Why the relative strengths of demand for labor by the high-wage sectors varied so much across countries is taken up in Chapter VI.

Chapter VI The Growth of Manufacturing Output

A. Introduction

In Chapter V it was argued that employment patterns in the postwar period reflected a rather passive response of labor supply to the relative strengths of demand for labor by the different subsectors. The rate of growth of employment in manufacturing was relatively high in Japan, Italy, Germany and France, for example, because the rate of growth of demand for labor in manufacturing was high. Conversely, it was low in the United Kingdom and the United States because there did not exist a strong demand for labor by manufacturers. The main task of this chapter is to try and account for these differences in demand for labor in manufacturing between countries. This amounts to an explanation of the differences in the demand for manufacturing output across countries since the demand for labor in manufacturing is simply a derived demand stemming from the relative strengths of demand for manufacturing output.

Section B provides a brief description of some studies of 'patterns of industrialization.' These comparative studies are helpful in the present context because of their concern with determining the forces influencing the development of the manufacturing sector. Sections C–E discuss the impact of the international diffusion of technology on growth of the manufacturing sector. Section C is preliminary in nature, the main concern being to define terms and give background material; Section D discusses the determinants of technological progress in a closed economy; while Section E outlines the manner in which a technology gap and the resulting diffusion of technology aid a country that can borrow technology. In Section F the intra-country rate of diffusion of a technology is taken up. Section G summarizes the model developed to explain rates of growth of manufacturing output, a model that is later tested in Chapter VIII. Section H is a summary of the findings.

While viewed as an extension of the model of the dual economy developed in Chapters IV and V, Chapter VI marks a change in emphasis from these earlier chapters in two senses. First, the earlier chapters focused on the labor input and the movements of labor in the growth process. In Chapter VI more attention is given to capital formation and its role in growth. Second,

Chapter VI begins a phase of the analysis where more emphasis is given to the changing patterns of output than to labor inputs as an economy grows.

B. Patterns of Industrialization

1. Fixed-growth elasticities

The study of the changing patterns of output as a country industrializes has been treated by the economics profession in a somewhat ambivalent way. On the one hand, this branch of economics has been treated with the utmost respect and attention by economists interested in applied problems and by government officials looking for clues in formulating successful export and industrialization policies. On the other hand, the results of the research in this area have been virtually ignored by modern growth theorists who have not been able to fit them into a balanced growth framework. However, work of this sort is especially useful here since an integral and important part of the studies of patterns of industrialization has been an attempt to explain the development of the manufacturing sector. One of the earliest studies, that by Colin Clark, highlighted the shift of production and employment from agriculture to industry, manufacturing and the tertiary (service) sectors both absolutely and relatively as per capita income rose during the early stages of industrialization.[1] Further industrialization and greater affluence was seen by Clark to result in an expanded role of the tertiary sector, at least in terms of employment, compared with both industry and agriculture. Since manufacturing was such a large part of the industrial sector this view suggested that one determinant of manufacturing output and its growth was the level of per capita income.

One explanation of the similarity in patterns of production as industrialization proceeded was the rather general notion that consumers in different countries have 'similar tastes.'[2] This similarity of tastes argument seems most persuasive when attempting to explain the consumption of manufacturing output as distinct from the production of manufacturing. For example, a country heavily endowed with resources that are especially suitable for agricultural production or the development of extractive industries might be expected to be highly specialized in the production of agricultural or extractive products at every level of per capita incomes because specialization followed by trade may well raise incomes compared with a greater diversification of production. At the same time, consumption patterns might very well resemble countries at the same level of per capita income who specialize in the production of manufacturing goods.

Nevertheless, studies by economists of patterns of industrialization stress the similarities in the composition of production for similar income levels

[1] Clark, op. cit.

[2] See, for example, S. Linder, *An Essay on Trade and Transformation*, Almqvist and Wiksell, Stockholm, 1961.

which suggests that, not only are patterns of consumption similar for countries with similar levels of per capita income, but patterns of imports and exports are as well. Chenery and Maizels, in attempting to account for these similarities in production patterns across countries at similar income levels, argued that the supply factors must also have been at work, since similarities in tastes were not strong enough to account for the results.[3] In Chenery's study, the impact of supply on production patterns was found through (1) the correlation of per capita income and the physical capital–labor and human capital–labor ratios and the influence of these, in turn, on patterns of trade, and (2) the economies of scale.

Theories of this sort are tested using either cross-section or time series data and specifying equations of the following sort (for production and imports);

$$\log q_i = \log a_{i0} + a_{i1} \log q + a_{i2} \log P \tag{1}$$

and

$$\log M_i = \log b_{i0} + b_{i1} \log q + b_{i2} \log P \tag{2}$$

where q_i and M_i are per capita value added in production and imports of the ith good, respectively, and q and P are per capita income and size of the population of a country, respectively.[4] The coefficients a_{i1} and b_{i1} are usually interpreted as 'growth' rather than 'income' elasticities since their size can be influenced by factor proportions of a country and relative price changes as well as consumer incomes. Their expected signs are positive. A variable measuring population size is cited as one of the determinants of outputs and imports of manufactured goods primarily because of economies of scale in production. The larger is P, for a given level of per capita income, q, the lower will be costs of production and the greater the likelihood of import substitution. Thus, the expected sign of a_{i2} is positive and that of b_{i2} is negative. A successful testing of the model by the usual statistical criteria is then considered support for the view that patterns of manufacturing and industrial output can be explained in terms of per capita income and population size.[5]

As any number of investigations have shown, growth elasticities for manufacturing and industry are relatively large (and greater than one) while those for, say, agriculture were relatively low (and much less than one). Within manufacturing goods, growth elasticities have been found to be high for metals, metal products and chemicals and low for textiles and food, bever-

[3] See A. Maizels, *Growth and Trade*, Cambridge University Press, 1970, pp. 44–5, and H. Chenery, 'Patterns of Industrial Growth,' *American Economic Review*, September 1960.

[4] See Maizels, op. cit., p. 52. The lack of comparable export figures usually precludes extending the regression analysis in this direction.

[5] Naturally, when using cross-section data it is necessary to assume that the results function as indicators of temporal growth functions within a country.

ages and tobacco.[6] To use a different nomenclature, high growth elasticities were found for producer durable equipment and consumer durables.[7]

2. Variable growth elasticities

Transforming the variables in equations (1) and (2) into rates of growth gives

$$\dot{q}_i = a_{i1}\dot{q} + a_{i2}\dot{P} \tag{1a}$$

and

$$\dot{M}_i = b_{i1}\dot{q} + b_{i2}\dot{P} \tag{2a}$$

where a_{i2} and b_{i1} are again the respective growth elasticities and $\dot{q}_i$, $\dot{q}$, $\dot{P}$ and $\dot{M}_i$ are the rates of growth of production of the *i*th good, per capita income, population and imports of the *i*th good, respectively. While models of the sort discussed so far allow for income or growth elasticities to vary from one good to the next, the estimating procedures suggested by equations (1) and (2) do not allow growth elasticities of demand to vary as per capita incomes grow.

A large body of literature in demand and development analysis has grown up around this notion of variable income (or growth) elasticities and the findings are certainly relevant here. For example, when manufacturing output is disaggregated at the two-digit level, it is possible to classify these sectors as 'early,' 'middle' and 'late' industries depending upon the range of per capita incomes during which their contribution to the expansion of manufacturing output is most pronounced. Thus, textiles were found to be important at low levels of per capita income but increased their share of GNP very little beyond per capita income levels of $200. On the other hand, middle industries, e.g. rubber products, doubled their share of GNP at lower levels but showed little change after income levels of $400–$500. Finally, the late industries, e.g. metal products, consumer durables and investment goods, typically doubled their share of GNP in the late stages of industrialization.[8]

The notion of a variable income elasticity of demand has also been developed in what has come to be known as the 'Engel Curve' analysis. Thus write

$$q_i = f_i(q, p_1 \ldots p_n)$$

where q_i is the quantity demanded of some commodity, q is the income of

[6] See Maizels, op. cit., p. 53.

[7] Chenery, op. cit., Table 5. Of particular interest is the finding by Chenery on the relative importance of import substitution compared with the growth of final and intermediate demand on the growth of manufacturing and industrial output. The former influence is appreciably greater, treating output in the aggregate, and is especially important in explaining the growth of 'investment and related goods.'

[8] See H. Chenery and L. Taylor, 'Development Patterns: Among Countries and Over Time,' *Review of Economic and Statistics*, November 1968, pp. 412–13.

some consumer and the p's represent prices of the n goods. Holding prices constant, demand becomes a function only of the consumer's income, the consumer's Engel (demand) Curve for the ith good. The form of the Engel Curve is then specified in such a way that the function is able to represent luxuries and necessities or, alternatively, a good that is a luxury at some income levels (where the income elasticity of demand is greater than one) and a necessity at others (where the income elasticity of demand is less than one). A special case of this function is one in which a particular good is a luxury at low levels of income, becomes a necessity at higher levels of income and finally reaches some maximum saturation level of consumption.

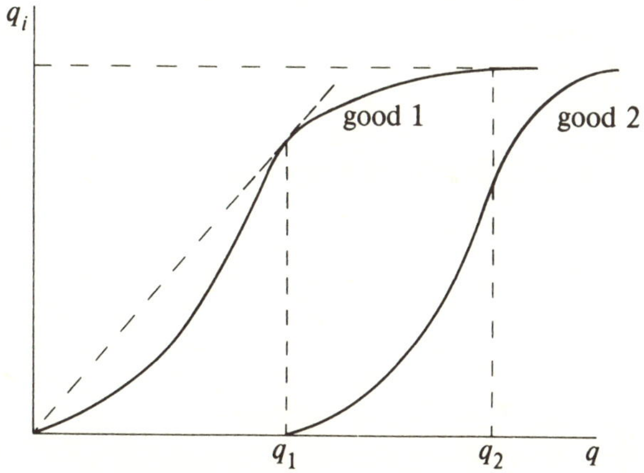

Diagram 6.1. A hierarchy of goods

In Diagram 6.1 a lognormal Engel Curve is shown for a 'normal' good. To the left of $q=q_1$ the good is a luxury and to the right it is a necessity, reaching a saturation point (prices held constant) at $q=q_2$. Given the distribution of consumer incomes, the aggregate demand for the ith good can be computed. For certain assumed distributions of income, the effect of rising per capita incomes is to cause the rate of growth of aggregate demand for the good to rise at first, then taper off and finally decline to zero.

Diagram 6.1 depicts a function that goes through the origin requiring some consumption by the consumer at even very low levels of income. Studies of consumer demand, especially for durables, have introduced the notion of a 'tolerance' level of income defined as that level of income that is just sufficiently large to induce the consumer to buy the good.[9] Until income reaches this level ($q=q_1$ in Diagram 6.1 for good 2), the good is not consumed. Given certain assumptions about the distribution of tolerance incomes and the distribution of actual incomes for the population, it is then possible to determine the expected proportion of the population that will

[9] See A. Brown and A. Deaton, 'Models of Consumer Behavior: A Survey,' *Economic Journal*, December 1972, p. 1225.

purchase the good (or will have purchased the good, in the case of durables).[10]

Finally, Diagram 6.1 helps to illustrate the idea of a hierarchy of goods or a priority ranking of goods in the consumer's (and the economy's) intertemporal budget plans according to the tolerance level of income at which they are purchased and consumed. For example, good 1 precedes good 2 in the hierarchy of the consumer as the tolerance level for good 1 is zero income and an income of q_1 for good 2. The analogy with early, middle and late industries mentioned earlier easily suggests itself.[11]

This same approach can be taken with manufacturing output as a whole, allowing for the possibility that the elasticity of demand may vary with per capita income. However, rather than deal with the complications introduced by using a rather complicated form of the Engel Curve and then aggregating, a useful simplification is to use the level of per capita income, q, along with the growth rate of per capita income, $\dot{q}$, and population, $\dot{P}$, or simply the rate of growth of total income, $\dot{Q}$, to explain the rate of growth of manufacturing output, $\dot{Q}_{\mathrm{m}}$. Thus;

$$\dot{Q}_{\mathrm{m}} = f_1(\dot{q}, \dot{P}, q) \qquad (3)$$

or

$$\dot{Q}_{\mathrm{m}} = f_2(\dot{Q}, q). \qquad (4)$$

Given the range of per capita income in the postwar period of the countries considered here, the expected sign of q is negative.[12] The higher is per capita income, the greater will be the tendency for consumers to spend relatively more on services and relatively less on manufactured goods.

C. Technical Change as an Endogenous Process

1. Introduction

An entirely different approach to the question of why rates of growth of manufacturing output differ relies on differences across countries in the size of a 'technology gap' between the industrial leader (e.g. the United States) and the various countries in question. The usual approach is to assume that per capita income in some country relative to per capita income in the industrial leader is a measure of technological gap that exists for that country. It is then hypothesized that an inverse relation exists between the size of this gap and the amount of technology that a country can borrow and,

[10] See D. Ironmonger, *New Commodities and Consumer Behavior*, Cambridge University Press, 1972, Chapter 4.

[11] See G. Pyatt, *Priority Patterns and the Demand for Household Durable Goods*, Cambridge University Press, 1964.

[12] Taking Cripps and Tarling's sample of twelve developed economies, per capita incomes range from $249 for Japan in 1953 to a figure over $3000 in the United States by the end of the 1960s, all figures in constant 1963 dollars – see Cripps and Tarling, op. cit.

therefore, the rate of growth of manufacturing output.[13] The patterns of industrialization and technology gap explanations of growth are complementary in the sense that the former concentrates on the demand for manufacturing output while the latter highlights supply or productivity aspects.

In Chapter III expressions for the rate of growth of total factor productivity or technical progress and labor productivity were developed. Again, write

$$\dot{A}_{\mathrm{m}} = \dot{Q}_{\mathrm{m}} - w_1\dot{K}_{\mathrm{m}} - w_2\dot{L}_{\mathrm{m}}$$

where $\dot{A}_{\mathrm{m}}$, $\dot{Q}_{\mathrm{m}}$, $\dot{K}_{\mathrm{m}}$ and $\dot{L}_{\mathrm{m}}$ are the rates of growth of technical progress, output, capital stock and labor, respectively, in manufacturing and the w's are the weights assigned to the two inputs, i.e. the output elasticities. Rearranging terms and subtracting $\dot{L}_{\mathrm{m}}$ from both sides leads to

$$\dot{Q}_{\mathrm{m}} - \dot{L}_{\mathrm{m}} = \dot{A}_{\mathrm{m}} + w_1\dot{K}_{\mathrm{m}} - (1 - w_2)\dot{L}_{\mathrm{m}}$$

an expression for the rate of growth of labor productivity in manufacturing. The technology gap analysis can be viewed as one of several attempts to explain differences in the rate of technical progress between countries and, therefore, labor productivities. Briefly, the technology gap or diffusion of technology approach accepts the notion that the rate of technical progress is the most important determinant of growth rates. Its special contribution is to stress the importance of the international flow of inventions and innovations in determining the rate of technical progress and labor productivity.[14] In so doing emphasis is placed on the endogenous nature of technical progress. Since so much emphasis throughout the remaining chapters will be given to the importance of this technology gap and the endogenous nature of technical progress in explaining differences in growth (and export) performances, the analysis must be developed with some care.

2. *Technology – some definitions*

The technology of a country at any point in time is the stock of knowledge that pertains primarily to the production of goods and services.[15] It defines what goods can be produced and the processes available for producing them. The operational part of this technology or stock of knowledge consists of a set of techniques, each technique defined as a set of actions and decision rules, for transforming inputs into outputs. Maximum or potential output of an economy at some point in time is a function of the stock of this knowledge, i.e. the technology, the extent to which the technology is embodied in the labor force, the organizational structure of the economy includ-

[13] See S. Gomulka, *Inventitive Activity, Diffusion, and the Stages of Economic Growth*, Aarhus University, Aarhus, 1971.

[14] Technical progress can be embodied in new consumer goods. This aspect is downplayed in the text which emphasizes technical progress embodied in new production processes.

[15] This section relies heavily on R. Nelson, M. Peck and E. Kalachek, *Technology, Economic Growth and Public Policy*, The Brookings Institution, Washington, DC, 1967, Chapters 1 and 2.

ing the entrepreneurial abilities of organizational leaders, and the stock of physical capital and other material resources, due account being taken of the quality of these inputs.

This complicated functional relationship is often summarized in the form of a simple aggregate production function of the type discussed in Chapter III. For a given technology, the level of factor inputs determines the level of output. If the technology advances, the production function shifts. Much of the early literature on the sources of shifts in the production function distinguishes between technological and technical progress or advance. The former refers to the discovery of new techniques, product designs or ideas, i.e. inventions, that have a potential commercial value. The latter refers to the commercial application of the invention in production. The notions 'know why' versus 'know how' and 'invention' versus 'innovation' are often used to capture the thrust of the distinction. Both technological and technical knowledge are part of the technology of a country as the words are used here. However, it is technical knowledge that leads to shifts in the production function. Finally, in all this analysis the concern is, implicitly at least, with the nature and shifts of production functions for the usual sort of commercial product. This can be contrasted with a production function for inventions and innovations to be discussed presently.

The diffusion or spread of technologies in general and their international diffusion in particular have become important subjects of discussion in the profession in recent years, particularly as sources of technical progress and productivity growth.[16] The nature of the diffusion of a technology, including its measurement, can be viewed in many ways. For example, one can refer to the diffusion of a good or a process, although this distinction is not so clear-cut since many processes are really little more than capital goods. Second, one can distinguish between the diffusion of the use of a good (or process) and its production. Thus, inter-country trade allows goods or processes to be used in some country where they are not produced and vice versa. Third, a distinction between the diffusion of technological knowledge or inventions and technical knowledge or innovations is often helpful. Finally, it is possible to distinguish between intra-firm, inter-firm and inter-country diffusion. In Section E attention is focused on the latter, the international diffusion of inventions and innovations. In this and the other parts of the chapter, interest is confined to developments within a country.

The rate at which the diffusion of technical change proceeds has important implications and can be measured in different ways. A simple measure refers to the time interval between the initial adoption of the production of a good or process by the innovator and the initial adoption by the imitator. This time interval has been given the name of the 'imitation lag'

[16] See for example, E. Mansfield, *The Economics of Technological Change*, Norton, New York, 1968, and L. Nabseth and G. Ray (eds.), *The Diffusion of New Industrial Processes: An International Study*, Cambridge University Press, 1974.

in trade theory and has played a key role in product life-cycle explanations of trade patterns.[17] It is also possible to measure the speed of diffusion in terms of the percentage of output of a firm or industry produced by a certain process, the percentage of firms in an industry that have adopted the new good or process to whatever extent, the value of production attributable to some new process in a firm or industry, etc.

3. An extended sequence

The distinction between technological and technical knowledge, while useful in some problems, suggests a much too simple and clear-cut sequence of developments from the additions to the stock of technological knowledge to shifts in the production function. Limiting the analysis to this two-stage sequence is also incomplete because it fails to stress that much of technological and technical progress is the outgrowth of conscious activity on the part of firms, individuals and non-profit-making organizations. Furthermore, it fails to consider that innovations may be widely or narrowly adopted or diffused and that the extent of this diffusion of innovations can be considered an important determinant of the rate of technical progress. To remedy this partially, define research and development activity (R and D) as the conscious application of resources to develop inventions into a form that has commercial value. Then in the absence of an ability to borrow technology abroad, the sequence of developments ultimately resulting in technical progress and a shift in the economy's production function (and growth of labor productivity) can be broken down into four steps: (1) technological progress as just defined resulting from some initial R and D effort; (2) development of the invention into something commercially feasible, i.e. the 'innovation'; (3) modification of the innovation as a result of a learning process; and (4) the diffusion of the innovation throughout the industry and economy.[18]

Both steps (2) and (3) should be viewed as a more or less continuous process of a reworking, testing, evaluation and modification of the original design of an invention. However, it is useful to think that step (3) differs from step (2) (and step (1)) in that substantial investment outlays take place at this stage and not before. As will be argued shortly, the actual diffusion of the innovation will also involve relatively large investment outlays.

While very simple, the sequence of developments just outlined is suggestive if for no other reason than that it challenges the view that technological and technical progress are the result of 'manna from heaven' and instead stresses their endogenous character. Thus, R and D expenditures and investment outlays are parts of a process that is a deliberate attempt to exploit the existing technology and expand its frontiers. The actual diffusion or spread in the use of a new technology is also clearly of this character. By

[17]See Chapter X.

[18]This is the sequence suggested in Nabseth and Ray, op. cit., p. 4.

increasing R and D expenditures, scientific knowledge can more rapidly be developed into inventions and, together with larger investment outlays, these inventions can be more rapidly developed into innovations and more widely diffused throughout the economy. At every step, deliberate purposive action induced by economic events is being undertaken. Section D discusses in more detail the first step in this four-step sequence.

D. The Determinants of the Rate of Technological Progress in a Closed Economy

1. The demand for inventive activity

R and D activity undertaken by firms is clearly motivated by a desire to expand sales and profits of the firms. This suggests that the extent and direction of R and D inventive activities can, in turn, be related to past, current and expected demand performance. This view is seen most clearly in the writings of Schmookler who has attempted to relate the amount and direction of inventive activity to the relative strength and direction of demand for different goods and services.[19] Using both cross-section and time series data, Schmookler found that, when inventions, as recorded in patents, are classified by industry of use (rather than by industry of origin), there was a strong correlation between the size of lagged investment outlays by the industry in question and the number of patented inventions used in that industry. The relationship was such that Schmookler was able to link up the rate of growth of output of some industry or market with the number of patented inventions used by that industry. The key link in this sequence was the behavior of firms in the capital goods industry in their quest for profits. These firms were viewed as allocating their major inventive efforts in perfecting and developing techniques toward those industries that can most benefit from technical improvements, i.e. those that have invested heavily and expanded rapidly in the recent past. An implication of this was that, as per capita incomes rise and the distribution of demand shifts, the distribution of inventive activity shifts toward those industries experiencing rapid growth of demand. The distribution of innovations and the sectoral rates of growth of technical progress and productivity correspondingly respond.

2. The supply of inventions

The Schmookler view has been much admired as a corrective to the intellectually unsatisfactory 'manna from heaven' view of technical progress. It has, however, met with criticism for its unwillingness to consider the rate of technological progress as the outcome of two sets of forces, demand and

[19] See J. Schmookler, *Invention and Economic Growth*, Harvard University Press, Cambridge, 1966.

supply – the same two that determine the rate of output of goods and services in general.[20] According to this latter view, greater demand for inventive activity, because of the greater rewards generated by expanding markets, is a force to be considered, but supply considerations cannot be overlooked since the elasticity of the supply of inventions is not infinite in every industry. In some cases the supply elasticities may be so small that the costs of inventions become prohibitive.

In this more comprehensive view, this supply curve of inventions is derived from a special kind of production function for the 'inventions sector' with inventions the output and with inputs composed of the number of people capable of engaging in inventive activity, the number and quality of capital and material inputs that can be used to produce inventions and the stock of available technological knowledge that can be used to think them up.[21]

Within the context of a closed economy with no possibility of borrowing technology it is useful to think of the stock of technological knowledge in the inventions sector being augmented from two sources: (1) a general learning process emerging from the production process itself; and (2) developments in the various sub-branches of science, both pure and applied, where the basic knowledge is developed. Developments of both sorts increase the elasticity of supply of inventions. In general, a 'learning by doing' process at the production line is sufficient for generating the additional technological knowledge ultimately required for minor improvement of some product or process. The larger and more rapidly growing is some industry, the greater the amount of learning and, therefore, the greater the rate of technological advance developed for the expanding industry.

This kind of technology response to demand conditions is a special case of the Schmookler view and would be generally acceptable to his critics.[22] However, major technological advances often (and increasingly) depend upon previous developments in the sub-branches of science. The view that previous scientific breakthroughs are required in many areas before substantive technological advances are possible has assumed increased emphasis in the twentieth century. The growth of the engineering profession and the growth of industrial and government research laboratories are cited as two factors promoting this greater dependence upon science.[23] And while it is

[20] See N. Rosenberg, 'Science, Invention and Economic Growth,' *Economic Journal*, March 1974. Nelson *et al.*, op. cit., and Mansfield, op. cit., Chapter II, are also relevant in this context.

[21] Nelson *et al.*, op. cit., Chapter 2. For additional factors that might be important see Mansfield, op. cit., Chapter II and Nabseth and Ray, op. cit., Chapters 2 and II. The inventions sector can be thought of as the R and D sectors of each and every firm.

[22] See Mansfield, op. cit., p. 18, and J. Tilton, *International Diffusion of Technology: The Case of Semiconductors*, The Brookings Institution, Washington, DC, 1971, pp. 34–8.

[23] Mansfield dates the rising importance of science for technological progress around 1850 while Nelson sets a somewhat earlier date. See Mansfield, op. cit., p. 44, and Nelson *et al.*, op. cit., p. 33.

seldom if ever maintained that there is any one-to-one correspondence between some scientific breakthrough and a major invention, the postwar developments in, say, the electronics and chemical industries are often cited as industries where major inventions and ultimately technical progress were highly dependent upon the previous development of a broad scientific base.

If the supply of inventions in a closed economy is to be highly responsive to demand pressures, as Schmookler has argued, then developments in the sub-branches of science must also be responsive to demand considerations (along with the requisite labor and materials supplies). However, if developments in science have a life of their own to some extent, then greater demand pressures and greater profit incentives for developing inventions in certain industries may only result in scientific failures. The history of science is replete with examples of demands for the discovery of scientific knowledge that could solve some practical need which have met with no such supply response.[24] Thus, considerations on the supply side act as constraints which influence the direction, timing and allocation of inventive activity along with demand factors. When the supplies of technological knowledge, skilled workers, etc. which are available differ across industries, this naturally leads to differences in the real cost or supply price of inventions (and their ultimate commercial development) in different sectors of the economy. All of this is of great importance in determining the importance of an international technology gap for relative rates of growth of output, a matter to be taken up now.

E. The Technology Gap and the Elasticity of Supply of Inventions and Innovations

1. The potential benefits

With these preliminary remarks out of the way it is possible to proceed to the main task: an understanding of why the existence of an international technology gap is conducive to more rapid rates of growth of manufacturing output. To anticipate the conclusions, what is to be argued is that productivity growth will be higher in manufacturing, other things being equal, if it is possible to borrow technology because the elasticity of supply of inventions and innovations is greater for imitators compared with the technology leaders (i.e. the high income countries). This arises because to a large extent the inventions and innovations have already been produced. This view will be discussed here. In Section F it is argued that productivity growth will be higher in manufacturing for countries borrowing technologies also because imitators will have greater flexibility in their choice of technologies, other things being equal. As will be clear, the operative expression is 'other things being equal,' since some imitators may not avail themselves of the opportunity to borrow technology for one reason or another.

The earlier discussion emphasized the endogenous nature of technological

[24] See Rosenberg, op. cit.

progress and the importance for growth of directing resources toward producing more inventions. However, it was stressed that the output of inventions should not be viewed as determined solely by demand considerations. As per capita incomes rise and demand shifts, industries experiencing increased demand pressures will seek improvements in their technologies in order more easily and more inexpensively to satisfy this growing demand. The demand for commercially feasible inventions will certainly rise. However, if the supply of inventions does not respond to the demand, because it is partly and importantly dependent on autonomous developments in the more basic sciences, the elasticity of supply of new inventions with respect to their costs may be extremely low. As a result, the rate of technical progress and productivity growth in these lines will be very low.

One of the potential benefits of being able to borrow technologies is easily formulated. Section B above emphasized the similarities of patterns of industrialization between countries. Holding per capita income levels constant, the composition of output was found to be quite similar for a large number of countries. To put matters differently, various studies have suggested that as incomes rise demand patterns shift in a predictable way as the different countries go through a similar hierarchy of goods. This means that countries with lower per capita incomes, whatever the cause of their 'starting late' in the industrialization and modernization process, not only may be able to borrow technologies from those countries with higher income levels, but will very likely want to borrow such technologies. As long as the patterns of demand for innovators (early starters) varied in the past in a way that closely resembles the manner in which demand patterns will vary for the imitators (late starters), the elasticity of supply of inventions should be more elastic for the latter because to a large extent they are already there.[25]

The amount of technological knowledge available for innovation in the imitating country is to a large extent determined by the extent of licensing agreements and patent sales and the creation of subsidiaries by multinational corporations in the countries industrializing late.[26] The relative importance of these channels for the borrowing of technology depends primarily on: (1) the attitude of the importing (of technology) country towards foreign corporate ownership; and (2) the attractiveness of the foreign market in the eyes of the firm having the option of selling patents or working out licensing arrangements or setting up production in the foreign country. For example, if, as was the case in Japan in the postwar period, the local government takes a very unfavorable attitude toward

[25] '... knowledge is expensive to produce but cheap to reproduce.' See W. Nordhaus, *Invention, Growth and Public Policy*, The Brookings Institution, Washington, DC, 1967, Chapters 1 and 2. 1969, p. 36.

[26] It should be noted that World War II, with its widespread destruction of physical capital in many countries, led to something very similar to a late start in industrializing in those countries suffering damage.

foreign ownership while foreign firms find the market too risky for setting up subsidiaries, licensing arrangements become the predominant channel for the diffusion of technology.

Provided these channels of international diffusion of technologies are available, the supply of inventions available to a borrowing country will be measurably more elastic than it was to the industrial leader.[27] To be sure, commercially feasible inventions in one country are seldom borrowed and used without modification in the imitating country.[28] But in varying degree, depending upon the nature of the invention borrowed, a higher rate of demand for a particular invention will find supply more responsive for a borrowing country. Fortunately for imitating countries in the postwar period, the industrial leaders, especially the United States, were particularly motivated to transfer technological knowledge in one form or another.[29]

Much of what has just been said about the borrowing of technological knowledge through licensing arrangements or outright sales of patents applies when discussing the transfer of technical knowledge. The elasticity of supply of innovations not previously used in the borrowing country should be greater for an imitating country than for an innovating country that had to develop inventions into commercially successful products at some earlier date. Furthermore, provided patterns of industrialization are such that countries go through a similar hierarchy of goods, late starters will have a desire to borrow technical as well as technological knowledge developed abroad.

2. The realization of benefits

However, if borrowed, inventions and innovations are seldom adopted without modification, and this requires large numbers of people possessing the knowledge needed to innovate together with the necessary materials, capital goods and other components[30] The earlier discussion referred to a pro-

[27] Certainly, many inventions are first developed in countries that were not the industrial or technology leaders as these latter terms are defined here. But there are any number of cases where the innovations based on these inventions were carried out by the high-income countries, especially the United States, e.g. cellophane, jet engines, etc. The explanation of this sequence in many cases was simply a lack of a broad enough market in the relatively low-income country for the commercial application of the invention but a ready market in the high-income countries. In these cases, the supply of inventions is then more elastic to the high-income country that borrows the invention, but the supply of innovations is more elastic to the low-income country that eventually borrows the innovation. See Tilton, op. cit., pp. 160–3 for a related phenomenon.

[28] See T. Ozawa, *Japan's Technological Challenge to the West, 1950–1974: Motivation and Accomplishment*, MIT Press, Cambridge, 1974, Chapter 3; and Y. Tsurumi, *Technology Transfer and Foreign Trade: The Case of Japan, 1950–1966*, unpublished doctoral dissertation, Harvard, Graduate School of Business and Administration, 1966, Chapter IV.

[29] See Ozawa, op. cit., pp. 24–9.

[30] Ozawa has well documented the relationship between 'technology purchase contracts,' i.e. the purchase of patents and licenses, and investment, using both cross-section and time series data for Japan. See ibid., Chapters 2 and 3.

duction function for the inventing sector. A more common notion in the literature on the production of technology is that of a production function for the 'technology sector,' a function that describes the relationship between inputs and the output of both inventions and innovations.[31] The technology sector, like the inventions sector, plays a key role in determining the extent to which the potential benefits of being able to borrow technology are realized.

In the introduction to Section C above it was pointed out that the technology gap has usually been measured in terms of relative income levels.[32] In the absence of a better data, per capita income levels were seen as the best available measure of levels of technology because of their close relationship to average labor productivity levels. However, it is incorrect to assume that the relationship between per capita income in a country relative to the high-income country and the realization of the benefits of the technology gap is a simple inverse one. Per capita income levels also serve to measure the level of development of the technology sector of an economy. At low levels of per capita income, when a country has yet to emerge from an underdeveloped status, the technology sector can be expected to be similarly primitive. This means that such economies lack a skilled body of workers and entrepreneurs and the necessary materials and capital equipment needed to produce inventions and innovations. In such a situation, relative income levels would not be expected to have a significant effect on rates of growth of productivity and output in manufacturing. The absolute level of income of a country must obviously exceed some critical level before the relative income effect becomes operative. As is clear from the discussion in earlier chapters, this study has been confined to a group of economies with a relatively high degree of development and which are above some threshold absolute income level.[33]

Given, then, the existence of technology sectors in various stages of development (but all above some critical stage), various other conditions required for the realization of the potential benefits of borrowing technology should be stressed. First, there is the importance of the growth of the technology sector itself. As stressed throughout this study, the growth process is an unbalanced process with demand and production constantly shifting as income levels rise. This requires the continuous development of new technologies. Late starters, it is being argued, receive a bonus in the sense that a relatively elastic supply of inventions is available under circum-

[31] See, for example, Gomulka, op. cit.

[32] See ibid., Chapter IV. Alternatively, the level of per capita income in some country has been used in regression work to 'pick up' the influence of this technology gap. See *Economic Survey of Europe 1969, Part I*, United Nations, New York, 1970, Chapter 3.

[33] Gomulka, op. cit., p. 67, suggests that maximum benefits from borrowing technologies occur when per capita incomes in the imitating countries vary from one-tenth to one-half that of the industrial leader. At the beginning of the 1950s per capita income in Japan, the poorest of the market economies studied here, was approximately 12 per cent of that in the United States.

stances such as prevailed in the postwar period. A relatively elastic supply of innovations is to be expected also. However, even if the latter is not significantly different for the late starter because, say, borrowed innovations must be greatly modified for the local market, late starters are in the enviable position of being able to concentrate their inputs in the technology sector in the production of innovations.[34] As a result a very rapid expansion of the output of the technology sector can be expected relative to the expansion of inputs.

The last point emphasizes again the importance of investment for growth. Earlier chapters concentrated on the impact of high investment on the additional flexibility given to an economy as it sought to redirect production in response to changes in demand. The discussion of borrowing technology and modifying the borrowed technology indicates the importance of investment for expanding the absorptive capacity of the imitating country.[35]

Having stressed the importance of borrowed technology and investment for growth, it remains clear that, if the benefits of the technology gap are to be realized, there must be an entrepreneurial class that desires to borrow the inventions (and innovations) available abroad. This obviously must be based on a desire to expand markets and profits which will be strengthened by the general economic picture in the country being considered. In other words, in keeping with the emphasis in earlier chapters on the importance of strong aggregate demand pressures for reducing macroeconomic risks, it can be argued that in the postwar period, because of a strong commitment by authorities in the various market economies to maintain high levels of employment, the incentives for borrowing technology abroad were greatly strengthened. However, there obviously will be important and persistent differences across countries in their eagerness to import these technologies. The point being argued here is that this propensity to import technologies is one of the most important indications of a high level of entrepreneurship.

Given an entrepreneurial class willing to make licensing arrangements and eager to obtain the venture capital needed to finance investment in new lines of production on a broad scale, the position taken here is that the realized benefits of a technology gap will be very large indeed. And these benefits are likely to be realized over a fairly lengthy period of time. For the ability to borrow technology from the industrial leaders is not a 'one-shot' affair but involves a more or less prolonged process in at least two senses. First, the borrowing process can continue as an imitating country goes through a hierarchy of goods, provided its pattern of industrialization is similar to that of the leader(s). As each industry develops, different inventions and innovations can be borrowed abroad and modified to fit the needs of the

[34] This is brought out clearly in Ozawa, op. cit., Chapters 2 and 3.

[35] This is clear in Nabseth and Ray's study of the international diffusion of process technologies. Only one out of eleven processes, the application of gibberellic acid in malting, required small amounts of investment in its adoption. See Nabseth and Ray, op. cit., p. 304.

home (and export) market. Second, the analysis above may suggest that, when borrowing some technology, each separate technique borrowed is immediately adopted and completely diffused throughout some industry in the borrowing country. What must be emphasized is that the adoption of a new technology can be a more or less extended process depending upon the rapidity with which firms in some industry adopt the technology. What remains to be argued is that the rate of diffusion of a new technology within a country is likely to be more rapid for the imitating countries.

F. The Technology Gap and the Intra-Country Rate of Diffusion of Technology

1. An alternative measure of diffusion

One measure of the speed of diffusion of a technology mentioned in Section C above was the interval of time between the adoption of some innovation in the innovating country and its subsequent initial adoption in the imitating country. This interval has been termed the imitation lag in discussions dealing with the inter-country diffusion of technology. However, the international diffusion process also involves another dimension: the spread of the new technology within the borrowing or imitating country. It has been argued that it is the speed of the diffusion of technology in this latter sense that is the prime determinant of the rate of technical progress in any country.[36] It has also been argued that a technology gap confers an additional benefit on an imitating country to that discussed in Section E above. Not only are the supply curves for inventions and innovations more elastic, but it has also been argued that there is greater flexibility in the choice of production processes the imitator can borrow, should it so choose.[37] If so, then, this raises the likelihood that the intra-country diffusion of best practice techniques will be more rapid for a borrowing country should the latter opt for borrowing technology abroad. Such an outcome also strengthens the argument that an international technology gap gives rise to a substantial productivity bonus to those countries willing to avail themselves. Furthermore, it suggests that a country may be an imitator in the initial adoption of a new technology but a pioneer in the widespread and rapid diffusion of the same technology.[38]

2. The relationship between two diffusion processes

An international study of the diffusion of process technology sought to discover whether there was any relation between the length of the lag between the time that a new process was first introduced in an imitating country and

[36]ibid., p. 4.

[37]See Nelson, *et al.*, op. cit., pp. 99–105; M. Frankel, 'Obsolescence and Technological Change in a Maturing Economy,' *American Economic Review*, June 1955; 'Comment' and 'Reply,' *American Economic Review*, September 1966; and A. Lamfalussy, *Investment and Growth in Mature Economies*, MacMillan, New York, 1961.

[38]See Tilton, op. cit., Chapter 7.

when it was previously introduced in the innovating country (i.e. the imitation lag), and the number of years it took before a certain percentage of output was produced by the new process in the imitating country.[39] Using a sample of six European market economies and covering seven different production processes, regression results indicated that in five of the seven processes there existed a negative correlation between the latter measure of the speed of diffusion and the length of the imitation lag. Pooling the data for the five processes that seemed to indicate this negative relationship, a regression was run giving;

$$y = 10.776 - 0.764x \quad R^2 = 0.560 \tag{5}$$

where y is the number of years needed to reach some percentage of output produced by the new process and x is the time lag in years in the introduction of one of the processes behind the international industrial leader. This relationship is illustrated by Diagram 6.2.

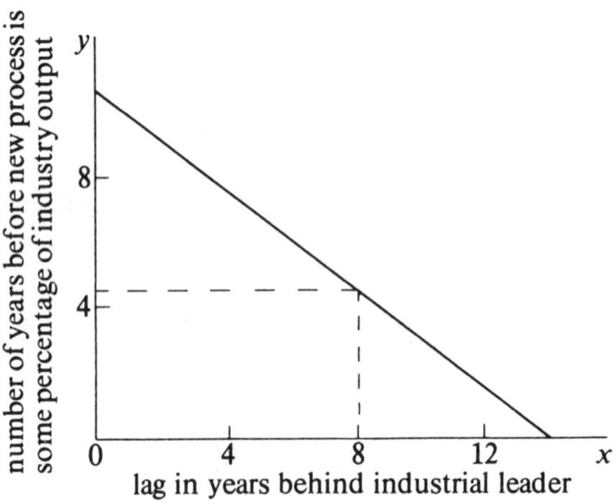

Diagram 6.2. The imitation lag and diffusion within the borrowing country

For example, for the industrial leader ($x = 0$) equation (5) and Diagram 6.2 indicates that it will take 10.776 years before a new process will produce a certain percentage of industry output. However, a late starter in the adoption of a process (say, $x = 8$) can achieve the same results in 4.664 years. Since it is reasonable to assume that the new process was superior to that which it replaced, it can be expected that the rate of growth of productivity in some industry was higher the later the initial adoption of the new process since it took less time to reach a certain level of adoption or diffusion.

[39] Nabseth and Ray, op. cit., Chapter 2.

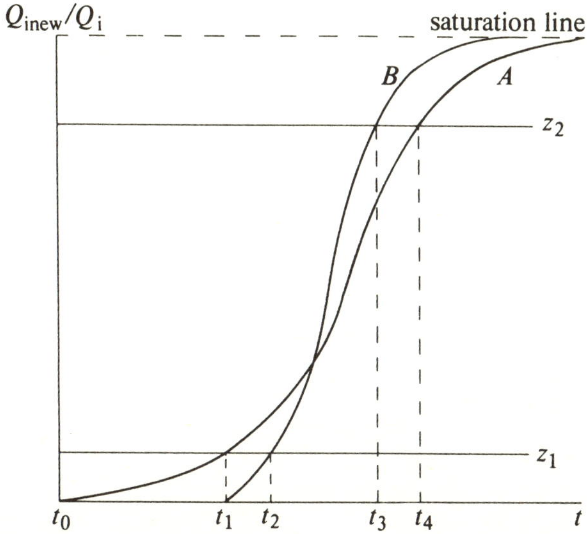

Diagram 6.3. The intra-country diffusion of technology

3. The speed of diffusion and profitability of innovation

The rate at which a new technology spreads or diffuses throughout some industry is a function of the speed at which firms in the industry adopt the new technique (the inter-firm rate of diffusion) and the speed with which any given firm replaces the old with the new technology (the intra-firm rate of diffusion). It has been found that very similar models can explain both the rate of inter-firm and intra-firm diffusion.[40]

Diagram 6.3 provides a useful picture and a measure of the speed of diffusion of some productive process for some industry. On the vertical axis is measured the percentage of output of the *i*th industry produced by a new process, $Q_{i\,new}/Q_i$. As such this measures the total impact of inter-firm as well as intra-firm diffusion. Time is measured on the horizontal axis.

Curves *A* and *B* are drawn in such a way that it takes a longer period of time to reach any level of diffusion in some industry if diffusion follows the *A* pattern rather than the *B*. For example, using curve *A*, it takes t_0t_1 to reach a level of diffusion equal to z_1, while curve *B* depicts a situation where $t_1t_2 < t_0t_1$ is required.

The patterns of diffusion in both examples in Diagram 6.3 follow that of a logistic function whereby diffusion is first slow, then accelerates and finally ceases.[41] The rationale for this pattern runs in terms of an initial

[40] E. Mansfield, *Industrial Research and Technological Innovation: An Econometic Analysis*, Norton, New York, 1968, Chapters 7 and 9.
[41] ibid.

aversion to experimenting by most firms until more information is available plus a possible need for modification of the original design of the process after its early adoption. This is followed by a period of rapid adoption as information becomes available more widely and design problems have been eliminated, followed in turn by a phase of increased resistance to the adoption of the process as it becomes increasingly ill-suited to the production needs of firms in the industry.

Several studies have attempted to determine why the diffusion process is more compact, i.e., why the S-curve is more squeezed (such as B compared with A), for one situation compared with another. As might be expected, one of the more important determinants of the degree of compression of the S-curve is the profitability of the innovation. The profitability of an innovation is viewed as a stimulus, the intensity of which determines the speed of diffusion. Thus (other things being equal), the greater the profitability, the shorter the time taken to reach some level of diffusion, say z_1, or the greater the increase in the level of diffusion per time period.[42] For example, it would be expected that profitability would be correlated with the rate of growth of demand for the output produced by a new technique. Curves *A* and *B* could then be used to depict situations of slow and rapid growth of demand, respectively, for the output of the industry in question.

4. Profitability and 'transition costs'

However, while demand conditions are an important determinant of profitability, the issue here concerns the impact of costs on profitability and the reason why the costs of some techniques are lower in imitating countries. Therefore, let curve *A* represent the diffusion of some technique in an industry in country α while curve *B* represents the intra-country diffusion process for the same technique in country β. As seen in Diagram 6.3, this technique is introduced earlier in time in country α. Assume this to be the case because per capita incomes are higher in country α than in β and there is no demand for the output of the particular industry in country β until t_1. The question arises as to why it would be expected that the profitability of the technique in question would be perceived as higher and, therefore, the S-curve more squeezed in country β than α.

It would be expected that the rate of inter-firm diffusion of the technique in country β would be more rapid for reasons suggested in Section E above. Much of the research and development work has already been done by time period t_1 by firms in the innovating country, thus reducing the cost and increasing the profits of the technique for the late starter or user of the technique. In other words, the elasticity of supply inventions and innovations involved in this particular process is greater for firms in country β when demand patterns in country β justify developing a new industry or market.

[42]See, for example, ibid., for additional variables influencing the speed of inter-firm and intra-firm diffusion.

However, there are additional factors at work raising the profitability of the technique in country β. These involve what has been termed 'transition costs or frictions' involved when new techniques or innovations must replace and compete with existing techniques of production.[43] To see this, assume that, beginning in period t_0, two processes for producing a good were available in country α and because of certain technical problems the process whose diffusion is depicted in Diagram 6.3 was not the more profitable one during the interval from t_0 until t_1. Furthermore, suppose that by time t_1 many of the 'bugs' involved in using this previously rejected technique that had not been widely adopted in country α before t_1 had somehow been eliminated. The question arises then as to why, from time t_1 onward, the rate of diffusion in country α of the process adopted by the same industry in country β is not nearly as rapid as in country β. Why for example does the industry in country β move from a level of diffusion z_1 to that of z_2 in the period t_2t_3 while the same industry in country α takes $t_1t_4 > t_2t_3$ to achieve the same result?

One answer frequently cited is that the new capital goods that would embody the now improved technique must, by period t_1, compete with capital goods that embodied the alternative technique adopted in country α during the interval t_0t_1. Such competition is not present in country β. As a result there arise the transition costs and frictions mentioned earlier, which reduce the expected profit generated by switching over to the improved technique in country α.

These transition costs and frictions are of several kinds. Two are worth citing.[44] First, existing techniques involve capital goods already purchased, familiar production layouts and labor forces with certain rather specific, already acquired, skills. With respect to replacing these capital goods, innovation is profitable only if the cost of the innovation plus its operating cost is less than the operating cost of the old capital goods plus their resale value. Innovations of a given purchase price will, therefore, be less likely to be widely adopted in a mature industry in country α than in the same industry in country β where the market and industry are just developing. With regards to labor, retraining costs involved will similarly act as a deterrent to the diffusion of the improved technique in country α compared with country β.[45]

Secondly, individual items of the capital stock of a firm, industry and country are usually interrelated in the sense that the components of a production process are technically interconnected. As a result a kind of indivisibility is introduced so that piecemeal introduction of cost-saving innovations is often not possible. Naturally in fast-growing industries this is less

[43] Nelson *et al.*, p. 100.

[44] See references in fn. 37 of this chapter.

[45] Critics of this line of reasoning invariably adopt a perfect foresight or certainty model in rebuttal. However, the reasonableness of the text position can only be decided within a framework that allows for a good deal of uncertainty.

of a problem. But if the production (and distribution) of a product is, in fact, a rather extended sequence, then it is very likely that that ownership will be fragmented among parts of this sequence. This, in turn, necessitates inter-firm and even inter-industry cooperation before innovations can be introduced.[46] At the very least this will act to retard the rate of introduction of new techniques in those countries, industries and firms that have developed earlier utilizing alternative techniques. While there are other factors at work, this view of the intra-country diffusion process does provide support for the empirical findings summarized in Diagram 6.2. In so doing, it also gives credence to the view that the technology gap acts to stimulate growth, provided the opportunity is not missed.

5. The hierarchy once more

What holds for one industry can be assumed to hold for a series of industries. Consider the following simplified example. Assume a hierarchy of goods or a similar pattern of industrialization such that any low-income country or 'late starter' will eventually follow a similar consumption, production and investment pattern as a high-income country or 'early starter.' Then, as per capita incomes rise in the low-income country and the pattern of demand shifts toward high-income (or growth) elasticity goods, the distribution of manpower, raw materials, capital and managerial skills will shift in response. At the same time, entrepreneurs, in response to these new growing demands, must decide what technology to use. According to the discussion above, the late starter is more prone to adopt the 'best practice' technique, not in the sense that the early starter will never opt for such techniques, but in the sense that the rate of diffusion of the new technique in the late starting country will be much quicker. The imitator does this because the profitability of the best technique is more apparent because the costs of this technique are less. Because the speed of adoption of the technique or innovation is more rapid in the relatively low-income country, the rate of growth of productivity in the particular industry will be higher in the low-income country than it was for a comparable stage of development in the high-income country.

The process repeats itself as long as the late starter repeats the consumption and production patterns of the early starter. At each successive stage it opts for the best practice technique more rapidly than the early starter did. As a result the rate of growth of productivity is higher in each successive industry for the late compared with early starter. Given the assumption, this continues to be the case as long as per capita incomes differ and as long as the early starter is the innovator for each successive technology.

[46] See especially Frankel, op. cit.

G. A Model for Explaining the Rate of Growth of Manufacturing Output

The analysis of Sections B–E can now be summarized in the form of a model designed to explain why rates of growth of manufacturing output differ. Given the assumption that the supply of labor responds passively to the relative demands for labor in the manufacturing sectors of the different economies, differences in the rate of growth of employment in manufacturing between countries follow immediately.

Section B approached the issue of the determinants of manufacturing output from the 'patterns of industrialization' approach. The rate of growth of manufacturing output was explained essentially in terms of demand factors as seen by;

$$\dot{Q}_{\mathrm{m}} = f_1(\dot{q}, \dot{P}, q) \tag{3}$$

or

$$\dot{Q}_{\mathrm{m}} = f_2(\dot{Q}, q) \tag{4}$$

The rate of growth of per capita income, $\dot{q}$, and population, $\dot{P}$, in equation (3) and the rate of growth of aggregate income, $\dot{Q}$, in equation (4) were used to pick up the growth elasticity of demand for manufacturing output. The level of per capita income was included as an approximation of a more elaborate specification designed to allow the growth or income elasticity of demand for manufacturing to vary depending upon the level of development. Given the range of values for q during the postwar period, it was hypothesized that there would be an inverse relation between q and $\dot{Q}_{\mathrm{m}}$ as rising levels of per capita income would lead to a substitution of services for goods.

The technology gap explanation of growth emphasized supply factors and, thereby, served to complement the demand approach just summarized. The problem for investigators has been how to measure a technology gap between countries. It was suggested in Section E that as long as the analysis was confined to a sample of countries that had achieved some minimum level of industrialization, a useful approximate measure of the level of technology of a country was its per capita income.[47] A measure of the size of a technology gap facing a country was, then, the ratio of per capita income in some country compared with that of the high-income nation(s). Other things being equal, the rate of growth of manufacturing output and the ratio of per capita income in a country relative to the industrial leader(s), q_{r}, should be negative.

[47] See Gomulka, op. cit. Obviously relative income and productivity levels are imperfect measures of relative levels of technology and, therefore, the size of the technology gap. Those studies that employ this measure assume a correlation between income levels and such things as educational levels, research and development expenditures, the stock of human and physical capital and the like, in other words the very things that determine the output of what was termed the technology sector or industry in the text. For a discussion of these latter factors see *Gaps in Technology: Analytical Report*, OECD, Paris, 1970.

Throughout this chapter emphasis has been placed on the importance of investment in developing technologies, whether borrowed or not. Let, then, the ratio of investment to output in manufacturing $(I/Q)_m$, represent a measure of the effort made to develop borrowed and indigenous technologies. Combining the patterns of industrialization approach (equation (4) version) with the technology gap view leads to an explanation of the rate of growth of manufacturing output given by equation (6):

$$\dot{Q}_m = f[\dot{Q}, q, q_r, (I/Q)_m] \tag{6}$$

where all other variables have their previous meanings. Lags, either distributive or discrete, can be introduced to take account of some of the recursive properties of the market economies. For example, using annual or quarterly data, it would be expected that there would exist a lag in output growth in manufacturing behind investment. In addition, interactions between any of the variables can be allowed for, etc.

In Chapter V it was concluded that differences in growth of employment of labor in manufacturing could be explained in terms of differences in the rate of growth of manufacturing output. From equation (6) it is clear that differences in the latter can be attributed to income levels, both q and q_r, growth rates of aggregate output, $\dot{Q}$, and the ratio of investment to value added in manufacturing, $(I/Q)_m$. In Chapter VIII some regression results are summarized which include estimates of the model of growth of the manufacturing sector specified in equation (6). There the technology gap is measured by the ratio of per capita income in some country relative to that in the United States. The regression results are interesting in their own right, but they also serve the purpose of tying together and laying out in as clear a manner as possible the basic structure of the model developed up to that point.

H. Summary

Throughout the chapter the general notion of similar patterns of industrialization across countries has been stressed. Different levels of technology and industrialization (as imperfectly measured by per capita incomes) tend to be associated with certain distributions of output (and resources) in a fairly regular way. This was the basis for arguing that an important influence on the rate of growth of manufacturing output was the level of per capita income. These were influences on the demand side.

On the supply side, a factor contributing in an important manner to the rate of growth of manufacturing output was a large stock of technology developed by the industrial leaders, which could be borrowed. Some countries greatly availed themselves of this opportunity (e.g. Japan, Germany and Italy) and as a result productivity and therefore output grew rapidly. The rate of investment was cited as the best measure of the 'effort' different countries made to avail themselves of this technology. Various studies were cited to support the view that new technologies require substantial investment outlays if they are to be implemented.

The ability to borrow technology was singled out as a cause of rapid growth because technological and technical knowledge can often be costly to obtain. The fact that firms in high-income countries had spent time and money in 'searching' for new and better technologies was seen as a real advantage for those who later wanted to borrow the results of this search. Specifically, it meant that new processes were more profitable for those who did not have to incur the costs involved in experimenting, screening, modifying, etc., the new technologies.

Some of the implications of the analysis are worth re-emphasizing. It is of little help in comparative growth analysis to try and explain why growth rates differ while at the same time assuming that knowledge is a free good that falls like manna from heaven. Technological knowledge, technical progress and productivity growth are very much the results of a concerted effort on the part of the economic actors involved to alter technologies and are best viewed as something that is to a large extent endogenous. Second, the importance of investment for growth in its role of adopting and modifying new technologies and the importance of the latter in explaining why rates of growth of manufacturing output differ across countries and over time cannot be overemphasized. Third, it is important that there be an entrepreneurial or managerial class orientated to exploiting the available stock of technology if rapid growth is to result. Fourth, while nothing has been said about the determinants of the investment ratio, the notion that the investment ratio is something determined by the desires of entrepreneurs is certainly consistent with the analysis just presented. In contrast, in neoclassical analysis, the rate of investment is determined by the propensity of the economy to save and not the other way around. The entrepreneurial function in neoclassical analysis is a passive one, that of coordinating the given factor supplies while accepting as given the rate of savings (= investment). However, once growth and the production process are viewed as a process of change and transformation, of developing new goods, processes and markets, the notion of a passive adaptation of investment to savings is not acceptable.

In summary, the rate at which manufacturing output grows is best seen as the outcome of the extent to which an entrepreneurial class searches for new and better ways to expand markets. For most countries, this involves borrowing new technologies. In the process, a deliberate, sustained effort is made to find and organize the capital and labor resources necessary for the task. Before attempting to tie the model together and test it in Chapter VIII, Chapter VII considers one additional, important part of the model; the relationship between the manufacturing sector and the rest of the economy.

Chapter VII The Manufacturing Sector as the Engine of Growth

A. Introduction

A brief recapitulation of what has been said in the last few chapters is useful at this point. Recall, in Chapter IV a generalized model of the dual economy was developed that stressed the importance of sectoral differences in rates of growth of employment and output throughout the growth process. In the majority of the countries studied, employment expanded more rapidly in manufacturing than in the economy as a whole while output in manufacturing grew more rapidly than overall output in every country. Chapter V sought to discover whether differences in employment patterns in the different market economies could be explained in terms of important differences in the elasticity of supply of labor to the manufacturing sector. The conclusion reached was that differences in employment patterns were explicable in terms of cross-country differences in the demand for labor by the manufacturing sectors of the different countries.

Chapter VI attempted to push the analysis back one stage further by seeking to discover why the demand for labor in manufacturing differed across countries. The demand for labor was treated there as a derived demand, one derived from the demand for manufacturing output. Differences in the rate of growth of manufacturing output were then explained in terms of differences in the growth of total output, the stage of industrialization, the accumulated stock of technology that could be borrowed and the effort made to borrow the technology of the industrial leaders of the postwar period.

Recall that, by bisecting or disaggregating the economy, dual model-builders were able to better emphasize the importance of surplus labor in one or more sectors of the economy together with the importance of other sectors (i.e. industry or manufacturing) in providing what was termed the technical dynamism that drives an economy. However, in Chapter V it was argued that in no country was the expansion of manufacturing output constrained by a shortage of surplus labor. This would seem to indicate that the presence of surplus labor in some sector is not something worth highlighting in explaining growth performances in these countries. Accordingly, the stress on elements of dualism appears to lose some of its force in explaining why growth rates differ.

However, dual models also emphasize the importance of certain sectors in propelling the rest of the economy. If, then, an argument can be made that it is the relative rates of growth of sectoral outputs that matter for growth and, in particular, that, the more the growth of manufacturing exceeds the growth of the rest of the economy, the more rapid is overall growth, then the dual model approach to growth retains much if not most of its value.

Chapter VII has one main function, and that is to justify the emphasis given to the manufacturing sector throughout the study. Hence, the expression 'engine of growth' in the title of this chapter. Section B is a review of ideas concerning the manner in which manufacturing acts as an engine of growth. Section C argues for the importance of economies of scale in manufacturing. Section D discusses the impact of growth of output in manufacturing on the rate of growth of productivity in non-manufacturing sectors, and Section E concludes the discussion.

B. The Importance of Manufacturing

The view that differences in the rate of growth of manufacturing output can be explained in terms of differences in the rate of growth of labor supply has been rejected. Various kinds of evidence were offered in Chapter V to support this rejection. This does not necessarily imply that growth of labor supply in manufacturing was not essential for the expansion of manufacturing output; only that, when there was an increase in the demand for manufacturing output, the expansion of manufacturing output was not thwarted by a lack of labor. A separate issue from that of labor supply, and one of at least equal importance, is whether growth of the manufacturing sector is in some sense the key to growth and transformation of the whole economy. This view has a long history in economics and support has been based on the recognition of certain events that were common in the industrialization process of a large number of countries.[1]

First, as already pointed out, productivity levels are higher in the manufacturing sector than in those sectors that tend to decline in importance, relatively and absolutely, as real incomes rise. In the extreme case, the disguised unemployment case, productivity rises even in the declining sector, which only magnifies the impact on productivity growth of the transfer of resources. This interpretation of the notion that growth of the manufacturing sector is the driving force behind rapid growth of aggregate and per worker (or per capita) output is the one usually associated with the models of the

[1] See, for example, Maizels, op. cit., Chapter 1.

dual economy as sketched in Chapter IV. Indeed, this interpretation was the basis for categorizing patterns of employment in Chapter IV when the economy was divided into more than two sectors. One of the criteria adopted for the application of the dual model there was formulated in terms of the growth of employment in manufacturing compared with the total economy because such a criterion suggested focusing on employment shifts as a source of economic growth.

Various attempts to quantify the importance of this source of growth have not found it to be one of the more important.[2] Unfortunately, these estimates all suffer from the same shortcoming; they assume that the level and rate of growth of productivity in the sector expanding inputs and output are independent of the expansion process itself. This rules out the possibility of various economies of scale in manufacturing and is, therefore, question-begging. However, there is an additional way of interpreting the view that growth of the manufacturing sector is the engine of growth, and that involves stressing the importance of the growth of its output irrespective of the implications of this for patterns of employment.[3] Such an expansion may or may not require an expansion of employment in manufacturing, but that is a separate issue and is discussed in Chapter VIII below.

A very simple way of expressing this notion of the manufacturing sector as the engine of growth is seen in Table 7.1, which summarizes the findings of three studies of market economies in the postwar period. Here, the

Table 7.1. Manufacturing as the engine of growth

$\dot{Q} = 1.153 + \underset{(0.040)}{0.614}\,\dot{Q}_m$	$R^2 = 0.96$	(Kaldor)	(1a)
$\dot{Q} = 1.295 + \underset{(0.037)}{0.603}\,\dot{Q}_m$	$R^2 = 0.899$	(Cripps and Tarling)	(1b)
$\dot{Q} = 1.12 + \underset{(\text{n.a.})}{0.60}\,\dot{Q}_m$	$R^2 = 0.94$	(UN)	(1c)

Sources: N. Kaldor, *Strategic Factors*, op. cit., p. 8; Cripps and Tarling, op. cit., p. 22; *Economic Survey of Europe, 1969, Part I*, United Nations, New York, p. 78.

dependent variable is the rate of growth of total output, $\dot{Q}$, and the independent variable is the rate of growth of manufacturing output, $\dot{Q}_m$. This

[2] See *The Growth of Output, 1960–1980*, op. cit., p. 38, and W. Beckerman, *The British Economy in 1975*, Cambridge University Press, 1965, pp. 23–5.

[3] The chief proponent of this view in recent times is Kaldor. See *Strategic Factors*, op. cit.; 'The Irrelevance of Equilibrium Economics,' *Economic Journal*, December 1972; and 'Economic Growth and the Verdoorn Law: A Comment of Mr. Rowthorn's Article,' *Economic Journal*, December 1975. See also *Economic Survey of Europe 1969, Part 1*, United Nations, New York, 1970, Chapter 3.

same relationship is shown graphically in Diagram 7.1. Using equation (1b) as an illustration, this relationship states that rates of growth of aggregate output are 'high,' i.e. greater than 3.26 per cent, only when the rate of growth of manufacturing output is greater than the rate of growth of total output. Alternatively, growth rates are high only when the rate of growth of manufacturing output exceeds that of non-manufacturing output, and the more by which growth in manufacturing exceeds the non-manufacturing sectors, the greater is the overall growth of the economy.

The relation summarized in equations (1a)–(1c) introduces a second relationship between the rate of growth of total and manufacturing output. In Chapter VI, the rate of growth of total output influenced the rate of growth of manufacturing output according to the income or growth elasticity of demand for manufacturing output. Here, as the notion 'engine of growth' suggests, the relationship is to be interpreted in a cause and effect sense with the causation running from right to left. Its importance in the explanation of why growth rates differ warrants further discussion of just what is involved.

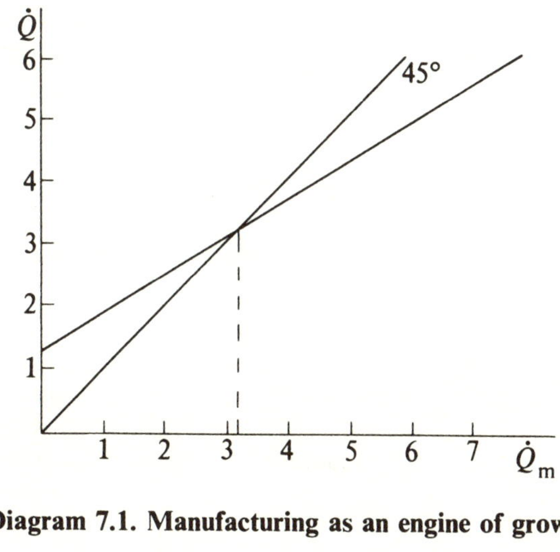

Diagram 7.1. Manufacturing as an engine of growth

Basically, those who stress the importance of the manufacturing sector in explaining the overall growth performance of an economy make two arguments: (1) the rate of growth of productivity in manufacturing is not something given exogenously but is dependent upon the rate of growth of manufacturing output; and (2) the rate of growth of manufacturing output is an important factor in determining the rate of growth of productivity in several non-manufacturing sectors as well as in manufacturing. Both arguments focus on the changing allocation or distribution of output rather than inputs, i.e. labor and capital, in their interpretation of the importance of the manufacturing sector. The remainder of this chapter will concern itself with this interpretation of the manufacturing sector as the engine of growth and the forces at work causing manufacturing to play this role.

C. Economies of Scale in Manufacturing

1. Verdoorn's Law

Following the usual definitions, a 'static' economy of scale refers to a reduction of unit costs (and an increase in average productivity) as output for a given production period increases. The traditional source of static economies of scale has been an increase in plant, firm or industry size. More recently emphasis has been given to longer production runs as a source.[4] Longer production runs within a given production period give rise to reductions of unit costs because they involve fewer halts in production and less 'downtime' for the adjustment of production to handle different models, and because they allow a reduction in inventories. A dynamic economy of scale refers to a more or less continuous reduction in unit costs (and continuous increases in productivity) owing to continuous increases in the output of a firm, industry or economy over time. These economies are often described as learning economies in that they are a function of cumulative output increases or cumulative gross investment and thus are partly a function of time itself.

A well-known model used to test for the existence of economies of scale has come to be known as 'Verdoorn's Law.' The emphasis in this approach is on the importance of the rate of growth of output in determining the rate of growth of productivity, rather than the level of output determining the level of average productivity. The observations used to test the model are either a cross-section of manufacturing or industrial subsectors within a country or a cross-section of manufacturing or industrial sectors of several economies.[5] Thus, letting $\dot{\rho}_m$ and $\dot{Q}_m$ represent rates of growth of labor productivity and output in manufacturing, respectively, write:

$$\dot{\rho}_m = a_0 + a_1 \dot{Q}_m. \tag{2}$$

Statistically significant results have been found by numerous investigators, whether cross-section or time series data are used. The results of several cross-section studies utilizing the manufacturing sectors of different market economies as observations are shown in Table 7.2. As equation (2) implies, since an increase in the rate of growth of manufacturing output increases

[4] See H. Grubel and P. Lloyd, *Intra-Industry Trade: The Theory and Measurement of International Trade in Differentiated Products*, John Wiley, New York, 1975.

[5] The interpretation of the results may differ depending upon whether the sample consists of industries within a country or the total manufacturing or industry sectors of several countries. See K. Kennedy, *Productivity and Industrial Growth*, Clarendon Press, Oxford, 1971, Chapter 6.

the rate of growth of productivity in manufacturing, it will increase the rate of growth of overall productivity and output as a result.

2. Some criticisms

Three kinds of arguments can and have been brought against this view that, in general, causation runs from output to productivity growth and that, in particular, statistical studies of the kind summarized in Table 7.2, therefore, support the engine of growth hypothesis. First, ordinary least squares regression estimates applied to models depicted by equations (2a)–(2d) give biased estimates of the parameters when the alleged independent variable, $\dot{Q}_m$ in this case, is not truly independent or predetermined. Partly in response to this criticism, a different kind of test has been put forward, and that is to regress $\dot{\rho}_m$ on $\dot{E}_m$, the rate of growth of employment in manufacturing.[6] However, evidence was presented in Chapter V indicating that the rate of growth of employment in manufacturing in the postwar period was determined by the rate of growth of output in manufacturing. Therefore, regressing $\dot{\rho}_m$ on $\dot{E}_m$ is, if anything, even less satisfactory. The problem of bias must remain unresolved.[7]

Table 7.2. Verdoorn's Law

$\dot{\rho}_m = 0.67 + 0.64\dot{Q}_m$ (n.a.)	$R^2 = 0.90$	(UN)	(2a)
$\dot{\rho}_m = 1.035 + 0.484\dot{Q}_m$ (0.070)	$R^2 = 0.826$	(Kaldor)	(2b)
$\dot{\rho}_m = 1.10 + 0.545\dot{Q}_m$ (0.055)	$R^2 = 0.710$	(Cornwall)	(2c)
$\dot{\rho}_m = 1.12 + 0.532\dot{Q}_m$ (0.059)	$R^2 = 0.804$	(Cornwall)	(2d)

Sources: *Economic Survey*, op. cit., p. 84; Kaldor, op. cit., p. 16; and Cripps and Tarling, op. cit. Equation (2c) is based on all twelve countries in Cripps and Tarling's sample, while equation (2d) is based on a sample of the six largest economies from their study. Cripps and Tarling's data were used in both regressions.

[6] R. Rowthorn, 'What Remains of Kaldor's Law?,' *Economic Journal*, March 1975.

[7] A comparison with the identification problem in consumption studies is helpful. Write $C = a_0 + a_1 Q$ and $Q = C + I$ where Q, C and I represent aggregate output, consumption and investment, respectively. It was early recognized that ordinary least squares regression of C on Q gave biased estimates of the parameters of the consumption function. Instead, by positing that I was a predetermined or exogenous variable, an unbiased estimate of the parameters of the consumption function was obtained by regressing C on I, and then by substitution the values of a_0 and a_1 could be determined (under certain conditions). Similarly, it might be though that in a model where $\dot{\rho}_m = a_0 + a_1\dot{Q}_m$ and $\dot{Q}_m = \dot{\rho}_m + \dot{E}_m$, it is preferable to regress $\dot{\rho}_m$ on $\dot{E}_m$. However, the main conclusion of Chapter V was that $\dot{E}_m$ (unlike I) cannot be treated as a predetermined or exogenous variable. It is an endogenous variable determined by $\dot{Q}_m$ just as $\dot{\rho}_m$ is determined by $\dot{Q}_m$.

A second argument brought against Verdoorn's Law is that, since by definition $\dot{Q}_m = \dot{p}_m + \dot{E}_m$, the alleged causal relationship illustrated by equations (2a)–(2d) may be spurious. To some extent this argument can be countered by determining whether a relationship between $\dot{E}_m$ and $\dot{Q}_m$ exists. If $\dot{E}_m$ and $\dot{Q}_m$ show a significant correlation, there is less likelihood that the correlation between $\dot{p}_m$ and $\dot{Q}_m$ is spurious. Repeated studies have indicated that $\dot{Q}_m$ is highly correlated with both $\dot{p}_m$ and $\dot{E}_m$. This is illustrated in Tables 8.4 and 8.5.[8]

A third challenge to Verdoorn's Law raises both important statistical and theoretical issues. This challenge asserts that, in the relationship between $\dot{p}_m$ and $\dot{Q}_m$, the direction of causation is from higher rates of growth of productivity to higher rates of growth of output. This interpretation is clearly at variance with the notion that the manufacturing sector is the engine of growth. Since the causal chain runs from (unexplained) productivity growth in manufacturing to growth of manufacturing output to growth of total output, whatever it is that determines productivity growth, it is not growth of the manufacturing sector. Thus, define as before technological progress as the production or discovery of inventions that can be applied in production should the economic incentives justify their application and technical progress as the application of inventions. If, then, it is assumed that technological progress is purely an exogenous phenomenon falling at random across industries within a country or across the manufacturing sectors of different countries, it is possible to develop a plausible argument that the rate of growth of productivity determines the rate of growth of output and not the other way around. The connecting links, of course, are that differential rates of technological progress allow for differential rates of technical progress and productivity growth, which in turn affect relative prices and, ultimately, relative rates of growth of output.[9]

While investigators acknowledge this possible chain of causation as one reason for the high and persistent correlation between productivity and output growth in industry and manufacturing, various arguments have been offered to show that this chain of events by itself would only lead to a rather weak association between the two variables. For example, the price elasticities of demand for output are not large enough to generate the strong association that has been found in fact.[10] Additional considerations lead to the expectation of a strong association between output and productivity growth, and these indicate a direction of causation from output to productivity growth.

[8] As Tables 8.4 and 8.5 indicate, the correlations are not likely to be spurious just because all variables might be a function of time. Regressing $\dot{p}_m$ on $\dot{E}_m$ is not a very strong test of causation since other variables undoubtedly influence $\dot{p}_m$ besides $\dot{E}_m$ (or $\dot{Q}_m$).

[9] Section C relies heavily on Kennedy, op. cit., Chapter 6.

[10] See Kennedy, op. cit., pp. 178–86.

3. Technological progress as an endogenous variable

By far the strongest theoretical justification for the chain of causation running from output growth to productivity growth has arisen from a better understanding of the way in which technological progress as well as technical progress responds to economic events, i.e. the extent to which they are endogenous variables. In particular, various studies have made economists increasingly aware of the importance of activity in the capital goods industry in transmitting the fruits of technological progress into rising productivity growth. As already seen in Chapter VI, Schmookler has argued that, if inventions are classified by industry of use (rather than industry of origin), then the rate of inventions (and eventually productivity growth) is a function of recent investments in the industry of use because these past investments are an indication of future sales of capital goods. For example, if the level of investment undertaken by the aircraft industry has been high in the recent past, the rate of inventions that may eventually be applicable in the aircraft industry will also be high. This arises because the capital goods industry will anticipate a high demand in the near future for capital goods by the aircraft industry, other things being equal. Since recent investment outlays by the aircraft industry are a function of recent rates of growth of output, the link develops between output growth, investment, demand, profit-induced inventions and productivity growth.

Similarly, following Arrow, it can be argued that productivity growth results from a learning process, in particular a learning process that takes place in the capital goods industry.[11] This rate of learning is embodied in new capital goods and can be maintained only by new investment. Since the level of productivity depends on the level of cumulative gross investment, the rate of growth of productivity is a function of the rate of growth of cumulative gross investment. If the latter is then shown to be a positive function of the rate of growth of output of firms and industries utilizing the new capital goods, the causal link from output growth to productivity growth is again established.

Most of the studies attempting to justify a causal relationship emanating from the rate of growth of manufacturing output to productivity growth stress the importance of output growth in some industry-inducing technological progress that is embodied in the capital goods used by that industry. Obviously, other forms of induced productivity growth are plausible, e.g. the importance of longer production runs just mentioned.[12]

[11] K. Arrow, 'The Economic Implications of Learning by Doing,' *Review of Economic Studies*, June 1962.

[12] See for example J. Cornwall, *Growth and Stability in a Mature Economy*, Martin Robertson, London, and John Wiley, New York, 1972, pp. 62–71.

D. The Impact of Growth in Manufacturing on the Rate of Growth of Non-Manufacturing Productivity

1. Backward and forward linkages

The importance of growth in the manufacturing sector on productivity growth elsewhere in the economy can be made clearer with the use of two helpful terms, backward and forward linkage effects.[13] A backward linkage effect is a derived demand for input effect whereby some economic activity in one sector of the economy induces activity in some other sector(s) of the economy that acts as a supply sector for the former. A forward linkage effect is a process whereby the economic activity of some sector that does not cater exclusively to final demand induces attempts by some other sector(s) of the economy to make use of its output. A higher rate of growth of some manufacturing industry inducing a higher rate of growth of demand for coal is an example of a backward linkage effect. A higher rate of growth of cotton production generating a higher rate of growth of cloth production is an example of a forward linkage effect.

The notion of linkage effects was first applied to developing economies, but there is no need to restrict its usage in this manner. Indeed, specialists in input–output analysis have found the notions helpful in describing the technology structure of developed capitalist economies.[14] One important difference in the use of the term when applied to input–output relations in developed economies arises from the application of the term to linkages between existing industries. Development economists clearly had in mind a causal relationship between the establishment of some industry and the induced creation of a previously non-existing industry or one in a rather primitive state of development. Linkages in the developed economy studies referred to different rates of growth of output in one existing industry inducing different rates of growth of output in one or more other existing industries. Nevertheless, the notions of forward and backward linkages within the context of existing industries has proved to be a useful one and is especially helpful in the present discussion.

Input–output tables break down aggregate economic activity into a number of different producing industries. They do so in such a way as to make explicit the relationships between final demand for output (consumption, investment, government and foreign demand) and the intermediate demands that are necessary to meet this final demand. An input–output table can thus be viewed as a technology matrix, whereby any row of the matrix indicates where the output of some one industry is allocated, in the form of either an intermediate product or a final product. Any column of the same matrix indicates the various inputs used by a sector.

[13] A. Hirschman, *The Strategy of Economic Development*, Yale University Press, New Haven, 1958, Chapter 6.

[14] See *Economic Bulletin for Europe*, Vol. 23, No. 1, United Nations, New York, 1971, Part II.

2. The triangulation of the input–output matrix

The triangulation of the technology matrix involves a rearrangement of input–output industries or sectors in such a way as to find a hierarchy depicting the one-way dependence or recursive structure of an economy. Thus, in the extreme case industries can be ranked such that each industry supplies only those industries from which it is not supplied itself; e.g., coal is supplied to the iron and steel industry (but not vice versa), iron and steel products are supplied to the auto industry (but not vice versa), and autos are supplied to final demand. A recent United Nation study of twelve OECD and several Eastern bloc countries indicated quite similar technology structures in the sense that industry rankings in the triangulation process were quite similar across countries.[15] For example, when each economy was disaggregated into nineteen sectors, 'coal mining, crude petroleum, and natural gas' and 'electricity, gas and steam production' were typically at the bottom of the triangulation arrangement, indicating that, while these two sectors supplied intermediate goods to other industries, they were not dependent upon these other industries for inputs. At the top of the rankings, and therefore closest to final demand, were (a) 'miscellaneous services;' (b) 'food, beverage and tobacco;' (c) 'footwear, madeup textile goods, leather and fur products;' (d) 'machinery' and (e) 'transport equipment.'

As just mentioned, the notion of a linkage between existing sectors or industries is something different than that in which one sector, in effect, brings into existence another industry. Nevertheless, the nature of the various inter-industry links between existing industries are important for growth. By detailing the linkages according to a triangulation process, indicating which industries are close to final demand and which industries supply intermediate products at various levels removed from final demand, input–output analysis does suggest other ways in which manufacturing functions as a sector propelling growth. This has both a demand and supply aspect.

3. Demand and the structure of causation

As just indicated, in the triangulation of the technology matrices for the different countries various important subsectors of manufacturing stood at the top of the rankings (along with miscellaneous services). Viewing the issue of which sectors drive or propel which others from the demand side, the issue is, in which sectors or industries do changes in output induce changes in the demand for output in the other sectors, and not the other way around?

Here the direction of causation is fairly clear. From a purely demand point of view, it would be difficult to argue that, say, the mining or iron and steel industry, by increasing the rate of growth of their output, could cause manufacturing sectors (and services) to speed up their rates of growth of output, which would somehow then lead to higher rates of growth of demand for

[15] ibid., pp. 62–5.

the outputs of the latter. Whether one believes that consumer sovereignty exists or that tastes are created to match production, it is largely production of goods for final output that induces production by industries producing further down the triangulation arrangement. Looked at, then, in terms of derived demands, it is clearly industries producing closest to final demand that are the engines of growth in the input–output sense described here.[16]

But what has just been said allows for the possibility that miscellaneous services could be the engine of growth since they, along with manufacturing, are found at the top of the triangulation scheme. There is the further possibility that some industry, producing an intermediate product for domestic production, is a heavy exporter. The issue of export-led growth will be postponed until Chapter IX. The question of whether miscellaneous services or the service sector in general can function just as well as the manufacturing sector as the engine of growth is best handled by turning to certain supply considerations.

4. Supply and the structure of causation

It can be argued that industries supplying intermediate products could, by expanding output, achieve economies of scale and lower costs. This could then induce industries higher up the triangulation ladder to expand their inputs of these cheaper intermediate products and, because of a fall in price of the products using the latter, industries closer to final demand expand output and sales. However, a more likely sequence is higher rates of growth of manufacturing output stimulating more rapid rates of growth of productivity in industries further removed from final demand because of increased activity in the capital goods industry. Thus, following Schmookler and Arrow, higher rates of growth of production in manufacturing induce higher rates of growth of derived demand and output further 'down the line.' This will generate more investment and inventive activity and longer production runs, all of which stimulate productivity in industries producing intermediate products (as well as those in manufacturing). However, rather than deny that industries producing intermediate goods can, by expanding output and increasing productivity, induce an expansion of output in industries closer to final demand, the issue can be more fruitfully resolved by considering other more important supply considerations at work, certainly during the postwar period.

The United Nation study just cited, and most other input–output studies, are limited to current flows of material goods and services treating new capital goods as a final output. Hence, the finding that the manufacture of

[16] A UN study came to the same conclusions. To support the view that the manufacturing sector was the engine of growth, various regressions were run of the form: $Q_i = e_0 + e_1\dot{Q}_m$ where $\dot{Q}_i$ represents the rate of growth of output in some non-manufacturing sector, e.g. public utilities. Then the rate of growth of productivity in the *i*th sector was regressed on the rate of growth of output in this sector. See *Economic Survey of Europe*, op. cit., Chapter 3.

machinery was at the top of the triangulation rankings, being supplied by most other sectors but not providing inputs to the latter. However, in some long-run sense, the economic systems become circular in that new capital goods become inputs in the various sectors. It is when viewing the economy in this long-run sense that the crucial importance of manufacturing sector is seen most clearly. Thus, not only does manufacturing generate a large number of backward linkages (as indicated by the triangulation of an input–output matrix dealing with current flows), but when the analysis is expanded to take account of physical capital flows, the (redefined) forward linkage effects become very evident. The manufacturing sector supplies a large part of all capital goods supplied.

To some extent this influence has already been covered in the earlier discussion in Section C. But the importance of the capital goods industry in generating productivity growth need not be limited to the induced productivity growth in the manufacturing sector. Rapid rates of growth of output in the non-manufacturing sectors of the economy can certainly be expected to induce inventions and a learning process that is beneficial to these sectors, provided that the latter employ capital in production. Because of this, it would be expected that the rate of growth of productivity in certain non-manufacturing sectors of the economy would show a positive correlation with the rate of growth of output in these same sectors. In this case, higher rates of growth of manufacturing output, to the extent that they measure higher rates of growth of output of capital goods destined for non-manufacturing sectors, generate more rapid rates of growth of non-manufacturing productivity and output.

However, this extended view of the interdependence of production activities is still too limited in spite of the fact that the analysis has been broadened to include capital goods. For what needs special emphasis in the postwar period are the forward linkages, not just of what has traditionally become known as the capital goods sector, but of what was referred to earlier as the technology sector. Traditionally, the capital goods industry has been viewed as the collection of firms producing machine tools or non-electrical equipment, and indeed much of the source of productivity growth for the economy in earlier times stemmed from activities in this sector. In the postwar period, the sectors responsible for introducing new technologies throughout the market economies include, in addition to the non-electrical machinery industry, the electronics (or electrical machinery) and chemical industries.

The importance of these industries is indicated somewhat in Table 7.3, which gives a breakdown of industrial production by sectors for the OECD countries as a group. The ISIC classification number is given in parenthesis after each sector title. Table 7.3 indicates a sizeable variation in growth rates between sector. The high growth rates for chemicals and metal products (which includes both electrical and non-electrical machinery) are particularly

Table 7.3. Annual average rates of growth of industrial production by sectors, OECD, 1955–73

	%
Total industrial production	5.3
Mining and Quarrying (21–9)	1.7
Manufacturing (31–9)	5.5
Food, Beverages and Tobacco (31)	4.0
Textiles, Clothing and Leather (32)	3.0
Chemicals (35)	8.5
Basic Metals (37)	4.0
Iron and Steel (371)	3.4
Non-Ferrous Metals (372)	5.0
Metal Products (38)	5.9
Non-electrical Machinery (382)	6.2
Transport Equipment (384)	4.7
Manufacturing n.e.s.	4.9

Sources: *Industrial Production Historical Statistics, 1955–1971*, OECD, Paris, 1973; and *Industrial Production, Quarterly Supplement to Main Economic Indicators*, OECD, Paris, 1975–4.

noticeable. Together these two sectors account for about one-half of manufacturing output in the OECD countries.

The chemical industry has been described as the 'Pandora's box of modern economic growth,' both because it is the source of development in processing methods and because of its development of substitute materials. The latter includes the development of plastics and synthetic materials which have resulted in significant technical improvements and cost reductions in a wide number of industries.[17] In addition, the chemical industry has provided fertilizers and insecticides for agriculture that have been an important source of productivity growth in that sector. In one sense these various goods can be classified as intermediate products, goods used in the processing of output closer to final demand. But a better perspective is offered if these outputs of the chemical industry are looked upon as new technologies developed in the chemical industry that are more similar to capital goods in their impact on the economy.

The impact of the electronics industry on the economy combines the influences traditionally imputed to the capital goods industry (in a manner described, say, by Arrow) with those attributed to the chemical industry. What has been cited as one of the outstanding characteristics of the development of the electronics industry is that it has led to a significant improvement in the quality of the capital goods produced.[18] This includes not only elec-

[17] See C. Freeman, *The Economics of Industrial Innovation*, Penguin, Harmondsworth, 1974, Chapter 3.

[18] 'The introduction of reliable and relatively low-cost electronic computers is perhaps the most revolutionary development of the post-war period, influencing almost every other industry and service.' See Freeman, op. cit. p. 108.

tronic computers but radio and telecommunication systems whose use has been widespread throughout the economy. Although the impact of these various influences of growth in manufacturing on productivity in other sectors is difficult to quantify, its overall effect appears to be substantial.

4. Conclusions

What emerges is a view of the manufacturing sector as a sector producing a large part of the output of goods and services destined for final demand. But in addition, a large part of the manufacturing sector is made up of industries that comprise what earlier was termed the technology sector. The technology sector develops inventions and innovations whose effects are later diffused throughout the entire economy. And while the technology sector is broader than the chemical, electronic and machine tools industries, these three industries certainly dominate the activities of the former. As a result, the manufacturing sector takes on importance as the sector propelling the rest of the economy not only because of the large number of backward linkages in the traditional input–output sense. In addition, important subsectors of manufacturing have been the main purveyors of technological and technical progress throughout much of the economy. However, as the various examples illustrate, these inventions and innovations are embodied in goods (both capital and intermediate) produced in the manufacturing sector to be used as inputs throughout the economy. Hence, growth in manufacturing output in these areas gives rise, in effect, to important forward linkages in the extended view of the interdependence of productive activities. To say this is but to say that the postwar period was a period when science-based, research-intensive industries dominated the development of new technologies and, thus, contributed so greatly to the growth of productivity throughout the economy.[19]

E. Summary

Chapter VII sought to develop the final building block in the model to explain why growth rates differ. The chief aim was to give credence to a view with a long history in applied economics; namely, that the development of the manufacturing sector is the key to the overall development of an economy. This view has been widely accepted among economists studying underdeveloped or semi-industrialized economies. What has been attempted here is to make a case that the manufacturing sector continues to play a key role for economies well on the way to modernity and affluence.

As indicated above, attempts to substantiate this position statistically are fraught with danger. Nevertheless, Section C, and to a lesser extent Section D, did argue that estimated relations that assume that the rate of growth of output determines the rate of growth of productivity (and employment)

[19] See Nelson *et al.*, op. cit., Chapters 2–4.

are not so ambiguous as to prove meaningless. Furthermore, the growth of the manufacturing sector not only stimulates productivity growth in manufacturing (and, therefore, overall) but stimulates productivity growth in the non-manufacturing sectors. The arguments have been quite general and the formal models expressing the engine of growth hypothesis very crude. But the relationship of manufacturing to the rest of the economy is no less real for all that. Chapter VIII will attempt, with the aid of some simple mathematical and econometric relationships, to highlight the various strands in the argument developed up to this point.

Chapter VIII The Simple Mathematics of Growth

A. Introduction

Chapter VIII attempts to pull together the various strands of the argument developed in the last several chapters. This will be done with the help of some simple mathematical and econometric models. The simplicity of the analysis is largely a matter of necessity. Until recently, there were no comparable data extending over a suitable length of time for the various OECD economies that would allow for even the simplest sort of statistical testing of the model developed in the earlier chapters. Cripps's and Tarling's cross-section–time series data allows a testing of the theory against twelve OECD countries in the period roughly 1951 to 1970.[1]

There are still serious problems when using these data for regression work. First, in an effort to eliminate the influence of cyclical movements on growth rates, their observations on growth rates of output, employment and productivity are peak-to-peak measures in each country. This allowed for three to four observations for each country. Because of this procedure, a good part of the lag structure at work in the different economies cannot be picked up. The second limitation results from the fact that data were collected on only a few important economic variables in their study. This was largely responsible for some of the rather simple regressions in Chapter VII, and will continue to limit the analysis. However, some effort has been made to supplement these data. Furthermore, there is one compensation in all this. The resulting model, simple as it is, does outline very clearly the basic growth mechanism that has been at work during the period up to the early 1970s. As such, it serves as a useful pedagogical device for sharpening and highlighting the main points of the earlier analysis.

Section B gives the results of the statistical testing of the models developed in Chapter VI to explain the rate of growth of manufacturing output. In Section C one of these models is combined with the simple engine of growth relation illustrated earlier in Diagram 7.1 to bring out some of the con-

[1] Cripps and Tarling, op. cit. At the time of this writing (Autumn 1976) very few data were available for extending the sample period into the 1970s.

vergence properties of the model. Even though the relations are extremely simple, the orders of magnitude of the parameter estimates are reasonable and justify deriving the long-run growth rates for the different countries. Section D estimates some simple demand for labor relations illustrating the findings of Chapter V that employment of labor in manufacturing up until the early 1970s was demand-determined. Some regressions determining the rates of growth of productivity in manufacturing, one of the underpinnings of the engine of growth hypothesis, are also shown. Section E attempts to give an over view by comparing two extreme situations – the Japanese and British patterns of growth, the latter a version of a de-industrialization process. Section F summarizes the workings of the model, emphasizing the 'causal chain' involved in explaining why growth rates differ.

B. Some Regression Results

Consider first the explanation offered for the growth of manufacturing output in Chapter VI. The rate of growth of manufacturing output, $\dot{Q}_m$, was assumed to be negatively related to per capita income, q, and to the ratio of per capita income in some country and the income of the industrial leader, q_r; and positively related to the ratio of investment to value added in manufacturing, $(I/Q)_m$, and to the rate of growth of total output, $\dot{Q}$. It was also suggested that certain interactions between some of the variables might exist.

Other things being equal, low levels of per capita income were associated with rapid rates of growth of manufacturing output for two reasons: (1) given the range of per capita incomes for the industrialized countries of the sample, the lower the level of per capita income the smaller the proportion of consumer budgets allocated to services and the larger the proportion spent on goods; and (2) the lower the level of per capita income relative to that of the industrial leader, the larger the stock of technological and technical knowledge to be borrowed. However, there was no *a priori* reason to expect that these two variables, q and q_r, would move together. Per capita income levels in any country can be expected to have an upward trend, but the ratio of any such income level to that of the industrial leader would depend upon relative rates of growth of per capita income in the two countries. Its behavior over time could, therefore, show widely different patterns. As a result, in the theoretical model of Chapter VI, q and q_r were both included in the model. The investment ratio was assumed to have a positive effect on the rate of growth of manufacturing output primarily because it measured the extent to which a country attempted to absorb new technologies, whether borrowed or otherwise. In addition, high investment ratios indicated the kinds of strong demand pressures that reduce macro-risks and have favorable stimulating effects on productivity. Finally, the rate of growth of manufacturing output was assumed to be positively related to the overall growth of the economy because a large share of manufacturing output is made up of consumer goods whose consumption will grow with the economy.

In seeking to test the model one basic change was made at the outset. In Chapter VII it was argued that the manufacturing sector should be viewed as the engine of growth. This view was summarized in Diagram 7.1 above. The explanation of the rate of growth of manufacturing output put forward in Chapter VI indicated a second relationship between these two variables, this time with the rate of growth of total output influencing the rate of growth of manufacturing output. This raises problems for the statistical testing of the model.

In an attempt to estimate parameters of models that involve simultaneous relations, such as the two between the rate of growth of total output and manufacturing output, econometricians have devised rather refined estimating techniques with certain desirable properties. However, this solution was not available in this study because of a lack of data on a significant number of variables, and a different approach had to be taken. Instead a simplification was introduced in the estimation of the equation for the growth of manufacturing output that emphasized the importance of the manufacturing sector in the whole growth process. The simplification entailed the specification of a 'structural' equation of the form (disregarding lags)

$$\dot{Q}_{\mathrm{m}} = f[q, \dot{Q}, q_{\mathrm{r}}, (I/Q)_{\mathrm{m}}].$$

Then, an engine of growth of equation such as

$$\dot{Q} = 1.153 + 0.614\,\dot{Q}_{\mathrm{m}} \tag{1a}$$

from Table 7.1 was substituted into this structural equation and $\dot{Q}$ eliminated, giving

$$\dot{Q}_{\mathrm{m}} = F[q, q_{\mathrm{r}}, (I/Q)_{\mathrm{m}}].$$

This last equation was then viewed as a reduced form equation whereby a set of exogenous variables determines the rate of growth of manufacturing output, which in turn determines the rate of growth of total output as seen in equation (1a) above. Using this form of the model for estimating purposes made explicit the importance of the manufacturing sector for growth.

In Chapter VI it was emphasized that the impact of investment on output growth was very likely lagged. The Cripps and Tarling method of computing growth rates from one cycle peak to the next did not allow these kinds of lags to be picked up. As a result, all the regressions related output growth (so measured) to investment during the same period. It is also true that output growth affects investment again with a lag. No attempt was made to estimate this relation in order to stress the basic recursive structure of the economies studied.

Preliminary regressions indicated that no satisfactory statistical results were possible if the per capita income variables, q and q_{r}, were both entered in any equation because of multicollinearity. In the regressions, q_r was always measured as the ratio of per capita income in some country to per capita income in the United States in constant dollars at the beginning of each (peak-to-peak) period. What happened during the postwar period was that both q and q_r had strong upward trends. The trend in per capita income in some country relative to that in the United States, q_r arose from the more rapid growth in per capita incomes in this and all other countries relative to growth rates in the United States.[2] As a result the model was re-estimated with one or the other per capita income variable supressed.

Three different forms of the model were tried. Thus;

$$\dot{Q}_m = b_0 + b_1 q_r + b_2 (I/Q)_m; \tag{1a}$$

$$\dot{Q}_m = c_0 + (c_1 + c_2 q_r) \cdot (I/Q)_m = c_0 + c_1 (I/Q)_m + c_2 q_r (I/Q)_m \tag{1b}$$

and

$$\dot{Q}_m = d_0 + (d_1 + d_2/q_r) \cdot (I/Q)_m = d_0 + d_1 (I/Q)_m + d_2 (I/Q)_m / q_r. \tag{1c}$$

In equation (1a), the expected sign of b_1 (and b_2) was positive. The reciprocal of the relative income variable was used to allow the influence of changes in q_r to diminish as q_r increases. In other words in a process of 'catching up' with the industrial leader, the bonus received for being a late starter declines rapidly during the early stages of catching up but less rapidly as the gap in income levels continues to narrow. Similar notions are implied by equation (1c). However, equations (1b) and (1c) allow the technology gap to influence growth rates through the former's impact on the productivity of investment by incorporating an interaction between q_r and $(I/Q)_m$. The expected signs of c_2 and d_2 are negative and positive respectively; i.e., the higher are relative income levels, the less productive is investment. Additional regressions substituted q for q_r and also included the rate of growth of population, $\dot{P}$.

The various regression results are summarized in Table 8.1 for the twelve countries in the sample and in Table 8.2 for the larger six countries. Additional regressions (not shown) were run with Japan excluded from the sample. The results indicated some sensitivity to the exclusion of Japan in the sense that the R-squares were lower and in some cases the investment variable became non-significant, but even without Japan the tests supported the model according to the usual statistical criteria.

It is clear from Tables 8.1 and 8.2 that the fit is better for the six large countries treated separately than when all twelve economies, large and small, are treated together.[3] The population variable was significant in one-half

[2] See Table 2.2.

[3] The six large countries in the sample were France, Germany, Italy, Japan, the United Kingdom and the United States. The remaining smaller countries were Austria, Belgium, Canada, Denmark, the Netherlands and Norway. For Italy it was necessary to use industrial output and investment rather than manufacturing output and investment.

Table 8.1. Regression models for the rate of growth of manufacturing output, all countries

	Constant term	$1/q$	$1/q_r$	$(I/Q)_m$	$q(I/Q)_m$	$(I/Q)_m/q$	$q_r(I/Q)_m$	$(I/Q)_m/q_r$	P	R^2
(1)	0.185		1.09* (0.211)	0.173* (0.059)						0.72
(2)	−0.955		1.21* (0.209)	0.155* (0.061)					1.12* (0.524)	0.73
(3)	3.75			−0.021 (0.088)				0.053* (0.009)		0.71
(4)	2.93			−0.032 (0.088)				0.055* (0.010)	0.850 (0.520)	0.73
(5)	2.64			0.369* (0.055)			−0.381* (0.106)			0.62
(6)	1.97			0.369* (0.052)			−0.501* (0.111)		1.54* (0.620)	0.67
(7)	0.078	2205* (449)		0.204* (0.062)						0.69
(8)	−0.760	2334* (449)		0.195* (0.061)					0.833 (0.538)	0.71
(9)	2.95			0.051 (0.084)		104* (21.2)				0.68
(10)	2.37			0.042 (0.083)		107.5* (21.2)			0.665 (0.539)	0.70
(11)	2.58			0.370* (0.054)	−0.00016* (0.0004)					0.63
(12)	1.87			0.372* (0.052)	−0.00018* (0.0004)				1.13* (0.60)	0.66

*Coefficient is significant at 5 per cent level.

Table 8.2. Regression models for rate of growth of manufacturing output, all big countries

	Constant term	$1/q$	$1/q_r$	$(I/Q)_m$	$q(I/Q)_m$	$(I/Q)_m/q$	$q_r(I/Q)_m$	$(I/Q)_m/q_r$	$\dot{P}$	R^2
(13)	−0.036		0.953* (0.286)	0.229* (0.083)						0.80
(14)	−2.54		1.07* (0.269)	0.213* (0.084)					2.40* (1.12)	0.82
(15)	2.77			0.086 (0.146)				0.042* (0.015)		0.74
(16)	0.812			0.074 (0.139)				0.045* (0.015)	2.02 (1.24)	0.78
(17)	2.16			0.403* (0.076)			−0.322* (0.154)			0.71
(18)	0.491			0.377* (0.065)			−0.540* (0.150)		3.86* (1.33)	0.80
(19)	−0.412	1961* (603)		0.265* (0.086)						0.77
(20)	−0.245	2127* (573)		0.253* (0.081)					2.13 (1.15)	0.81
(21)	1.92			0.153 (0.131)		83.5* (31.4)				0.73
(22)	0.295			0.141 (0.128)		87.6* (30.6)			1.80 (1.26)	0.77
(23)	2.26			0.400* (0.075)	−0.00014* (0.00006)					0.72
(24)	0.504			0.388* (0.068)	−0.00019* (0.00006)				2.97* (1.31)	0.78

*Coefficient is significant at 5 per cent level.

the regressions. The models that attempted to pick up the interaction between investment and income levels in the form $(I/Q)_m/q$ or $(I/Q)_m/q_r$ were the.least successful and will not be discussed further. The intercorrelation between these variables and $(I/Q)_m$ was very high, suggesting again a problem of multicollinearity. The ratio of per capita incomes in some country to that in the United States performed slightly better than per capita income alone. Since q_r can serve to pick up the influence of income levels on demand patterns as well as the technology gap, only models utilizing this variable will be discussed further.

Equations (13) and (17) in Table 8.2 illustrate the economic forces at work. Equation (13),

$$\dot{Q}_m = -0.036 + 0.953/q_r + 0.229(I/Q)_m$$

indicates that, for each one per cent increase in the investment ratio, the rate of growth of manufacturing output increases by a little less than 0.25 per cent. At the beginning of the postwar period, the ratio of per capita income in Japan to per capita income in the United States, i.e. q_r, was 0.118 compared with a value of 0.255 for the ratio of German to United States per capita income for the same period. Thus, the 'late start' in the industrialization (owing to World War II) added $0.953/0.118 = 8.08$ per cent to the Japanese growth rate in manufacturing but only $0.953/0.255 = 3.74$ per cent to the German rate. By the mid-1960s, as these and other countries closed the per capita income gap, the relevant relative per capita income values were 0.222 and 0.479 for Japan and Germany, respectively. The ability to borrow technology by this point in time, therefore, added $0.953/0.222 = 4.29$ per cent and $0.953/0.479 = 1.99$ per cent to the growth of output in Japan and Germany, respectively. The 'long-run' growth rate, i.e. if and when per capita incomes reach the American level and $q_r = 1$, is given by equation (13) as

$$\dot{Q}_m = 0.917 + 0.229(I/Q)_m.$$

Differences in growth rates in this situation depend only on investment or the 'effort' made to grow.

Equation (17) can be written

$$\dot{Q}_m = 2.16 + (0.403 - 0.322q_r)\cdot(I/Q)_m.$$

Using the earlier example of $q_r = 0.118$ for Japan and $q_r = 0.255$ for Germany, a one per cent increase in the investment ratio increased the rate of growth of output by $(0.403 - 0.038) = 0.365$ per cent in Japan and by $(0.403 - 0.082) = 0.321$ per cent in Germany at the beginning of the postwar period. However, by the mid-1960s, a one per cent increase in the investment ratio served to increase the rate of growth of manufacturing output by $(0.403 - 0.071) = 0.322$ per cent and by $(0.403 - 0.154) = 0.249$ per cent in Japan and Germany respectively. Thus, whether the model depicted by equation (13) or (17) in Table 8.2 is used, the bonus for starting late declines as the technology gap narrows.[4]

C. The Workings of the Model

1. Relative rates of growth of manufacturing and total output

Having derived some parameter estimates for the models explaining growth of the manufacturing sector, it is now possible to lay out in a simple fashion the basic causal structure of the model of the last few chapters together with some orders of magnitude and long-run implications for growth. First write

$$\dot{Q}_m = g_0 + g_1(I/Q)_m + k_1/q_r = k_0 + k_1/q_r \tag{I}$$

with $k_0 = g_0 + g_1(I/Q)_m$ as the model for explaining the growth of manufacturing output assuming $k_0, k_1 > 0$. Next write

$$\dot{Q} = e_0 + e_1\dot{Q}_m$$

for the engine of growth relation, $\dot{Q}$ again measuring the rate of growth of total output. Substituting equation (I) into this gives

$$\dot{Q} = e_0 + e_1\dot{Q}_m = e_0 + e_1k_0 + e_1k_1/q_r. \tag{II}$$

If it is assumed that $e_1 < 1$ (as indicated in Table 7.1), then $k_1 > e_1k_1$ and the graphs of equations (I) and (II) will always indicate a steeper slope for the $\dot{Q}_m$ line compared with the $\dot{Q}$ line with respect to q_r. The relative size of k_0 compared with $(e_0 + e_1k_0)$ determines whether or not $\dot{Q} = \dot{Q}_m$ at any q_r. Thus, assume that $k_0 < (e_0 + e_1k_0)$ (which ensures that $\dot{Q} = \dot{Q}_m$ at some positive growth rate). Then the graphs of equations (I) and (II) are given in Diagram 8.1 as lines $\dot{Q}$ and $\dot{Q}_m$. If $k_0 > e_0 + e_1k_0$, the two lines never intersect with $\dot{Q}_m > \dot{Q}$ for all q_r. This is shown by lines $\dot{Q}$ and $\dot{Q}_m$ in Diagram 8.2.

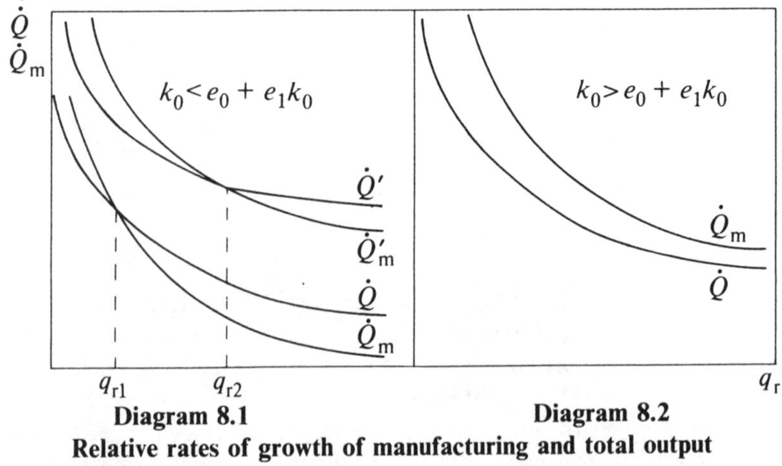

Diagram 8.1 **Diagram 8.2**

Relative rates of growth of manufacturing and total output

[4]The text stresses the ability to borrow from the United States. However, there is nothing to prevent, say, the Japanese from borrowing technology from the Germans as they undoubtedly did by the 1960s.

The workings of an economy other than the industrial leader that behaves according to equations (I) and (II) can be interpreted with the help of Diagram 8.1. To the left of income $q_{r1} = k_1(1 - e_1)/(e_0 + e_1k_0 - k_0)$, the rate of growth of manufacturing output exceeds the rate of growth of total output; to the right the inequality is reversed. At $q_r = q_{r1}$ we have a situation of (momentary) balanced growth. This result can be compared with the formulation depicted in Diagram 7.1 above where $\dot{Q}_m$ always exceeded $\dot{Q}$ provided $\dot{Q}_m$ grew above a critical rate; i.e., $\dot{Q}_m > e_0/(1 - e_1)$ as determined by equation (II), $\dot{Q} = e_0 + e_1\dot{Q}_m$. In the model here, $\dot{Q}$ and $\dot{Q}_m$ are both ultimately determined by q_r and $(I/Q)_m$. So long as $(I/Q)_m$ is such that $k_0 < e_0 + e_1k_0$, then, given $0 < e_1 < 1$, rising levels of q_r will lead to greater decreases in $\dot{Q}_m$ than $\dot{Q}$ until eventually $\dot{Q}_m < \dot{Q}$. In the case where $k_0 > e_1 + e_1k_0$ as in Diagram 8.2, $\dot{Q}_m > \dot{Q}$ for all q_r.

2. Equal effort–convergent growth rates

Diagrams 8.1 and 8.2 bring out some interesting aspects of the growth properties and patterns of the model. Assume that k_0, k_1, e_0 and e_1 are identical for all countries. Now,

$$\dot{Q} = e_0 + e_1k_0 + e_1k_1/q_r \qquad \text{(II)}$$

gives the rate of growth of aggregate output for every country other than the United States. Since $q_r = 1$ for the United States, its growth rate is given by

$$\dot{Q}_{US} = e_0 + e_1k_0 + e_1k_1.$$

Therefore $\dot{Q} > \dot{Q}_{US}$ as $e_1k_1/q_r > e_1k_1$ or $1 > q_r$. In other words, aggregate output always grows more slowly in the United States than in every other country as long as per capita incomes are higher in the United States, assuming k_0 (which is a function of the investment rates and, therefore, 'effort'), k_1, e_0 and e_1 are identical across countries. Whether or not rates of growth of per capita income are less in the United States than elsewhere, leading to an increase in q_r, depends upon population growth. Assume population grows at the same rate everywhere so that q_r rises initially over time. Then, given these assumptions, eventually all countries will grow at the same rate: $\dot{Q} = e_0 + e_1k_0 + e_1k_1$, a special kind of asymptote of equation (II). Late starters in the growth process may experience relatively rapid rates of growth at first, but over time differences in country growth rates will narrow.[5] If it could also be assumed that the relationship between rates of growth in the non-manufacturing sectors are also related to $\dot{Q}_m$, the patterns of growth also become increasingly similar over time.

[5] By assuming that k_0, k_1, e_0 and e_1 are identical across countries, the eventual convergence of growth rates is assured; the same results as the United Nations study (see *Economic Survey of Europe*, op. cit., Chapter 3). As is clear from the text, the model is only designed to handle those situations where $q_r \leq 1$.

3. Unequal effort–unequal growth rates

Next the parameter $k_0 = g_0 + g_1(I/Q)_m$ can be treated as a shift parameter in order to study the impact of changes in the investment ratio, $(I/Q)_m$. As is clear from equations (I) and (II), an increase in k_0 to k_0' has a bigger effect on $\dot{Q}_m$ than $\dot{Q}$ since $d\dot{Q}_m/dk_0 = 1$, while $d\dot{Q}/dk_0 = e_1 < 1$. An upward shift in k_0 is depicted in Diagram 8.1 by lines $\dot{Q}'$ and $\dot{Q}_m'$. Clearly, the shift allows high rates of growth to persist for long periods of time.[6] The level of per capita income at which $\dot{Q} = \dot{Q}_m$ is now higher, q_{r2} rather than q_{r1}.

The importance of investment for growth can be seen in another way. The assumption that $k_0 = g_0 + g_1(I/Q)_m$ is identical for all countries can be dropped and the actual values for $(I/Q)_m$ and q_r during the period for each country can be inserted into estimated equations of the type depicted by equations (I) and (II) to determine the impact of differences in these factors on growth rates. In Table 8.3 the six largest OECD countries in the sample are used to bring out these influences. Three pairs of growth rates are given, the actual, the predicted and the long-run growth rates of total and manufacturing output for the six big OECD countries. Columns (5) and (6) rank the countries from fastest to slowest on the basis of their actual postwar record up to 1969 or 1970. These rankings show an inverse relation with the ratio of per capita income of a country to per capita income in the United States, q_r, at the beginning of the postwar period, which is given in the last column.

Table 8.3. Short-run and long-run growth rates

	Long-run growth rates		*Predicted growth rates*		*Actual growth rates*		*Initial per capital income*[a]
	(1) $\dot{Q}$	(2) $\dot{Q}_m$	(3) $\dot{Q}$	(4) $\dot{Q}_m$	(5) $\dot{Q}$	(6) $\dot{Q}_m$	(7)
	%	%	%	%	%	%	
Japan	5.88	7.60	10.18	14.72	9.52	13.25	0.118
Germany	4.67	5.59	6.35	8.37	6.00	7.74	0.255
Italy	3.94	4.37	6.66	8.89	5.29	7.65	0.174
France	4.06	4.57	4.62	5.50	4.99	5.51	0.504
USA	3.45	3.58	3.45	3.58	3.54	3.73	1.00
UK	3.59	3.79	4.26	4.91	2.62	3.16	0.458

[a] Ratio of constant dollar figures.

Sources: *Labour Force Statistics*, OECD, Paris, and *International Financial Statistics*, International Monetary Fund, Washington, DC and Cripps and Tarling, op. cit.

[6] The two lines always intersect at $\dot{Q} = \dot{Q}_m = e_0/(1 - e_1)$ as long as $k_0 < e_0 + e_1 k_0$.

Columns (3) and (4) give the predicted values of $\dot{Q}$ and $\dot{Q}_m$ found by inserting into equation (13) from Table 8.2; i.e.,

$$\dot{Q}_m = -0.036 + 0.953/q_r + 0.229(I/Q)_m$$

– the average values of $(I/Q)_m$ over the whole sample period and the initial value for q_r for each country – and then inserting these predicted values of $\dot{Q}_m$ into equation (1b) from Table 7.1 above; i.e.,

$$\dot{Q} = 1.295 + 0.603\,\dot{Q}_m. \quad (1b)$$

The predicted growth rates give rankings similar to the actual growth rates except that the rankings of the United States and the United Kingdom, on the one hand, and Germany and Italy, on the other, are reversed. Using this method for computation, predicted growth rates for Japan, Italy and Germany are high partly because of a large technology gap bonus, i.e. a low initial q_r, but also because of a strong effort to borrow the technology. The predicted performance of the other three falls short of this because of a smaller bonus (zero for the United States) and a poor investment effort, especially in the case of the United States and the United Kingdom.[7]

Columns (1) and (2) give the long-run growth rates of each country, allowing q_r to go to one and assuming that the average postwar values of $(I/Q)_m$ for each country are maintained. In other words, columns (1) and (2) give the separate 'asymptotes' of the equations

$$\dot{Q}_m = -0.036 + 0.953/q_r + 0.229\,(I/Q)_m$$

and

$$\dot{Q} = 1.295 + 0.603\,\dot{Q}_m$$

for each country in the following sense. If the actual investment ratio of each country during the postwar period is maintained until per capita incomes in each country are equal to those in the United States, the long-run growth rate of manufacturing output is then given by

$$\dot{Q}_m = 0.917 + 0.229\,(I/Q)_m.$$

By inserting the different postwar values for $(I/Q)_m$ into this equation, the growth rates listed in column (2) are obtained. When this is inserted into the equation,

$$\dot{Q} = 1.295 + 0.603\,\dot{Q}_m$$

the growth rates listed in column (1) are determined.

Given the assumptions that $q_r = 1$ but $(I/Q)_m$ varies across countries, it is clear that the long-run growth rates $\dot{Q}$ and $\dot{Q}_m$ for each country are less than the postwar experience and the predicted values. But there is no longer a tendency for convergence of growth rates across countries as in the previous section. It is certainly true that a late start in the growth race can

[7] The annual average ratio of investment to output in manufacturing over the whole period was 29.17, 20.39, 15.08, 15.94, 11.63 and 12.55 for Japan, Germany, Italy, France, the United States and the United Kingdom, respectively. Data taken from Cripps and Tarling, op. cit.

partly explain higher growth rates, but a high investment ratio also helps to determine why growth rates differ. To put it another way, going to war against the industrial leaders and losing it may spur growth rates; but without a sustained effort to take advantage of the technological gap that exists following that war, long-run 'super' growth cannot be maintained.

D. Is Flexibility Still Important?

The discussion in Chapters I–VI stressed the importance of flexibility in determining the speed of the growth and transformation process. In particular Chapters IV and V focused on the importance of the availability of adequate supplies of labor for the manufacturing and industrial sectors should the demand for output be strong in these sectors. The reallocation of resources toward the industrial sectors was viewed as a possible important source of growth. Yet the emphasis in Chapter VII was clearly shifted toward the importance of the reallocation of output and not inputs in determining the rate of growth and transformation. The shift in emphasis from the reallocation of inputs to the reallocation of outputs served to emphasize that one of the merits of the dual model approach to growth is its singling out the importance of the growth of output of the manufacturing sector for growth of the economy. This remains true whatever the derived employment patterns.

Thus write as in Chapter VII

$$\dot{p}_{m} = a_0 + a_1 \dot{Q}_{m} \qquad (2)$$

where $\dot{p}_{m}$ and $\dot{Q}_{m}$ are, as before, the rate of growth of labor productivity and output in manufacturing, respectively. Since the rate of growth of manufacturing output must, by definition, equal the sum of the rate of growth of labor productivity and employment in manufacturing, $\dot{E}_{m}$ (i.e., $\dot{Q}_{m} = \dot{p}_{m} + \dot{E}_{m}$), then it follows that

$$\dot{E}_{m} = -a_0 + (1 - a_1)\dot{Q}_{m}. \qquad (3)$$

If $a_1 \geqslant 1$, the expansion of output in manufacturing can proceed at any rate without the expansion of employment; i.e., the elasticity of the demand for labor with respect to output, $(1 - a_1)$. is negative or zero. The belief that the manufacturing sector acts as the prime force in determining the overall growth performance of the economy is thus a separate issue from the belief that the reallocation of labor is a necessary condition for growth. Nevertheless, repeated estimates of the relationship between productivity and employment growth on the one hand and output growth on the other, of the type described in equations (2) and (3), have indicated that a_1 is substantially less than one. The expansion of output in manufacturing requires the simultaneous expansion of labor. Flexibility of labor supply has been found to be an important condition for growth in this sense.

Table 8.4. Verdoorn's Law again

$\dot{p}_m = 1.10 + 0.545\,\dot{Q}_m$ (0.055)	$R^2 = 0.710$	All countries	(2a)
$\dot{E}_m = -1.10 + 0.456\dot{Q}_m$ (0.056)	$R^2 = 0.627$	All countries	(3a)
$\dot{p}_m = 1.33 + 0.499\dot{Q}_m$ (0.090)	$R^2 = 0.461$	All countries except Japan	(2b)
$\dot{E}_m = -1.35 + 0.509\,\dot{Q}_m$ (0.090)	$R^2 = 0.467$	All countries except Japan	(3b)
$\dot{p}_m = 1.12 + 0.532\dot{Q}_m$ (0.059)	$R^2 = 0.804$	All big countries	(2c)
$\dot{E}_m = -1.09 + 0.468\dot{Q}_m$ (0.060)	$R^2 = 0.755$	All big countries	(3c)

Source: Cripps and Tarling, op. cit.

Table 8.4 gives the results for various samples for the period up to 1970, when the growth of both employment and productivity are regressed against the growth of output. The results are influenced by the exclusion of Japan but never in such a way as to lead to non-significant statistical results. Furthermore, dropping and adding other countries indicates that the results are not appreciably affected.

But the relationship between employment (and productivity) growth and output growth in manufacturing is seen to be even stronger when one important factor is taken into account: the marked acceleration in the rate of growth of productivity that took place over time during the postwar period.[8] Some account of this acceleration in productivity growth (and the related impact on the demand for labor) can be seen by allowing the elasticity of productivity growth with respect to output growth, and the elasticity of the demand for labor with respect to output growth, to be a function of time itself.

Thus write

$$a_1 = h_0 + h_1 T$$

where T takes values from 1 to 4, $T = 1$ being the first peak-to-peak period in the postwar period in some country, etc. This expression when substituted into equations (2) and (3) gives

$$\dot{p}_m = a_0 + h_0\dot{Q}_m + h_1(\dot{Q}_m T) \qquad (4)$$

[8] See the data in Table 2.2 above.

and

$$\dot{E}_m = -a_0 + (1-h_0)\dot{Q}_m - h_1(\dot{Q}_m T). \quad (5)$$

The regression results are shown in Table 8.5. The R-squares are appreciably larger in there than in Table 8.4 and the coefficients are very stable across samples.[9]

Table 8.5. The acceleration in productivity growth

$\dot{p}_m = 0.926 + 0.394\,\dot{Q}_m + 0.071(\dot{Q}_m T)$	$R^2 = 0.789$	All countries	(4a)
(0.062) (0.019)			
$\dot{E}_m = -0.921 + 0.605\dot{Q}_m - 0.070(\dot{Q}_m T)$	$R^2 = 0.724$	All countries	(5a)
(0.062) (0.019)			
$\dot{p}_m = 1.09 + 0.369\,\dot{Q}_m + 0.068(\dot{Q}_m T)$	$R^2 = 0.558$	All countries except Japan	(4b)
(0.095) (0.025)			
$\dot{E}_m = -1.12 + 0.636\,\dot{Q}_m - 0.066\,(\dot{Q}_m T)$	$R^2 = 0.556$	All countries except Japan	(5b)
(0.097) (0.025)			
$\dot{p}_m = 0.938 + 0.405\,\dot{Q}_m + 0.062(\dot{Q}_m T)$	$R^2 = 0.866$	All big countries	(4c)
(0.066) (0.021)			
$\dot{E}_m = -0.907 + 0.591\,\dot{Q}_m - 0.060\,(\dot{Q}_m T)$	$R^2 = 0.826$	All big countries	(5c)
(0.068) (0.022)			

Source: Cripps and Tarling, op. cit.

Equation (5a) can be written

$$\dot{E}_m = -0.921 + (0.605 - 0.07T)\dot{Q}_m. \quad (5a)$$

Allowing T to increase from 1 to 4 over the sample period (1951–70), the elasticity of the derived demand for labor declines from 0.535 to 0.325.[10] This, of course, is the result of the acceleration of productivity growth during the period indicated in equation (4a).

Incorporating time trends in the testing of a modified version of Verdoorn's Law and the derived demand for labor equation explains very little. There is evidence that what was taking place in the market economies during the postwar period was a kind of development familiar to specialists in developing economies. Thus, during the 1950s, it has been argued, a great deal of development of the infrastructure or social overhead capital in transportation, communication and distribution took place. The full fruits of

[9] As Table 8.5 indicates, the correlations are not likely to be spurious just because all variables might be a function of time. The relationships between the economic variables remain strong even after a time trend is introduced. The relation $a_1 = h_0 + h_1 T^2$ was also tried and gave highly significant results! Obviously, other (economic) variables could be introduced.

[10] The time trend takes values from 1 to 4 since there are three or four time series observations for each of the countries in Cripps and Tarling's study.

these developments gradually became available during the second half of the period and the productivity of other sectors, notably manufacturing, then accelerated.[11]

However, whatever the underlying economic process involved, Table 8.5 once again illustrates reasonably strong and stable relationships across samples between productivity and employment growth on the one hand and output growth on the other. But Table 8.5 also points out that, while expansion of labor might well be essential for the expansion of output in manufacturing during the period covered in the sample, it need not always be. Thus, setting equation (5a) in Table 8.5 equal to zero and solving for $\dot{Q}_m$ gives $\dot{Q}_m = 0.921/(0.605 - 0.070T)$. By the end of the sample period, $(T = 4)$, this expression gives $\dot{Q}_m = 2.83$, indicating that any growth rate of manufacturing output less than 2.83 per cent would actually lead to a decline in manufacturing employment. In contrast, during the first part of the postwar period $(T = 1)$, any growth rate of output above 1.72 per cent required an expansion of labor.

The results shown in Table 8.5, therefore, suggest a refinement of the assertion that flexibility of labor supply is an important condition for growth of output and transformation. Recall that in Chapter IV economies were characterized as conforming to the model of the dual economy according to one criterion, if the rate of growth of employment in manufacturing exceeded that for the whole economy. This was thought to be a useful way of distinguishing between employment patterns, because it focused attention on a possible source of output and productivity growth – that arising from a relative shift of labor between sectors. It was but another way of emphasizing the importance of flexibility as a determinant of the rate of growth of output and transformation.

The results of this chapter indicate that this distinction between patterns of employment is a useful one when its implications are properly interpreted. Thus, when employment growth was rapid in manufacturing relative to overall employment, this would be related to the relatively higher rates of growth of demand for manufacturing output. The latter, in turn, led to rapid rates of growth of productivity in manufacturing and throughout the economy. The induced rate of growth of productivity in manufacturing was always impressive, but rarely was it large enough to allow manufacturing output to grow without the use of additional units of labor; at least during the period 1950–70.[12] However, the results in Table 8.5 indicate that the

[11] See K. Kennedy and B. Dowling, *Economic Growth in Ireland: The Experience since 1947*, Gill and MacMillan, Dublin, 1975; and K. Allen and A. Stevenson, *An Introduction to the Italian Economy*, Martin Robertson, London, 1974.

[12] In the period up until 1970, only three observations out of the forty-five in the Cripps and Tarling sample show a rate of growth of employment in manufacturing that is negative. These were the final boom periods in Austria, the Netherlands and the UK. After 1970, a decline in the level of employment in manufacturing became more common. See Chapter XI below.

elasticity of the derived demand for labor decreased over the period. For example, differentiating equation (5a) with respect to time gives

$$\partial \dot{E}_m / \partial T = -0.070 \dot{Q}_m$$

which states that, for any given $\dot{Q}_m$, the rate of growth of the derived demand for labor, $\dot{E}_m$, declines by 7 per cent per period. This reduced demand can in turn be traced to the acceleration in productivity growth seen, for example, in equation (4a) in Table 8.5. Thus flexibility was important for growth, although the importance of being able to draw labor into manufacturing lessened in this sense over the period as productivity growth accelerated. Some of the implications of these results will be drawn out now.

E. The Industrialization of Japan and the De-industrialization of Britain

The results of the last three sections can be drawn together by contrasting a Japanese model of industrialization with a British model of de-industrialization. Japan and the United Kingdom represent the two extremes among the developed market economies in postwar growth and transformation performances; the former, easily the most dynamic economy among the industrialized market economies, the latter, one of the most stagnant. In Diagram 8.3 two graphs of the equation (13)

$$\dot{Q}_m = -0.036 + 0.953/q_r + 0.229(I/Q)_m$$

from Table 8.2 are given, one for the United Kingdom and the other for

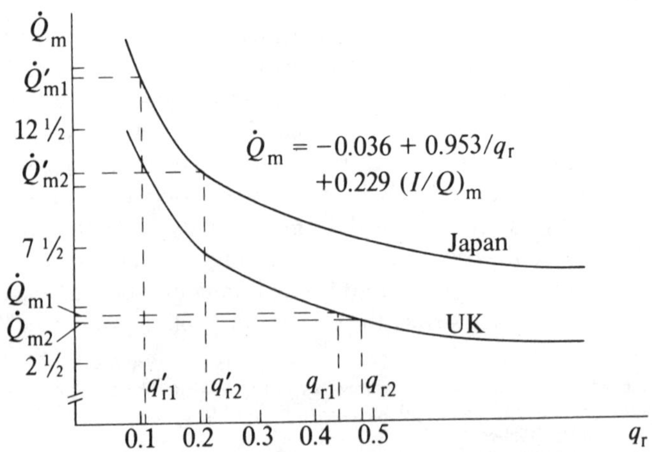

Diagram 8.3. Growth of manufacturing output in Japan and the United Kingdom

Japan. These curves are obtained by inserting the average value for the investment ratio in manufacturing for each country over the period from the early 1950s to the end of the 1960s, i.e. inserting $(I/Q)_m = 12.55$ per cent for the United Kingdom and $(I/Q)_m = 29.17$ per cent for Japan into equation (13) and plotting both relations. As is clear for any level of per capita income relative to the United States, the rate of growth of manufacturing output is higher for Japan because of the greater investment effort.

The expressions $q_{r1}' = 0.118$ and $q_{r2}' = 0.222$ represent the ratio of per capita income in Japan to that in the United States in 1953 and 1964, respectively, while $q_{r1} = 0.453$ and $q_{r2} = 0.483$ represent the ratio of per capita income in the United Kingdom to that in the United States in 1951 and 1965, respectively. The two earliest dates represent the first peak year in aggregate activity in each country and the later dates the initial year in the last peak-to-peak period for each. Given the initial values for per capita incomes, q_{r1} and q_{r1}', and the assumed values for investment, equation (13) predicts a rate of growth of manufacturing output of 14.79 per cent in Japan during the period 1953–57 and 4.82 per cent in the United Kingdom from 1951 to 1955. These are shown in Diagram 8.3 as $\dot{Q}_{m1}'$ and $\dot{Q}_{m1}$, respectively. Similarly, by inserting the actual values for q_{r2}' and q_{r2} for 1964 and 1965 into equation (13), along with the relevant investment ratios, the predicted growth rates for the period 1964–69 for Japan and 1965–69 for the United Kingdom are determined. These are shown by $\dot{Q}_{m2}' = 10.93$ per cent and $\dot{Q}_{m2} = 4.69$ per cent, respectively, in Diagram 8.3. From one period to the next, Japan and the United Kingdom both caught up to some extent with the United States. Because of this, rates of growth of output declined in both countries as there was less technology to borrow and as demand shifted relatively to services. But Japan continued to grow more rapidly than the United Kingdom because of a higher investment ratio and a lower per capita income.

Next in Diagram 8.4, two graphs of equation (5c) from Table 8.5 are drawn. Thus,

$$\dot{E}_m = -0.907 + 0.591\dot{Q}_m - 0.060(\dot{Q}_m T). \tag{5c}$$

with $T = 1$ in one case and $T = 4$ in the other. This derived demand for labor equation shifts over time because of the acceleration in the rate of growth of productivity, which acts to systematically reduce the demand for labor over time for any given rate of growth of manufacturing output. $\dot{Q}_{m1}'$ and $\dot{Q}_{m2}'$ are again the rates of growth of output of manufacturing for Japan and $\dot{Q}_{m1}$ and $\dot{Q}_{m2}$ their counterparts for the United Kingdom as just determined. The derived demands for labor for Japan are indicated by $\dot{E}_{m1}' = 6.95$ per cent and $\dot{E}_{m2}' = 2.93$ per cent and those for the United Kingdom by $\dot{E}_{m1} = 1.65$ per cent and $\dot{E}_{m2} = 0.74$ per cent. These are found by inserting $\dot{Q}_{m1}' = 14.79$ per cent and $\dot{Q}_{m2}' = 10.93$ per cent for Japan and

$\dot{Q}_{m1} = 4.82$ per cent and $\dot{Q}_{m2} = 4.69$ per cent for the United Kingdom into the equations;

$$\dot{E}_m = -0.907 + 0.531\,\dot{Q}_m \quad (T = 1) \tag{5c}$$

and

$$\dot{E}_m = -0.907 + 0.351\,\dot{Q}_m \quad (T = 4). \tag{5c}$$

The demands for labor fall for both countries from the first peak-to-peak period ($T = 1$) to the fourth peak-to-peak period ($T = 4$) and for two reasons; first, the rate of growth of output in manufacturing falls in both countries as just seen in Diagram 8.3; and less employment growth for any level of manufacturing growth is required because of the acceleration in the rate of growth of productivity in both countries between the two periods.

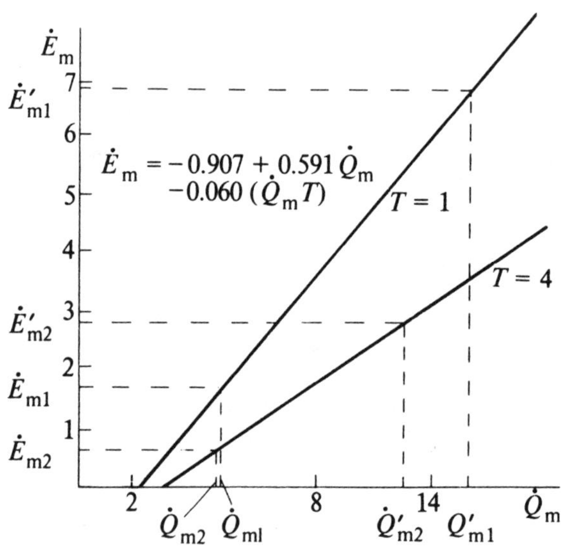

Diagram 8.4. The derived demand for labor in Japan and the United Kingdom

Finally, Diagram 8.5 graphs the equation

$$\dot{E}_w = -0.674 + \underset{(0.084)}{0.756}\,\dot{E}_m \quad R^2 = 0.87. \tag{6}$$

The variable $\dot{E}_w$ is the rate of growth of the ratio of employment of labor in manufacturing to total employment. A pooled cross-section–times series sample of the six large OECD economies from the early 1950s to the end of the 1960s was used to estimate the relationship.

Equation (6) implies that, for values of the rate of growth of derived demand for labor in manufacturing, $\dot{E}_m$, greater than 0.892 per cent, $\dot{E}_w$ is positive. In other words, labor will shift into manufacturing relative to total employment only when the derived demand for labor by manufacturers is sufficiently strong. When the rate of growth of employment in manufacturing is less than 0.892 per cent, a process of 'de-industrialization' will be said to have set in. The general sense of the model of de-industrialization (or industrialization) portrayed in equation (6) is as follows. Higher rates of growth of manufacturing employment are assumed to induce a greater economizing of labor in the non-manufacturing sectors through such means as induced productivity increases, thereby allowing the release of labor from agriculture, distribution and government service. Conversely, when the rate of growth of employment in manufacturing is low, the movement out of agriculture, distribution and government services slows down for reasons suggested in Chapter V.[13]

With this in mind, the postwar differences between Japan and Britain can be further illustrated with the help of Diagram 8.5. The values of $\dot{E}_m$, as

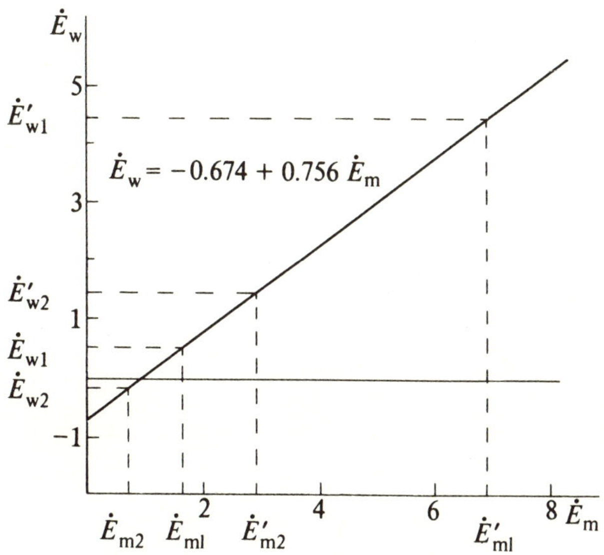

Diagram 8.5. The industrialization of Japan and the de-industrialization of Britain

measured in Diagram 8.4 on the vertical axis, are measured in Diagram 8.5 along the horizontal axis. For Japan the relatively large derived demands for manufacturing workers leads to positive rates of growth of $\dot{E}_w$; i.e., inserting $E_{ml}' = 6.95$ per cent and $E_{m2}' = 2.93$ per cent into equation (6) gives $\dot{E}_{wl}' = 4.57$ and $\dot{E}_{w2}' = 1.50$. For the United Kingdom, the corre-

[13] See Section E; Bacon and Eltis, op. cit. and; Sleeper, op. cit.

sponding figures are $\dot{E}_{w1} = 0.572$ and $\dot{E}_{w2} = -0.123$, found by inserting $E_{m1} = 1.65$ per cent and $E_{m2} = 0.74$ per cent into equation (6). In other words, by the end of the 1960s, the United Kingdom no longer conformed to the workings of the dual model in that the rate of growth of employment in manufacturing had fallen below the overall rate of growth of employment. This de-industrialization process that set in can be traced back with the help of Diagrams 8.3 and 8.4 to a failure of manufacturing output to grow rapidly and, ultimately, to a failure of Britain to invest a high enough portion of output. For example, if, by period $T = 4$, investment as a percentage of output in manufacturing had been 13.97 per cent (instead of 12.55 per cent), the rate of growth of manufacturing output according to equation (13) of Table 8.2 would have been 5.13 per cent. This, according to equation (5c), would have generated a rate of growth of employment in manufacturing of 0.892 per cent, enough to lead to $\dot{E}_w = 0$.

A final point before a summation. Recall that, in all countries listed in Table 4.4, the rate of growth of manufacturing output exceeded that of total output, while Table 4.3 indicated that there were a number of countries where the rate of growth of employment in manufacturing (and industry) fell below the overall rate of growth of employment.

$$\dot{E}_w = -0.716 + 0.672\,\dot{E}_m \qquad (6')$$

gives the results of a regression of the rate of growth of the ratio of employment in manufacturing to total employment on the rate of growth of manufacturing employment this time for twelve OECD countries from the early 1950s until the end of the 1970s. According to equation (6′), de-industrialization (i.e. $\dot{E}_w < 0$) sets in if $\dot{E}_m < 1.065$. Now, according to equation (5a) in Table 8.5, $\dot{E}_m$ grows at less than 1.065 per cent if $\dot{Q}_m < 6.11$ per cent ($T = 4$) or $\dot{Q}_m < 3.71$ per cent ($T = 1$). In other words, unless the rate of growth of manufacturing output exceeds the 6.11 per cent in the fourth or 3.71 per cent in the first period of the postwar period, $\dot{E}_w < 0$ and a country will not conform to one criterion for the application of the dual model. On the other hand, equation (7b) in Table 7.1, i.e.

$$\dot{Q} = 1.295 + 0.603\,\dot{Q}_m$$

indicates that $\dot{Q}_m > \dot{Q}$ when $\dot{Q}_m > 3.26$. In other words, as long as the rate of growth of manufacturing output exceeds 3.26 per cent, an economy satisfies the output criterion for application of the dual model. But as just indicated, growth rates of manufacturing output had to be greater than 3.71 per cent to satisfy the employment criterion for applicability of the dual model even in the early part of the postwar period.

The fact that all countries behaved in accordance with the dual model by the output criterion while several did not according to the employment criterion is now easily explained by the differences in the rate of growth of manufacturing output between countries. All the market economies experienced growth rates of output in the manufacturing sector that led to $\dot{Q}_m > \dot{Q}$. However, in some countries such as the United Kingdom and the United States, the rate of growth of manufacturing output and the resulting difference between the rates of growth of manufacturing and total output was not sufficiently large to prevent total employment from growing more rapidly than employment in manufacturing.

F. Summary

Chapter VIII has been essentially an exercise in simple econometrics and simulation. Single equation estimating techniques were employed to estimate the parameters of a simple mathematical version of the model sketched earlier in Chapters IV–VII. To be sure, the model was a very simple one, omitting a great deal of the complications, lags and interactions of the real world, and much needs to be done in the way of gathering better data, employing more sophisticated estimating techniques, etc. But the exercise seemed justified if for no other reason than that it laid out in an explicit form the basic mechanism that governed the growth processes of these economies. Moreover, the results were satisfactory given the usual statistical criteria, and the parameter estimates were reasonable. As a result, it was found useful to perform some simple simulation exercises, drawing out some of the dynamic implications of the model.

Section C brought out quite clearly the importance of investment for growth. It also indicated that, while the technology gap conferred a bonus on the different countries able to borrow technology, the importance of this factor declined for the different countries during the postwar period as per capita incomes grew rapidly relative to growth in the United States. By coupling the results of the model explaining the growth of manufacturing output with a simple engine of growth relation, it was possible to see clearly the factors that caused growth rates of total output to differ between countries in the postwar period. In addition, Section C allowed for a discussion of some of the convergence properties of the model.

Sections C, D and E taken together can be viewed as an attempt to explain (1) why patterns of employment varied across countries and (2) why employment patterns in some of the countries diverged from output patterns. Thus, the discussion in Section D clearly indicated that relative rates of growth of employment in manufacturing could be traced in the first instance to differences in the rate of growth of output in manufacturing, the conclusion drawn in Chapter V. But underlying the differences between countries in rates of growth of manufacturing output were differences in the technology gap facing each country, together with the effort made by the different countries to take advantage of this gap. Hence, the importance of investment and, ultimately, entrepreneurship and the technology sector discussed in Chapter VI.

Furthermore, the estimated relations were such that it was possible for the rate of growth of manufacturing output to exceed the rate of growth of total output in some country while the rate of growth of employment in manufacturing fell short of the growth of total employment. The difference, of course, could be traced to productivity growth in manufacturing. In order for an economy to conform to the workings of the dual model according to the employment criterion, not only was it necessary for manufacturing output to grow more rapidly than total output, but it had to do so by some critical amount.

The analysis of Sections D and E, particularly the finding of an acceleration in rates of growth of labor productivity over the period, lends itself easily to forecasts of employment patterns for the future. Thus, as per capita income levels rise, both absolutely and relative to the rich countries, it would be expected that rates of growth of manufacturing employment will decline absolutely and relatively leading eventually to a de-industrialization of all the market economies. At this point the transformation process envisaged by Svennilson may have reached a stage where the value of the dual model as a method of analysis may be questioned.

Moreover, in Chapter XI it is argued that, toward the end of the 1960s and beginning in the early 1970s, other structural changes were developing that were very likely changing the nature of modern capitalism in an even more profound manner. These reached a culmination with the traumatic 'shocks' that disturbed capitalism in 1973. The results, as will be argued, suggest that currently market capitalism may be undergoing a kind of transformation more dramatic than that envisaged by Svennilson and documented in the chapters thus far. Before undertaking to describe these shocks and the response of the different economies to them, a somewhat extended analysis of the relationship between trade and growth will be undertaken in Chapters IX and X. The reader willing to accept the general thrust of the arguments advanced to this point may proceed to Chapter XI. Those concerned that the role of exports in growth has been slighted and, particularly, with the possibility that differences in growth rates can be better explained in terms of differences in export performances will find Chapters IX and X of some interest.

Chapter IX **Export-Led Growth**

A. Introduction

In the regression model developed in Chapter VIII, the main instrument driving the economy was investment. Investment stimulated demand through the familiar multiplier process and added to the economy's capacity, especially in its role of implementing new technologies. At no point was any attention given to the importance (or lack thereof) of foreign trade. It is true that the rate of growth of manufacturing output can be divided into that destined for foreign markets and that produced locally for domestic consumption. Then, each of these could be related separately to the same set of factors that was used to explain growth of manufacturing output, i.e. investment, income levels and population growth. In Chapter X an argument is advanced that this procedure would be quite appropriate. But only in this limited sense has the analysis dealt with foreign trade.

In this chapter the analysis considers the foreign sector. This extension is important partly because balance of payments problems beset many economies in the postwar period and these difficulties were seen as one of the prime causes of a poor growth performance.[1] A more important reason for this extension is that many economists have stressed the important role exports play in growth. A large body of literature has developed which emphasizes the role of exports in 'driving' or 'leading' the economy.[2]

The main interest of this chapter will be to analyze the view that economic growth is export-led in some sense, primarily to see if the model summarized in Chapter VIII should at the very least be expanded to include a foreign sector. Section B discusses and rejects one criterion for determining whether growth is export-led or not. Section C discusses two alternative criteria. This is followed in Section D by the development of a simple model that incorporates the notion of a 'virtuous' or 'vicious' circle. Section E carries this analysis a step further by developing a more general model, one that takes more explicit account of the supply side. Section F attempts to

[1] The alleged adverse effects of what has come to be known as 'stop–go' policies have been worked out by several economists. See for example A. Lamfalussy, *The United Kingdom and the Six: An Essay on Economic Growth in Western Europe*, Richard Irwin, Homewood, Ill., 1963.

[2] Besides Lamfalussy, op. cit., two recent case studies emphasizing the importance of export-led growth are Allen and Stevenson, op. cit., and Kennedy and Dowling, op. cit.

draw out the basic distinction between export-led growth and 'homespun' growth within the context of models incorporating the notions of a virtuous or vicious circle. As such it sets the stage for Chapter X, which attempts to determine on *a priori* grounds whether growth is liable to be export-led or homespun. Section G suggests how the foreign sector might be grafted on to the model outlined in Chapter VIII, while Section H provides a summary. The analysis is carried out within the context of a system of 'relatively fixed' exchange rates.

B. Export-Led Growth and Market Shares

The view that economic growth is 'export-led' or 'export-determined' has a long history and many interpretations. For example, it has been argued that, if rapidly rising exports can be largely attributed to an enlarged share of different markets rather than to exporting the 'right' goods, i.e. goods with high worldwide growth elasticities, or exporting to the 'right' areas, i.e. those economies whose imports are expanding rapidly, then this is said to be evidence that growth is export-led. For the moment, let the correctness of this position go unchallenged. What has come to be known as the 'constant market share analysis' attempts to explain the export performance of a country by dividing up any change in the level of exports between two periods into components measuring the impact of growth in world trade, the changing commodity and area pattern of trade and the change in exports due to a change in the share of the market of each good in each area captured by the exporting country. This latter component is a residual which in some general sense is supposed to measure the competitiveness of a country's exports between two points in time and is usually termed the 'competitive effect.'[3]

As stressed in earlier chapters, as economies grow and per capita incomes rise, the composition of demand changes as a country works through a hierarchy of goods. Quite naturally, the composition of the demands for foreign goods changes also, partly as a result of the changing composition of demand itself and partly as a result of import substitution. The importance of the changing pattern of the area and commodity composition of trade for the relative export performance of any country arises from the fact that countries differ in their abilities to respond to these changing world demands for traded goods. The more flexible the economy, the better the export performance, other things being equal. Looked at worldwide, as growth proceeds large disparities in the relative growth of world demand for traded goods develop because of differences in the growth elasticities of demand for imports. For example, any number of studies indicate that machinery, transport equipment and chemicals have been the expanding export sectors

[3] See E. Leamer and R. Stern, *Quantitative International Economics*, Allyn and Bacon, Boston, 1970, Chapter 7, for an outline of this method of analysis.

in the postwar period while textiles have been stagnating.[4] Any country lacking the ability to channel its export efforts into industries with rapidly growing world demands will find its overall export performance hurt. Similarly, if a country develops special ties with certain countries or areas (because of, say, earlier developments of distribution and servicing functions in the importing countries), the inability or unwillingness to transfer export efforts to other areas may be disastrous if the growth of imports in the former countries is relatively slow.

Empirical studies of market economies in the postwar period indicate that that part of export growth of any country attributable to the changing structure of the area and commodity composition of trade is small.[5] Growth in world trade and the change in market shares of particular goods captured by each exporting country in the various areas account for most of the change in total exports. Still allowing that a large residual or competitive effect might be support for the export-led growth position, this would seem to be evidence for the export-led view. However, a few comments are in order.

First, since the change in exports attributable to the competitive effect is a residual, it must represent the impact of all aspects of competition, not just a relative price effect. These include the quality of after-purchase service, especially important with consumer and producer durables, the distribution system for promoting and facilitating the availability of the good, the length of delivery delays, credit terms and the various style and quality aspects that have become so important with finished manufactured goods. These various aspects of the competitive effect are clearly the same kind of things that determine the rate of growth of sales and output by local producers in local markets.

Second, it is important to stress that the size of the residual or competitive effect is very much a function of the level of disaggregation employed. For example, using the SITC classification system, disaggregation to the two-digit level makes no distinction between railway vehicles (731) and road motor vehicles (732). Similarly, proceeding to the three-digit level, the level of disaggregation fails to distinguish between passenger motor cars (732.1), lorries and trucks (732.3) and motorcycles, motorized cycles and their parts (732.9). Suppose, then, the world exports of passenger cars to be growing at a rate that far exceeds the rate of growth of world exports in general and world exports of road motor vehicles in particular. Then, if disaggregation is at the three-digit level in some constant market share study, a country whose exports of passenger cars has been exceptional will find, other things being equal, that this exceptional performance manifests

[4] Similar results are found when import functions are estimated. See H. Chenery, op. cit., Maizels, op. cit., Chapter 4, and Leamer and Stern, op. cit., Chapter 2.

[5] See Lamfalussy, op. cit., Chapter V; Maizels, op. cit., Chapter VIII; and R. Stern, *Foreign Trade and Economic Growth in Italy*, Praeger, New York, Chapter 2.

itself in a larger residual. The importance of exporting the right goods (passenger cars) is missed at this level of disaggregation since world exports of road motor vehicles is not exceptional.

Finally, there is no justification for the view that a rapid growth of exports which can be attributed to an exporting country's capturing a larger share of exports of different goods in different areas is proof of export-led growth, any more than alleging the same for a successful export drive that can be attributed to a relatively rapid expansion of exports of goods whose world-wide export sales are booming. As just stressed, when dealing with manufactured goods especially, the competitiveness of a country's exports has several aspects in a world of differentiated products. What both cases most likely indicate is superior entrepreneurship. Thus, the finding that changing shares of different goods in different areas account for a large part of the change in exports of a country cannot by itself be accepted as evidence that growth is export-led.

C. Export-Led Growth – Some Additional Considerations

A common and simple interpretation of export-led growth refers to nothing more than the fact that in developed market economies exports tend to grow more rapidly than the economy as a whole. As seen in Table 9.1, this fact is common to at least all the market economies treated in the regression study of Chapter VIII in the postwar period.

A related interpretation of the term revolves around the Keynesian multiplier process whereby the level and rate of growth of exports, determined by forces outside the economy, determine the level and rate of growth of aggregate output through the multiplier. Thus, assume some exogenously determined rate of growth of exports together with some kind of endogenous

Table 9.1. Annual average rate of growth of total exports ($\dot{E}_x$) and GDP ($\dot{Q}$) 1951–73 (in constant prices)

	$\dot{E}_x$	$\dot{Q}$		$\dot{E}_x$	$\dot{Q}$
	%	%		%	%
Austria	10.7	5.1[a]	Italy	11.7	5.1
Belgium	9.4	4.4[a]	Japan	15.4	9.5
Canada	6.9	4.6	Netherlands	10.1	5.0
Denmark	6.1	4.2[b]	Norway	7.2	4.2
France	8.1	5.0	United Kingdom	4.1	2.7
Germany	10.8	5.7	United States	5.1	3.7

[a]1955–73 [b]1954–73

Sources: *Monthly Bulletin of Statistics*, United Nations, New York, various issues; and those of Table 2.1.

mechanism, more or less complicated, which depicts an interaction between a generalized accelerator–multiplier mechanism that is damped. Then the rate of growth of output in the long run is equal to the rate of growth of exports. The greater is the latter, the more rapidly does demand and output grow, assuming there is no output constraint.[6] Further, if allowance is made for a progressive liberalization of trade, such as that which took place during the postwar period, the results depicted in Table 9.1 follow.

The view that growth is export-led because exports grow more rapidly than output, thereby providing all the demand stimulus needed for growth, is however, unhelpful for getting at the causes of why growth rates differ, for three reasons. First, government spending in all developed economies and investment in most grew more rapidly than output in the postwar period. Thus, by this kind of criterion, postwar growth could be termed government spending- or investment-led.[7] Second, this argument for export-led growth is phrased solely in terms of the impact on demand. Some consideration must be given to the impact of exports on supply or maximum output before it can be properly evaluated. Third, such views overlook the fact that the rate of growth of exports may be properly explained in terms of other economic (and non-economic) variables. As is argued below, these variables include those already stressed in this study as the determinants of growth. For these reasons, whether exports grow more or less rapidly than output is not a useful criterion for deciding whether growth is export-led.

Export expenditures are also considered important for growth because of balance of payments considerations. Thus, assume a world of fixed exchange rates and where a country's imports are always proportionate to aggregate output. Then a higher rate of growth of output always leads to a higher (and equal) rate of growth of imports. If capital movements and large holdings of foreign reserves are assumed away, then this higher rate of growth of output can be sustained only if the rate of growth of exports increases. If, initially, exports and imports are growing at the same rate but the rate of growth of output is less than some (given) rate of growth of full-employment output, then any attempt to inflate the economy in order to achieve full employment will be short-lived, as such a policy will push the rate of growth of imports above that of exports. In such a case the economy could grow at its maximum growth rate only if exports would grow more rapidly. Growth is export-led in the sense that exports place a ceiling on the rate of growth of demand and therefore output.

A related argument deals with the importance of export-led booms following a period of recession induced, say, by a policy response to balance of payments difficulties incurred during the previous boom. Here a distinction

[6] This is the familiar case in difference (or differential) equation models where the roots obtained from solving the homogeneous or endogenous part of the system are all less than one in absolute value. In this case the exogenous input(s) dominate the behavior of the model.

[7] See Table 2.5 for data on investment.

between consumer-led booms, fostered by expansionist fiscal and monetary policies, with export-led booms brought about, say, by a once-over devaluation is helpful. In the former case consumption and output rise and in so doing give a boost to imports. With no help necessarily forthcoming from exports, indeed with the possibility that exports may be squeezed out by an expanded domestic consumption of goods that might have flowed into the export markets, the payments position is liable to be further weakened. Furthermore, attempts to counteract this problem by depressing domestic consumption can weaken investment incentives which adversely affects productivity and international competitiveness. By contrast, export-led booms allow the authorities to depress domestic consumption without weakening investment. Alternatively, it can be said that, because of lags, the impact of stronger demand pressures on productivity growth are always delayed no matter what the source of increased demand. In the meantime, balance of payments problem can arise unless this source of additional demand comes from exports.[8]

The importance of exports in this sense, i.e. permitting the authorities to sustain demand pressures, is certainly beyond dispute. The 'stop–go' policies forced on the British government throughout the postwar period attest to the importance of a satisfactory export performance for prolonging boom periods. Basically, this position is a short-run version of the interpretation of export-led growth just given; namely, the faster income grows the faster imports grow and, therefore, the faster must exports grow, other things being equal. But while it is very likely true that a failure of exports to grow rapidly has choked off booms, it is harder to maintain that balance of payments considerations by themselves have determined long-run growth rates. The argument that, under a system of relatively fixed exchange rates, the growth of exports constrains, and therefore determines, the growth of output is acceptable only if such a constraint can't be removed. In the example given above, the economy cannot grow at its maximum growth rate with some given rate of exchange. But the postwar period was a period when exchange rate adjustments were permitted, especially in cases where unemployment was high, at a time that payments difficulties were serious. As a result such constraints could not be interpreted as something immutable. It will be argued further in Chapter X that the forces that lead to rapid growth of output also work to relieve a country of a payments constraint. In other words, those countries with reoccuring balance of payments difficulties were the slow growers, and both events can be attributed to the same causes.

[8] See N. Kaldor, 'Conflicts in National Economic Objectives,' in *Conflict in Policy Objectives*, Augustus M. Kelley, New York, 1971. An alternative policy, which Lamfalussy described as the key to France's ability to get on to the virtuous circle in the 1950s, was to stimulate demand by fiscal and monetary means, run down foreign reserves and then, when productivity has increased substantially, devalue. See Lamfalussy, op. cit.

D. The Virtuous Circle of Growth

A more fruitful approach to the whole issue of the role of exports in growth can be carried out within the context of what has become known as the virtuous or vicious circle of growth. This allows a fuller development of some of the arguments just presented as well as others, including their long-run implications. The notion of a virtuous circle of growth describes how an economy can find itself in a situation of rapid sustained growth of demand, maximum output and productivity while staying free of any balance of payments difficulties. The key, quite naturally, lies in the behavior of exports. If they grow rapidly, this helps overcome payments problems; but, in addition, rapid growth of exports leads to favorable effects on investment, productivity (and therefore maximum output) and a strengthening of a country's competitive international position. It is these additional effects of exports on the supply side that need further consideration. Unless otherwise indicated the analysis will be confined to the manufacturing sector and assumes relatively fixed exchange rates.

Let $\dot{p}/\dot{p}_f$, $\dot{\rho}_m$, $\dot{Q}_m$, $\dot{E}_x$, and $\dot{w}$ represent the ratio of the rate of growth of prices of domestic produced tradeable goods to the rate of growth of prices of foreign produced tradeable goods and the rates of growth of labor productivity, output, exports and money wages, respectively, in the manufacturing sector. Next write:

$$\dot{E}_x = a_0 + a_1(1 - \dot{p}/\dot{p}_f); \tag{1}$$
$$\dot{Q}_m = \dot{E}_x; \tag{2}$$
$$\dot{\rho}_m = b_0 + b_1\dot{Q}_m; \tag{3}$$
$$\dot{w} = c_0 + c_1(\dot{\rho}_m); \text{ and} \tag{4}$$
$$\dot{p} = \dot{w} - \dot{\rho}_m \tag{5}$$

where a_0, a_1, b_0, b_1, c_0, c_1 are parameters with $c_1 < 1$.[9]

Equation (1) attempts to explain export performance in terms of the competitive strength of a country's exports; i.e., relative rates of inflation. A decline (increase) in the rate of inflation in the local country compared to that in foreign countries leads to an increase (decrease) in the rate of growth of exports (the prices of exports and domestically consumed goods being the same). Equation (2) depicts the importance of export demand in driving the economy. Imports are not made explicit in the model but can be assumed to grow at the same rate as output and therefore, exports. Equation (3) is, as before, Verdoorn's Law; i.e., an example of dynamic economies of scale.[10] Equations (2) and (3) together indicate that, the greater is the rate of growth of exports, the greater is the rate of growth of productivity and, therefore,

[9] This is the model developed by W. Beckerman, 'Projecting Europe's Growth,' *Economic Journal*, December 1962.

[10] A simple amendment is to treat $(I/Q)_m$ as a function of $\dot{Q}_m$ and to allow the former to have a positive effect on $\dot{\rho}_m$. See Lamfalussy, op. cit. It is not incorporated into the text in order not to lose sight of the main issues.

maximum output. Equation (4) relates the growth of wages to productivity growth and equation (5) reflects a constant markup pricing policy of firms over average labor costs. If the rest of the world is treated as one identical competing country, then its export equation can be written

$$\dot{E}_{xf} = a_o - a_1(1 - \dot{p}/\dot{p}_f).^{11} \qquad (1')$$

For the rest of the model for the competing country, equations (2′)–(5′), the only alteration required is the use of the subscript f with each variable.

While the model is written in the form of a system of simultaneous equations, to see the actual workings of the model it is useful to introduce certain lags. Assume initially that $\dot{p} = \dot{p}_f$. Then from equations (1) and (1′) it is clear that $\dot{E}_x = \dot{E}_{xf}$ and, since exports and output always grow at the same rate, $\dot{Q}_m = \dot{Q}_{mf}$. Furthermore, with identical equations for the growth of productivity, wages and prices, this means that each of these variables grows at the same rate in both countries. In other words, if initially neither country shows superior competitive strength, the situation will perpetuate itself and growth rates of all variables including output will proceed at the same rate in both countries.

Now, introduce an outside disturbance such as will lead to a rate of inflation of export prices that is lower for the country in question, i.e. $\dot{p} < \dot{p}_f$, and allow for the workings of certain lags in the model. Then, the assumed differential rates of inflation leads to $\dot{E}_x > \dot{E}_{xf}$ and, therefore, to $\dot{Q}_m > \dot{Q}_{mf}$. Moving down through equations (3)–(5), and bearing in mind that equations (3′)–(5′) of the model for the competing country are identical to equations (3)–(5), it follows that $\dot{\rho}_m > \dot{\rho}_{mf}$, $\dot{w} < \dot{w}_f$ and, eventually, $\dot{p} < \dot{p}_f$. In other words, by introducing a 'shock' to the model such that $\dot{p} < \dot{p}_f$, it is apparent that, once a country achieves any superior competitive advantage, it perpetuates itself.

In this example, the local country is now said to find itself in a virtuous circle of (relatively) rapid growth of exports, demand, output and productivity which feeds back into the model as a relatively low rate of inflation of (export) prices. Rapid growth of output is led by rapid growth of exports in the local country, induced by some unexplained increase in competitive strength. This makes the process self-sustaining as the competing country, caught in a vicious circle of slow growth of exports, output and productivity, etc., increasingly suffers a loss of competitive strength.

This illustrates a situation of divergence of growth rates which can be traced back to superior competitive strength in export markets.[12] An initial competitive advantage generates relatively rapid rates of growth of exports, output and productivity for a country, which feed back to reinforce the initial

[11] The change in sign is required since the relative rate of inflation variable remains p/p_f.

[12] See B. Balassa, 'Some Observations on Mr Beckerman's "Export-propelled" Growth Model,' *Economic Journal*, December 1963, and the subsequent discussions in *Economic Journal*, December 1963, March 1963 and September 1964.

advantage. These long-run divergence properties of the model follow primarily from the special nature of equation (4), the relationship explaining the behavior of money wages. The model also illustrates one of the simplest kinds of circular causal chains that, as just seen, may be virtuous or vicious depending upon the initial conditions. The first possibility is depicted in Diagram 9.1. The arrows between any two variables indicate the direction of causation, while the arrows alongside each variable give the sign of the induced change. In the example just given, the sequence is initiated by breaking into the circular chain at the $\dot{p}/\dot{p}_f$ link, altering the initial conditions and simply assuming the local economy has achieved a competitive advantage, i.e. $\dot{p} < \dot{p}_f$. A vicious circle is easily depicted by reversing the direction of the arrows beside each variable.

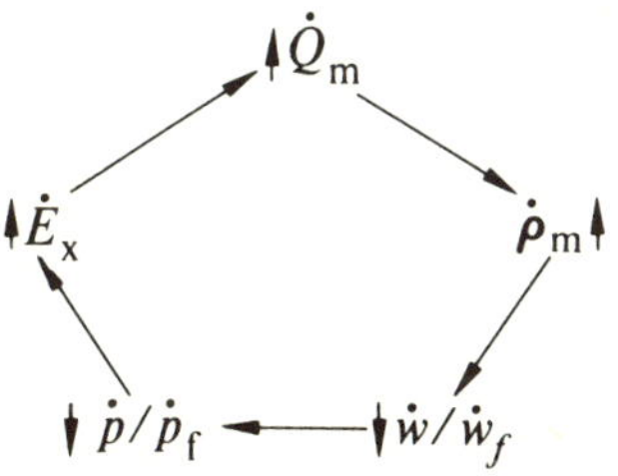

Diagram 9.1. The virtuous circle

E. The Role of Labor Supply

The model just developed for illustrating an interpretation of export-led growth incorporates a productivity or supply response to demand as well as a feedback effect that allows sustained growth of exports, demand, output and productivity. As such, it presents a fuller notion of what might constitute export-led growth and also a possible alternative explanation to that offered in earlier chapters of why growth rates differ. However, the model as outlined introduces some restrictive assumptions about the nature of the supply response to demand. This can be seen primarily in the specification of the wage equation, (4): $\dot{w} = c_0 + c_1(\dot{\rho}_m)$. Here the rate of growth of money wages depends on the rate of growth of productivity and not on conditions in the labor market as measured by, say, the unemployment or vacancy rate. Now, it is generally accepted that the behavior of money wage rates is affected by conditions in the labor market. Therefore, the only justification of this specification of the money wage equation is that the workings of the economy are such that the net effect of demand and supply pressures in the labor market are always constant; e.g., the unemployment rate is constant. This can arise in two situations: (1) the parameters of the model are such that the unemployment rate is constant throughout the growth process; or

(2) whatever the rate of growth of demand for output and, therefore, labor in manufacturing, labor supply responds in such a way as to maintain a relatively constant rate of unemployment in manufacturing. Since the first possibility is of little analytical or practical interest, the analysis will take up only the second.[13]

Much of the discussion in the earlier chapters stressed the responsiveness of labor supply in manufacturing to the derived demand for labor, at least to the early 1970s. The stress there centered on the ability of the manufacturing sectors of the various market economies to obtain surplus labor (from various sources) whenever the demand for manufactures warranted it. In such a situation it would be expected that the unemployment rate in manufacturing would remain more or less unchanged. This can be developed more fully with an extension of the model just discussed.[14] Write:

$$\dot{E}_x = a_0 + a_1(1 - \dot{p}/\dot{p}_f) \quad (1) \qquad \dot{Q}_m = \dot{E}_x \quad (2)$$
$$\dot{\rho}_m = b_0 + b_1\dot{Q}_m \quad (3) \qquad \dot{w} = g_0 + g_1(\dot{\rho}_m) - g_2U \quad (4')$$
$$\dot{p} = \dot{w} - \dot{\rho}_m \quad (5) \qquad \dot{u} = dU/U \quad (6)$$
$$\dot{u} = \dot{L}_m + \dot{\rho}_m - \dot{Q}_m \quad (7) \qquad \dot{E}_m = -b_0 + (1 - b_1)\dot{Q}_m \quad (8)$$

Equation (4′) allows the unemployment rate, U, to influence the rate of change of money wage rates. Equation (6) defines the rate of change of the unemployment rate, $\dot{u}$, while equation (7) relates the rate of change of the unemployment rate to the rate of growth of maximum output, $\dot{L}_m + \dot{\rho}_m$, where $\dot{L}_m$ is the rate of growth of the supply of labor to manufacturing, and the rate of growth of actual output, $\dot{Q}_m$. Equation (8) is the mirror image of equation (3), relating the rate of growth of employment, $\dot{E}_m$, to the rate of growth of output. Since by definition $\dot{Q}_m = \dot{E}_m + \dot{\rho}_m$, equations (3) and (8) determine the relative importance of the two sources of growth of manufacturing output. The rest of the model is unchanged. The eight endogenous variables are $\dot{E}_x$, $\dot{p}$, $\dot{\rho}_m$, $\dot{Q}_m$, $\dot{w}$, U, $\dot{E}_m$ and $\dot{u}$ with $\dot{p}_f$ and $\dot{L}_m$ exogenous.

However, if it is accepted that the supply of labor in manufacturing always responds to demand, $\dot{L}_m$ becomes an endogenous variable and an additional equation is added:

$$\dot{L}_m = \dot{E}_m. \quad (9)$$

Substituting Equation (9) into (7) gives

$$\dot{u} = \dot{E}_m + \dot{\rho}_m - \dot{Q}_m \quad \text{or} \quad \dot{u} = 0 \quad (7')$$

which can be verified by substituting equations (3) and (8) into equation (7′). In this case the unemployment rate, U, remains unchanged whatever the growth rate of demand and output in manufacturing, and equation (4′) may be written

[13] The first possibility is a kind of 'razor's edge' situation.

[14] This extension borrows heavily from Balassa, op. cit.

$$\dot{w} = (g_0 - g_2 U) + g_1(\dot{\rho}_m) \qquad (4')$$

or

$$\dot{w} = c_0 + c_1(\dot{\rho}_m) \qquad (4)$$

with $(g_0 - g_2 U) = c_0$ and $g_1 = c_1$.

To see the workings of this model, assume as before a situation where the two competing economies are growing at the same rate; i.e. $\dot{p} = \dot{p}_f$, but in addition $U = U_f$. Now allow for the competing country to experience an increasingly inelastic supply of labor while conditions in the local economy are such that $\dot{L}_m = \dot{E}_m$ continues. Then U_f must fall, leading to tighter labor markets in the competing country; i.e. $U_f < U$. This results in $\dot{w}_f > \dot{w}$ and, therefore, $\dot{p}_f > \dot{p}$, which then affects relative export, output and productivity performances in the two countries. The country with surplus labor is now on the virtuous circle while the country experiencing labor shortages is caught in a vicious circle and must respond somehow to correct balance of payments difficulties.[15]

This amended form of the virtuous circle is seen in Diagram 9.2. This is the same as Diagram 9.1 except two additional links have been added; the derived demand for labor link and the impact of a labor supply response on wages. As with Diagram 9.1, 9.2 illustrates a case of a virtuous circle. Starting from a situation where inflation and unemployment rates are identical in both countries, the competing country is assumed to run short of surplus labor. This causes relative wages and prices to fall in the local country, which boosts exports, output and productivity, as indicated by the arrows alongside these variables. Naturally, this continues to strengthen the competitive advantage of the local country with each successive loop through the causal chain.

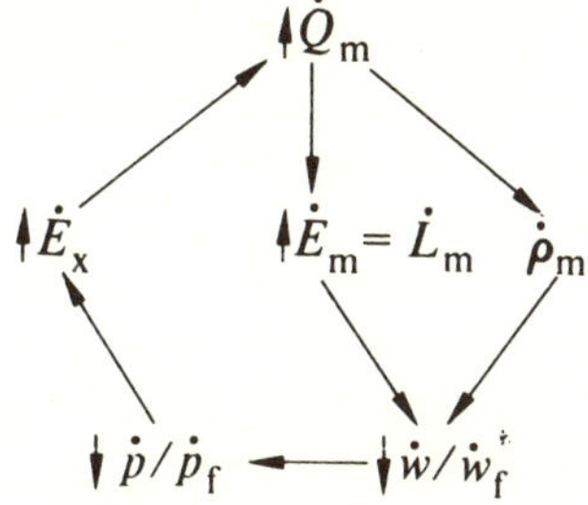

Diagram 9.2. The virtuous circle and labor supply

[15] Kindleberger, in particular, stresses the importance of surplus labor for these reasons. See Kindleberger, op. cit.

This amended model offers an explanation of why growth rates differ; namely, differences in the elasticity of supply of labor to manufacturing. As such it is certainly superior to the first model, which bases differences in growth rates on the assumed initial conditions. The model cannot, however, be considered a model solely of export-led growth. The driving force on the demand side is exports, to be sure; but the growth of exports is ultimately conditioned by the elasticity of a labor supply. If labor supply is perfectly elastic, then export demand determines output, which feeds back through productivity growth and export prices to exports. But once the supply of labor becomes inelastic the impact is fed back into the system in the form of rising export prices, which cuts back demand and growth. In this sense the model offers a more elaborate version of supply-determined growth, a view rejected earlier.

Now, while it is surely a simplification to assume, as in Chapter V, that the elasticity of supply of labor to the manufacturing sector was more or less the same in every country, there seemed to be no strong evidence that any country was hampered seriously by such shortages. In other words, if the arguments of Chapter V are correct, then differences in growth rates in the postwar period cannot be explained in terms of differences in labor supply whether this works directly or by first affecting the competitive position of a country. This in turn means that even a simple model like that discussed in Section D, which ignored the labor supply constraint, cannot be rejected out of hand. However, what is required is a closer analysis of just what are the important distinctive features of export-led growth.

F. Export-Led versus Homespun Growth

The mechanism outlined in Diagrams 9.1 and 9.2 allows rapid rates of growth of demand and output to be sustained once the process has started because of the favorable effects of the growth of export demand on the rate of growth of productivity and, therefore, on maximum output. Following the increase in demand led by exports, the feedback effect on productivity and relative export prices frees an economy from the operation of a balance of payments ceiling over extended periods of time so that the growth of demand can proceed uninhibited by any other force save the growth of exports themselves.[16] These associations between rapid growth in exports, output, productivity and declining relative export prices are often cited as the essence of export-led growth.[17]

Unfortunately, the same associations are to be expected from an entirely different explanation of growth of output and exports, one that entails a

[16]Provided, of course, there is an elastic supply of labor.

[17]See Allen and Stevenson, op. cit., Chapters 2 and 3; and Kennedy and Dowling, op. cit., Chapter 4. It should be added that these writers include a link between output growth and investment and between the latter and productivity. As pointed out in fn. 12 earlier, this amendment was deliberately left out of the text.

different interpretation of the structure of causation. Thus, it is often argued that it is rapid rates of growth of domestic sales that generate rapid rates of growth of exports, through economies of scale obtained from the (previous) development of the home market. Once the home market expands sufficiently to allow for economies of scale, the decline in average costs of production that results allows local producers to expand their sales in foreign markets. Sales and production 'spill over' into foreign markets. This latter expansion, in turn, feeds back into the system in the form of greater demand and productivity growth which strengthens the export position further. This form of growth will be referred to as 'homespun' growth.

This notion of a spillover from one market to another suggests incorporating a feature in the export-led models that could be emphasized in order to draw out the distinctive feature of this class of models. As just mentioned, homespun growth can be defined as a situation where local markets are the first to be exploited. Once successful, attempts are made to capture larger shares of foreign markets. Export-led growth, on the other hand, can be seen as a process where entrepreneurs first develop sales abroad and then (if at all) exploit the local markets.

These two different views of which market drives a capitalist economy are shown graphically in Diagrams 9.2a and 9.2b, where two different kinds of virtuous circles are depicted. Again, for simplicity, the derived demand for labor link is suppressed in both diagrams. Since the issue is one of the direction of the spillover between two distinct markets, the rate of growth of manufacturing output, $\dot{Q}_m$, is divided into two parts, the rate of growth of exports, $\dot{E}_x$, and the rate of growth of domestically produced and consumed goods, $\dot{Z}$.

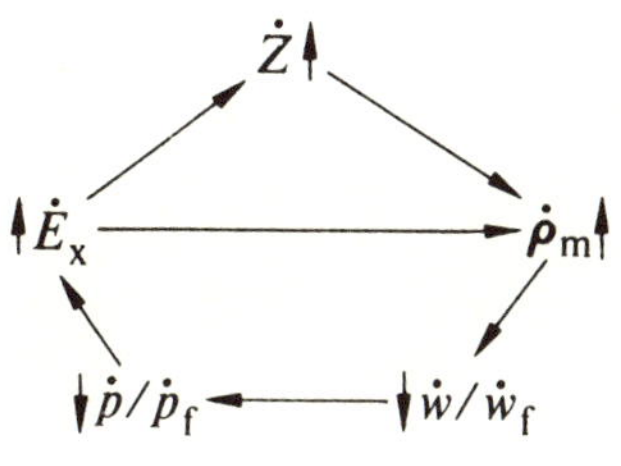

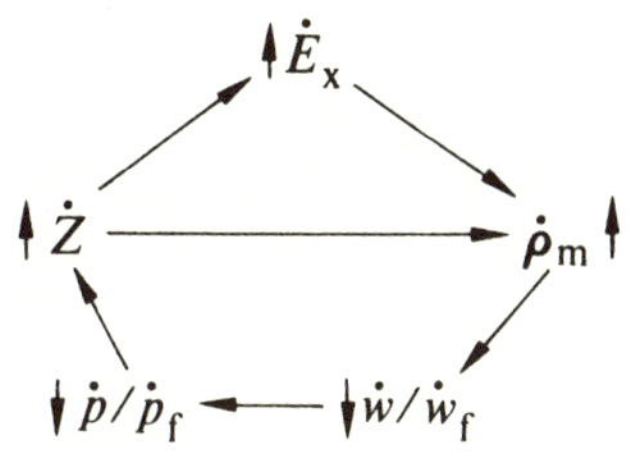

Diagram 9.2a. Export-led growth

Diagram 9.2b. Homespun growth

Diagram 9.2a differs from Diagram 9.1 in that a direct link from the rate of growth of exports to the rate of growth of productivity is incorporated. This is done to emphasize that there is something special about rising export demand and its effects on productivity. For example, it could be argued that rapidly growing exports have an especially favorable effect on entrepreneurial expectation. Thus, aware that demand is being propelled by exports, entrepreneurs can expect the authorities to allow demand pressures to continue strong and to grow because payments difficulties will be minimized. This will induce them to undertake 'enterprise' investment, which leads to rapid productivity growth.[18] Because of factors such as these, the tie between exports and productivity growth (and investment) is especially strong, allowing the direct link to be drawn between the two variables in Diagram 9.2a. The direct link also serves to emphasize the feedback effect envisaged by proponents of the export-led growth view that assert that once exports begin to boom they will continue to do so. Since, it was argued in Chapter VIII that it was the rate of growth of total manufacturing output that determined the rate of growth of productivity, both spending categories, $\dot{Z}$ and $\dot{E}_x$, are linked up with the rate of growth of productivity in the diagrams.

The link between the rate of growth of relative prices and the rate of growth of exports in Diagram 9.2a is matched in Diagram 9.2b by a link from the former variable to the rate of growth of domestically produced and sold goods, $\dot{Z}$. This can be interpreted as indicating the ability of an economy to remain on the virtuous circle because the more favorable relative price effect allows higher demand pressures to be sustained. In other words, it depicts a situation where producers, while primarily orientated toward their local markets, don't have to worry about the external balance because the induced greater productivity growth takes care of these matters.

G. An Evaluation

Diagram 9.2a illustrates a useful way in which to depict export-led growth. Not only does it incorporate the notion of rising export demand initiating the growth process, but it allows for this rising demand to set in motion a chain of events that sustains this process. Thus, higher rates of growth of exports induce an expansion of domestic sales and production in the same product lines. Together, growth in these outputs induce a supply response in the form of higher productivity growth which feeds back through relative wages and prices to sustain the process.

As depicted in Diagram 9.2a, the explanation of export-led growth is more satisfactory than that of homespun growth in at least one important sense. There is in the export-led model a plausible explanation of the sustained higher growth of export demand and, therefore, the whole growth process. Continued export success is explained in terms of relative price effects. The relative price variable does not play this role in Diagram 9.2b for homespun

[18] The term 'enterprise' investment is from Lamfalussy, op. cit., and refers basically to investment that expands capacity at the same time as it cuts labor costs. A stimulation in demand coming from a larger budget deficit would not have as favorable an effect on productivity growth because much of the rising demand would be for services of one kind or another.

growth. The variable $\dot{p}/\dot{p}_f$ was linked up with $\dot{Z}$ to indicate merely that balance of payments problems were minimal in a situation where economies of scale (generated by expanding domestic markets) led to a strong competitive position in foreign markets. Unlike the export-led model, the model of homespun growth has no explanation of what generates growth of demand.[19]

However, some remarks made earlier concerning the many dimensions to what is referred to in trade theory as the 'competitive effect' are relevant here. As pointed out more fully in Chapter X, historically growth in international trade has been accompanied by an increased sophistication in the kinds of goods traded. Not only has there been a shift toward trade in manufactured goods by market economies, but there has also been a shift toward trade in highly complex manufactured goods. This means that increasingly all the elements of non-price competition that come with trade in differentiated products must be included in any explanation of export success. In terms of Diagram 9.2a, this entails a rather broad interpretation of the relative price variable, $\dot{p}/\dot{p}_f$. In other words, sustained export success requires not just that productivity growth be rapid enough to keep product prices from rising relative to one's competitors; it also requires that styles, delivery dates and distribution and servicing facilities be appealing. Not only that, as pointed out in Chapter X, the composition of trade in manufactures has altered quite dramatically in the postwar period, pointing up the need for continuous adaptation of production to an ever-changing composition of world demand.

What is misleading about the process of export-led growth as pictured in Diagram 9.2a is the suggestion that sustained export success is almost automatic once started. Once on the virtuous circle, the depicted feedback effects generate an effortless continued success. The missing link in all this (and in the Diagram 9.2b as well) is some indication of the importance of a continuous adaptation to the changing needs and requirements for export success. Recall that in Chapter VIII the regression results indicated that the rate of growth of manufacturing output, $\dot{Q}_m$, could be explained in terms of the investment ratio in manufacturing, $(I/Q)_m$, and relative income levels, q_r. The investment ratio was included primarily because it indicated the effort made to adapt and modify new technologies. Unfortunately, no lags could be allowed for. This relation, together with the other one developed there, can be set down in the form of four equations:

$$\dot{Q}_m = f_1[(I/Q)_m, q_r] \quad (1) \qquad \dot{E}_m = f_2(\dot{Q}_m, T) \quad (2)$$

$$\dot{p}_m = f_3(\dot{Q}_m, T) \quad (3) \qquad \dot{E}_w = f_4(\dot{E}_m) \quad (4)$$

[19] Partly this arises because the analysis has so largely ignored the role of imports. If, instead of assuming that imports are always proportionate to total output (and, therefore, grow at the same rate as total output), relative price effects are allowed to affect imports, a tighter link between $\dot{p}/\dot{p}_f$ and $\dot{Z}$ develops. A decline in the ratio of the inflation of domestic prices to foreign prices stimulates growth of domestically produced and consumed goods through import substitution.

What will be asserted here and justified in Chapter X is that the rate of growth of exports and the rate of growth of domestic production sold at home can also be explained largely by these variables; i.e.,

$$\dot{Z} = f_{1a}[(I/Q)_m, q_r] \tag{1a}$$

and

$$\dot{E}_x = f_{1b}[(I/Q)_m, q_r]^{20} \tag{1b}$$

Success in achieving rapid growth in exports and domestic sales of home-produced goods is to be related to a progressive entrepreneurial class and labor force eager to adapt production to current and future foreign and domestic demands. As argued beginning in Chapter VI, this was largely reflected in a high investment ratio. All that is missing from the model described by equations (1a), (1b), (2), (3) and (4) and included in Diagrams 9.2a and 9.2b is the feedback effect from productivity growth to wages and prices and eventually $\dot{E}_x$ and $\dot{Z}$. Neglecting the time trend in equation (3) and the lags actually involved, and omitting equations (2) and (4), Diagram 9.3 indicates that, if necessary, this amendment is easily incorporated.[21]

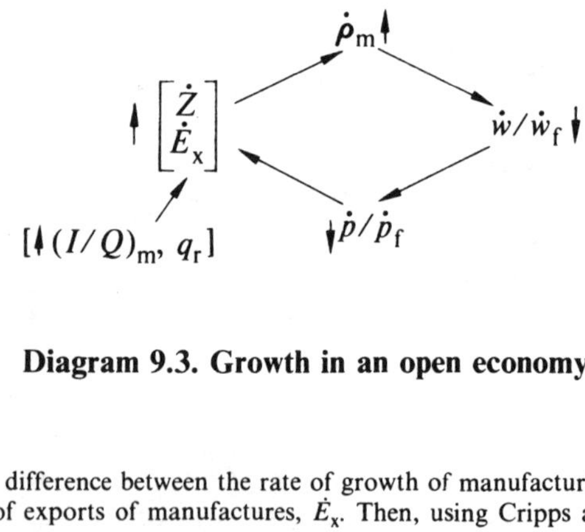

Diagram 9.3. Growth in an open economy

[20] Define $\dot{Z}$ as the difference between the rate of growth of manufacturing output, $\dot{Q}_m$, and the rate of growth of exports of manufactures, $\dot{E}_x$. Then, using Cripps and Tarling's twelve country sample,

$$\dot{Z} = 2.41 + \underset{(0.055)}{0.187}(I/Q)_m - \underset{(0.0003)}{0.00013}q(I/Q)_m - \underset{(0.054)}{0.725}\dot{E}_x \quad R^2 = 0.86$$

and

$$\dot{E}_x = 2.87 + \underset{(0.058)}{0.327}(I/Q)_m - \underset{(0.00004)}{0.00016}q(I/Q)_m - \underset{(0.085)}{1.146}\dot{Z} \quad R^2 = 0.90$$

where q is per capita income. Clearly, rates of growth of domestic and foreign sales compete with one another. For example, a one per cent increase in the rate of growth of exports leads to a 0.725 per cent decline in the growth of domestic sales. But both growth rates depend upon a common set of other variables as well.

[21] Diagram 9.3 depicts higher investment leading to more rapid growth. More rapid growth also induces more investment, a point suggested throughout the study, but neglected in the diagram.

H. Conclusions

The chief purpose of this chapter was to decide in what useful way it might be said that growth was export-led. Once having decided that issue, the next logical step was to see whether an export-led growth view might not be superior in explanatory power to that developed in earlier chapters. Section E argued that the most useful way to look upon export-led growth was within a context of a virtuous circle in which export sales spill over into the local market. This could then be contrasted with a virtuous circle in which the causation goes from success at home to forays into the export markets. No resolution of the question of which direction of causation dominates was undertaken in this chapter; that is a task assigned to Chapter X. However, what did emerge from the analysis was that whether growth is export-led or homespun is a somewhat secondary, peripheral matter in this study. In either case it was asserted that it is possible to push the analysis back further to reveal that the factors leading to rapid growth of both exports and domestic sales are one and the same and are the ones stressed throughout the study. Once this is recognized, Diagram 9.3 revealed that it was a simple matter to take explicit account of the foreign sector (and a virtuous circle).

Chapter X attempts to give some justification to the assumption that export sales and home sales depend basically on the same kinds of influences and also strives to indicate whether the more immediate causes of growth are homespun or export-led in nature.

Chapter X A Consistent View of Export and Output Growth

A. Introduction

Chapter IX was basically preliminary in nature, seeking to clarify the issues. More particularly, the discussion was intended to set the stage for this chapter, which considers two issues. First, some attempt is made to support the position that the same kinds of influences are at work in determining export and growth performances for some country. Second, the question of whether growth can be said to be export-led, homespun or, more likely, a mixture of the two is taken up. This chapter attempts to deal with these is issues by seeking out the sources of 'competitive advantage' in exports, factors that lead to strong export performance over time. Following some preliminary remarks in Section B, Section C describes the most widely used theory of international trade and comparative advantage today, the Heckscher–Ohlin theory. Some criticisms of this theory, both as an explanation of comparative advantage and as a theory for answering the central question of this chapter, are offered. Section D discusses some of the merits of several challenges to the Heckscher–Ohlin doctrine of comparative advantage. The neotechnology theory of trade is generally accepted here as the more profitable way in which to explain export patterns and success. Section E is a brief look at the Japanese experience, while Section F concludes the discussion.

B. Some Preliminary Remarks

In Table 10.1 figures for selective years give the proportion of world export sales in manufactured goods for different categories of goods. What stands out is the uneven growth of exports of the different groups. This changing composition of exports to a large extent mirrors the changing composition of output that took place during the same period.[1] The table illustrates a

[1] See *Economic Survey of Europe in 1971. Part I: The European Economy from the 1950s to the 1970s*, United Nations, New York, 1972, pp. 51–9.

Table 10.1. Commodity patterns of world exports in manufactures, 1955–70[a]

	1955	*1960*	*1965*	*1970*
	%	%	%	%
Chemicals	10.8	11.1	11.6	11.2
Textiles	9.9	8.1	6.8	5.6
Iron and Steel	10.2	10.8	9.1	8.6
Non-ferrous metals	5.0	4.7	4.2	4.0
Metal Manufacturers n.e.c.	5.3	3.5	3.7	3.4
Non-Electrical Machinery	16.0	18.5	20.0	20.3
Electrical machinery	6.8	7.5	8.8	9.5
Transport	15.6	16.7	16.1	18.4
Other	19.5	19.1	19.7	19.0

[a]Countries include Austria. Belgrium–Luxembourg, Canada, Denmark, France, Germany, Italy, Japan, Netherlands, Norway, Sweden, United Kingdom and the United States. Figures are ratios of current price estimates.

Source: *Yearbook of International Trade Statistics, 1958, 1961, 1967, 1970–71*, United Nations, New York.

point made in Section G of Chapter IX; i.e., that getting on some virtuous circle of growth and remaining there is not an automatic process. With the composition of exports changing constantly, to a large extent in response to growth in the importing countries, export success becomes very much a matter of channeling resources into profitable lines, i.e. industries with high growth elasticities of demand.[2] And the more rapidly resources are reallocated within the exporting country, the more rapidly exports would be expected to grow. Earlier chapters have stressed the importance of such things as flexibility and entrepreneurial ability in determining the rate at which resources are reallocated in organizing production for the home market. There is no reason to assume that these factors are any less important for organizing production for export.

The data in Table 10.1 together with other empirical findings reveal another important fact, an increasing complexity in the kinds of goods exported. Thus, Table 10.1 indicates a relative shift in exports from textiles to machinery, a category that includes both consumer and producer durables. An earlier study by Maizels showed that in developed economies the ratio of exports of finished manufactured goods to total exports tends to rise with per capita incomes.[3] In both cases, this suggests that the use of price variables alone to pick up changes in a country's competitive position or strength are increasingly inadequate. With the shifts in the composition

[2]Recall in Section B of Chapter IX the critique of the findings of 'constant market share' analysis. The findings that part of export growth attributable to the changing area and commodity pattern of trade was small may simply be due to a failure to disaggregate.

[3]See Maizels, op. cit., Chapter 3, Table 3.3.

of exports just described, various non-price qualities of the goods become increasingly important, e.g. delivery dates, ability to obtain spare parts and servicing (in the case of durables) and style and quality aspects. As also mentioned in Chapter IX, this reinforces the view that export success, once achieved, requires continuous efforts if it is to be maintained.

The changing patterns of exports depicted in Table 10.1 argue that the usefulness of any theory explaining the sources of export success would be enhanced if it was able to allow for a continuous change in the relative importance of the different exported goods, and if it could take explicit account of monopolistic elements. There are, however, additional considerations that are relevant to a theory of competitive advantage. First, the postwar period has been one of increasing liberalization of trade. At the same time, it has been a period where intra-industry trade was expanding much more rapidly than total and inter-industry trade. In other words, during this period there has been a relative expansion in trade that involved a simultaneous exporting and importing of goods belonging to the same industry, compared with the expansion of total trade and with trade between industries.[4] Any discussion of the sources of competitive advantage and the patterns of trade should certainly take this finding into account.

Second, as Chapter VI indicated, the borrowing of technologies has been a persistent and important element in the development of the market economies in the postwar period.[5] This is but another way of stating that production functions across countries are not and never have been either fixed within a country or identical across countries. The process of growth of output and exports can be described as a never-ending attempt to duplicate the technologies and production functions of the industrial leaders, while the behavior of the leaders can be described in terms of an attempt to develop new technologies in the production of new goods. These considerations strongly suggest the need to develop a theory of competitive advantage within a context that allows for differences between countries in the technologies used to produce any good.

Third, the arguments of Chapters VII and VIII attempted to support the view that economies of scale are an important part of the production process. Their inclusion in the analysis of the sources of competitive advantage therefore seems justified.

What has been listed are some of the more important features of postwar developments in the area of foreign trade.[6] Taken together, they strongly suggest what would be a proper orientation, emphasis and direction in an explanation of the sources of competitive advantage. Following a discussion

[4] See Grubel and Lloyd, op. cit., Chapters 2 and 3.

[5] Borrowed technology as a source of export success is a reoccuring theme in studies of the Japanese economy. This is especially so in Y. Tsurumi, op. cit.

[6] The importance of economies of scale is not something directly verifiable as, for example, the growth of intra-industry trade. It is, however, consistent with the facts.

of the Heckscher–Ohlin theory of trade, the study takes up a more recent alternative explanation.

C. The Neoclassical Theory of Trade

1. The basic assumptions

Traditional trade theory explains patterns of exports in terms of comparative costs or comparative advantage. This can be defined in various equivalent ways: a country will export a good whose relative cost is less; or, in somewhat more detail, if the price of a good A in terms of another good B is lower at home than abroad, then the country will have comparative advantage in the production of good A. As a result, if trade opens up, the country in question will find a market for good A abroad and a net benefit will result if the country transfers resources out of the production of good B into the production of good A and exports the latter. It will be noted that the doctrine is formulated in terms of the prices of the goods and not of non-price aspects of competition since, as will be clear shortly, the doctrine is derived from the competitive, neoclassical model.

Trade theory as it has developed in the last hundred years is designed to determine the patterns of, the terms of and the gains from trade. The special feature of the Heckscher–Ohlin theory, the modern version of traditional trade theory, is its explanation of the sources of comparative advantage. The Heckscher–Ohlin or neoclassical trade theory differs from earlier trade theories in that it explains comparative advantage in terms of relative factor endowments. Thus, since different goods require different inputs and since different countries have different relative factor endowments, relative costs will differ among countries. These relative costs will differ in such a way that under certain conditions a country will have a comparative advantage in the production of a good that makes relatively most use of its abundant factor. If it will export this good and import the good that requires relatively more of its scarce factor, real income will increase. For example, until the postwar period it was felt that America was well endowed with physical capital compared with other countries and as a result would have a comparative advantage in the export of goods that were relatively capital-intensive in their production, importing goods that were relatively labor-intensive.

The theorem that the exports of a country will make most use of or will use intensely its abundant factor rests on several assumptions.[7] A set of sufficient conditions for the theorem to hold are:

(1) identical fixed production functions throughout the world for each good;

(2) production functions that are linearly homogenous, i.e. exhibit con-

[7] J. Bhagwati, 'The Pure Theory of International Trade: A Survey,' *Surveys of Economic Theory: Growth and Development* (New York), August 1965.

stant returns to scale with diminishing marginal products for each factor;

(3) non-reversibility of factor intensities;

(4) identical consumer utility functions across countries, implying that at a given set of prices all goods are consumed in the same proportion across countries whatever the income level;

(5) perfect markets, free trade, no transport costs and complete international immobility of productive factors;

(6) each unit of capital and labor is identical with each other unit of capital and labor both within a country and across countries.

For some time it has been agreed that these various assumptions are 'unrealistic.' Partly as a result of this recognition, various studies have attempted to relax the different assumptions one at a time. The results have shown that, while this list may comprise a set of sufficient conditions, it is certainly not a list of necessary conditions. Unfortunately the list of minimal necessary conditions has not been formulated. Therefore, with this in mind and without belaboring the obvious the following points are worth making:

(1) As stressed in Chapter VI, production functions and technologies are not identical or fixed across countries. The large amount of importing of technologies in the postwar period indicated both differences in production functions across countries and a constant process of change and adaptation of technologies. All of this involved high costs in terms of time and money in the efforts to absorb new, previously unavailable technologies.

(2) A large part of the discussion of Chapter VII was devoted to indicating the importance of various kinds of economies of scale available to producers.

(3) Non-reversibility of factor intensities refers to a situation where, if a good makes most use of, say, its abundant factor for some range of relative input prices, it does so for all relative input prices. The realism of this assumption is still a matter of debate but the arguments that follow do not depend upon any particular resolution.

(4) Chapter VI only scratched the surface in its discussion of the various studies that stress the changing composition of consumption patterns as per capita incomes rise. The share of different classes of goods in total consumption changes fairly radically as incomes rise, as is implied by Table 2.4. The assumption of homothetic preference functions, i.e. that all goods have an income elasticity of demand of one, is necessary for the Heckscher–Ohlin theorem if pre-trade domestic price ratios are to reflect relative factor endowments and not demand conditions as well.

(5) The rising sophistication in the production and fabrication of manufactured goods as incomes rise has been accompanied by the development and stress of various non-price aspects of competition. These monopolistic elements in competition include emphasis on style and quality differences, servicing, credit terms and so on. As a result, export success cannot be ex-

plained solely in terms of comparative advantage, i.e. differences in relative prices. Hence the introduction of the terms 'competitive advantage' or 'export advantage' to convey the notion that export success is the outcome of both price and non-price aspects of competition. Chapter V strongly questions the realism of the assumption of labor immobility. The assumption that physical and financial capital are similarly immobile is also questionable.

(6) Chapter IV indicated the vast differences in the quality of inputs of each of the factors of production. In addition to recognizing the importance of these 'non-competing' groups, there is likely to exist complementary as well as competitive relationships between units of some factor.

2. The static nature of the analysis

In any discussion of the role of exports in growth, the focus quite naturally is on the behavior of exports over time. Probing further, the analysis must concern itself with the factors determining the success or failure of some economy in its export drive. As might be expected, the static and comparative static framework of the Heckscher–Ohlin theory is ill-suited for explaining such intertemporal performances. Given the relative factor endowments of two countries and the removal of some artificial barrier to trade, the pattern of specialization and trade and the possible long-run gains from trade is easily derived within the Heckscher–Ohlin framework. Similarly, comparative statics techniques can be employed to study once-over changes in the basic data, i.e. tastes, factor endowments and factor efficiencies.[8] Whether exports would grow more rapidly in one country compared with another and why is not a problem studied for reasons just mentioned.

In an effort to remedy this shortcoming, dynamic neoclassical trade models have been developed. The models are very similar in nature to the neoclassical models described in Chapter III, the main difference being that they are by necessity multi-sector neoclassical models, each sector corresponding to an industry producing some good in each country.[9] As might be expected, dynamic neoclassical trade models differ from the usual static trade models in the ability of the former to incorporate continuously changing factor endowments by allowing both the labor forces and capital stock to grow over time. Dynamic Heckscher–Ohlin models usually retain the two-country, two-factor and two-goods framework of most static analysis, which has the advantage of bringing out the determinants of trade patterns most clearly. Comparative advantage in some versions of these models turns out to be a function of the relative size of the savings ratio in the two countries. The country with the highest savings ratio ends up

[8] See, for example, G. Meier, *International Trade and Development*, Harper & Row, New York, 1963, Chapter 2.

[9] One of the earliest was that by P. Bardhan, 'Equilibrium Growth in the International Economy,' *Quarterly Journal of Economics*, August 1965. See also C. Smallwood, 'Economic Growth and the Pure Theory of International Trade,' *Scottish Journal of Political Economy*, June 1975.

with a (dynamic) comparative advantage in the production of capital goods. The other country specializes in the production and export of consumer goods. Exports of each country grow at the same rate, a rate equal to the rate of growth of total output, with the latter determined by the rate of growth of the labor force plus any allowance for a positive rate of growth of technical progress. Again the similarity to the results of Chapter III should be obvious. In these models the rate of growth of exports and output are determined by supply factors, i.e. the 'natural' rate of growth, and in this sense it cannot be said that growth is in any sense exported. While dynamic neoclassical trade models do allow for changing relative factor endowments, most of the same questioning of the realism of the assumptions given above remains.

3. The 'Leontief Paradox'

While it has long been recognized that the various assumptions upon which the Heckscher–Ohlin theory of comparative advantage was based diverged in various degrees from conditions in the real world, this was not necessarily considered to result in 'bad' theory, provided this lack of realism of the assumptions did not systematically and significantly bias the conclusions of the model.[10] For an extended period of time the model was thought to be able accurately to predict the nature of trade patterns because it was thought to generate unbiased results. The confidence of the economics profession in the ability of Heckscher–Ohlin theory to perform as 'good' theory in this sense was profoundly shaken by an important development in the postwar period. This was the finding by Leontief that American exports appeared to be more labor-intensive than American imports.[11]

Leontief's findings led for a reformulation of the Heckscher–Ohlin theory to include labor skills within the concept of capital; the so-called neofactor proportions theory of trade and comparative advantage. The rationale behind this extension was the notion that the acquisition of labor skills was an act of investment in human capital and that relative factor endowments of human capital are relevant in determining comparative advantage and, therefore, trade patterns. The reformulation was developed essentially within the two-goods, two-country, two-factor framework. One approach was to assume an equalization of rates of return on physical capital through the international mobility of capital. This allowed the analysis to proceed as if the only two factors of production were skilled (endowed with human capital) and unskilled labor. Alternatively, a combined measure of physical and human capital was used along with some measure of 'labor.'

[10] R. Baldwin, 'Determinants of the Commodity Structure of U.S. Trade,' *American Economic Review*, March 1971.

[11] W. Leontief, 'Domestic Production and Foreign Trade: The American Capital Position Re-examined,' *Proceedings of the American Philosophical Society*, September 1953; and 'Factor Proportions and the Structure of American Trade: Further Theoretical and Empirical Analysis,' *Review of Economics and Statistics*, November 1956.

The reformulated Heckscher–Ohlin model theorem has been confirmed in the sense that American exports were found to be more capital-intensive than imports, when natural resource-based goods were excluded from the sample of traded goods.[12] However, there are some difficulties. As advocates of what has come to be known as the neotechnology theory of trade argue, the fact that American exports involve relatively large amounts of human capital is explained within their non-neofactor theory of trade. Thus, the neotechnology theory of trade predicts that American trade advantage will be found in those industries most actively engaged in R and D and the development of new products and technologies.[13]

Second, while it may be true that American exports are more human capital-intensive than imports on a quantity basis, i.e. have a higher skilled to unskilled labor content, a recent study by Morrall indicates that they may not be so on a price basis.[14] In other words relative factor abundance (or shortage) can be defined either in physical or in economic terms. In physical terms, a country A is said to be more human capital-abundant than country B if the aggregate skilled–unskilled labor ratio is greater in A than in B. On the other hand, country A is more human capital-abundant than B in economic terms if the factor price ratio between wages of skilled workers and wages of unskilled workers is less in country A than B. Morrall's recent study showed that on an economic basis America is relatively abundant in unskilled labor and, according to the neofactor proportions theory of trade, should be exporting goods making most use of unskilled labor. The trade patterns of the United States may, therefore, be inconsistent with the neofactor proportions theory.

The issues involved here are exceedingly complex and as just indicated the empirical evidence can be used to support more than one explanation of trade patterns. However, in Section B above it was argued that there were certain characteristics of trade in manufactures in postwar period that cannot be overlooked in evaluating alternative explanations of trade patterns. And it is because Heckscher–Ohlin theory cannot explain these characteristics at all well that the present study must turn to alternative theories of trade patterns for guidance. These theories are discussed next.

D. The New Theories of Export Advantage

1. Intra-industry trade

A second and more recent finding that challenges the adequacy of Heckscher–Ohlin theory has been the rapid expansion of intra-industry

[12] See Baldwin, op. cit.

[13] See W. Gruber, D. Mehta and R. Vernon, 'The R and D Factor in International Trade and International Investment of United States Industries,' *Journal of Political Economy*, February 1967.

[14] J. Morrall, *Human Capital, Technology and International Trade*, University of Florida, Gainsville, 1972.

trade mentioned earlier.[15] On the basis of the Heckscher–Ohlin analysis it would be expected that any liberalization of trade would be accompanied by greater national specialization in the production and export of goods of certain industries by each country. In contrast, the postwar expansion of trade between industrial countries, partially in response to a liberalization of trade, has seen a relatively rapid growth in trade that involved a simultaneous importing and exporting of goods belonging to the same industry. This suggests that the Heckscher–Ohlin approach does, in fact, 'systematically and significantly' bias the conclusions of the model.

This finding, together with the long-recognized need to take account of elements of monopolistic competition, the additional evidence for the existence of scale economies and a general desire to provide a truly dynamic framework, has given rise to several alternative explanations of the determinants of trade patterns in manufactures. The expressions 'demand similarity,' 'technology gap,' 'product life cycle' and 'availability' theories of comparative advantage suggest some of the flavor of the stress and emphasis of these theories.

The value of these theories in accounting for one of the more important 'stylized facts' of postwar trade developments, the rapid expansion of intra-industry trade, has been pointed out by Grubel and Lloyd.[16] Their study was to a large extent motivated by a desire to discover the reasons for the persistent bias of the Heckscher–Ohlin theory in its 'predictions' of the patterns of trade. The Grubel–Lloyd procedure was to drop one or more of the assumptions of neoclassical trade theory and to study the implications for trade patterns.

For example, consider a world of two countries, A and B, each producing two similar but not identical goods before trade utilizing identical production functions across countries for each good. If, in addition, the possibility that each good can be produced under conditions of increasing returns in each country is allowed, a source of comparative advantage arises in each of the two countries.[17] Furthermore, the existence of intra-industry trade is not difficult to explain. If country A specializes in the production of good X and country B specializes in good Y, both achieve economies of scale in production and a comparative advantage in the production of one of the goods. As a result, each successfully exports its respective speciality. Note that, because the same two goods were available in each country before trade, competitive advantage is unambiguously defined in terms of relative prices; i.e., comparative advantage adequately explains export success.

[15]Grubel and Lloyd found that between 1959 and 1967, 80 per cent of the total increase in export plus import trade was due to an increase in intra-industry trade. Equally important, this growth could not be traced to the use of data at too high a level of aggregation. See Grubel and Lloyd, op. cit., p. 42 and Chapter 4.

[16]ibid.

[17]See Chapters VII and VIII.

The explanation of which goods will be exported by which country can then be explained in terms of the relative strength of demand within each country before trade. In the example just given, if country A consumed a greater proportion of good X relative to good Y than country B before trade, that would provide a reasonable explanation of A's comparative advantage in good X. In other words, countries end up exporting differentiated products that are most popular at home, and importing those that appeal to a minority.

Differences in tastes between countries may be due to differences in non-economic factors or incomes. In the latter case, the model resembles one formulated by Linder.[18] Thus, assume that good X is a higher-quality good than Y in some sense and that consumers choose between X and Y on the basis of their incomes; i.e., higher-quality goods are consumed by high-income groups. If, then, average per capita income in country A is greater than per capita income in country B but the income distributions overlap, country A will specialize and export the higher-quality good X to the wealthy of country B. Similarly, country B will specialize and export good Y. This simple model not only explains the existence of intra-industry trade, i.e. the trade in 'similar' goods; it provides an example of homespun growth. Through the relatively greater development of the domestic market for good X (Y) in country A (B) a comparative advantage develops which spills over into exports once trade opens up.

Next consider the case where production functions differ between countries but scale economies are absent. Recall that in Chapter VI the choice of technique of production was seen as the end result of a search process, a search for information and 'know-how' that costs time and money. Going further, there is no reason to assume that production functions are ever identical in different countries since these search costs and profits will vary from one country to another. Thus, firms everywhere are looking for new products to develop and for ways in which to modify existing products and improve their production processes; but it may not even pay to look for new products, new styles or better techniques because of these cost considerations. Suppose that not only are inventions influenced by demand conditions in a manner suggested by Schmookler, but improvements in general are as well. In particular, allow the size of the market for the output of a technology and its rate of growth to influence the rate of innovation and improvement in technology. This is to be expected because the size and growth of a market increases the 'payoff' for what might be obtained from additional search. Finally, suppose that search costs rise as the distance from the market increases and, therefore, that firms in their production and sales plans first exploit the domestic market. This could be justified by the know-

[18] Linder, op. cit. It should be noted that Linder applied his theory to trade in manufactures and believed that the Heckscher–Ohlin theory adequately explained trade in primary products.

ledge that, in the development of a successful product, a good deal of feedback between consumer and producer is required before the product design and consumer tastes coincide. This should be especially true during the early stages of product development. Distance makes this feedback effect take longer and therefore costs more.

This is the setting for a model also made familiar by Linder and leads to specialization and trade as before.[19] Thus, assume that country A is again the high-income country and that income distributions overlap between A and B. Because it is the high-income country, there is a large domestic market for good X, the high-quality good, in country A. Similarly a larger domestic market for good Y, a good similar to X, develops in country B. If then, before trade, country A was denied the possibility of producing good Y and country B was similarly denied the possibility of producing good X, i.e. if production functions are not identical across countries, then upon the opening up of trade country A will again export good X to the wealthy of country B and country B export good Y to the poor of country A. Naturally, if economies of scale are also allowed, this reinforces the tendencies at work for greater intra-industry trade and for trade to spill over from domestic production. Finally, it should be noted that export success cannot now be attributed to comparative advantage since the lack of availability of one good in each country, i.e. the differences in technologies between countries, does not allow for the functioning of relative prices.[20]

2. The product life cycle and trade

The title 'neotechnology theory of trade' is given to those theories of trade that emphasize international differences in technologies or production functions and economies of scale as causes of trade and sources of export success.[21] As the two examples in the previous section illustrate, the neotechnology theory of trade is not only consistent with the views that (a) growth in particular markets is homespun and (b) the same kinds of factors ensure sales success in domestic and foreign markets; it emphasizes these notions. In addition, stress is often given to the importance of research and development (R and D) activity in creating differences in technology between countries. Neotechnology theorists have tended to concentrate their atten-

[19] S. Linder, 'Trade and Technical Efficiency' in J. Bhagwati *et al.* (eds.), *Trade, Balance of Payments and Growth*, North Holland, Amsterdam, 1971.

[20] Since comparative advantage is defined in terms of relative prices, it becomes difficult to use the expression outside of the context of the competitive, Heckshher–Ohlin model. Thus, once product differentiation enters it seems better to talk in some general sense about 'competitive advantage' or 'export advantage' or some such notion as in the text. Grubel and Lloyd argue that increasing returns to scale in industries characterized by products with only minor differences between them is the most important explanation of intra-industry trade. See Grubel and Lloyd, op. cit. p. 84.

[21] A summary of the many strands is provided by L. Wells, 'International Trade: The Product Life Cycle Approach,' in *The Product Life Cycle and International Trade*, Harvard University, Cambridge, 1972, as well as several studies found in R. Vernon (ed.), *The Technology Factor in International Trade*, Columbia University Press, New York, 1970.

tion on the United States, the country with the highest per capita income for most of the postwar period. Thus, when industries are classified by the percentage of scientists and engineers in the total work force or by the R and D expenditures as a percentage of net sales, chemicals, non-electrical machinery, aircraft and parts, and professional and scientific instruments are usually found to be the most R-and-D-intensive product groups. It has also been found that these industries accounted for the overwhelming share of American exports.[22] However, this approach to trade is easily extended to other countries with additional emphasis given to the borrowing of technology and the application of R and D to this borrowed technology, as in Chapter VI.

What has become known as the product life cycle theory of trade can be looked upon as a special case of the neotechnology theory. Not only does it incorporate differences in technologies and economies of scale, and the notion of a spillover of sales from domestic to foreign markets; it provides a framework for accommodating the changing pattern of trade in manufactured goods. In particular, it provides an explanation of why trade advantages might be quite temporary in nature.[23] Thus, while the examples in the previous section allow for a plausible explanation of intra-industry trade within a framework that allows for monopoly elements, they do not allow for developments of trade patterns over time, especially developments whereby patterns of exports change in a manner suggested by Table 10.1. These examples also tend to suggest that, once a country has established a competitive advantage in the production of some good or has obtained a monopoly position, such conditions become somehow fixed. These shortcomings are easily remedied.

The last example of intra-industry trade in the previous section was confined to two similar goods, one of which was not available in each country before trade. Trade in pharmaceuticals closely resembles the model just outlined. Most examples of trade based on differences in technologies or technology 'gaps' are similar but the product life cycle explanation lays heavy stress on the newness of the good. For example, because of, say, a scientific breakthrough, let country A, a high-income country, develop a technology for producing a good that is not available elsewhere or is likely to be produced elsewhere since it is a high-quality good. Alternatively, because of patent restrictions the technology cannot be borrowed. Then, country A will have a monopoly on the production and export of the good at least for the life of the patent.

However, the discussion in Chapter VI suggested that patent purchases and licensing arrangements were an important part of the international exchange and diffusion of technology in the postwar period, indicating that

[22] Gruber, *et al.*, op. cit.

[23] For one of the earliest studies see R. Vernon, 'International Investment and International Trade in the Product Cycle,' *Quarterly Journal of Economics*, May 1966.

a temporary monopoly position for the innovator is very likely. The product life cycle theory of trade patterns emphasizes the temporary nature of this monopoly or limited availability aspect of a good in the country originating the innovation. In the product life cycle theory, product development, trade, demand and production are seen as a dynamic process of change through three stages; early, growth and mature.[24] In the early stages of development of a new good, there exists a great deal of uncertainty about the characteristics of the good from the point of view of both consumers and producers. Customers buying the good are even described in the literature as 'innovators,' who will purchase the good in spite of a lack of any basis for comparison with other goods or for evaluating the good itself. Producers are at the same time experimenting with product design, attempting to find those designs that will have the greatest growth and profit prospects. The importance of skilled labor and entrepreneurship is greatest at this point. And because of the large number of alternative designs, production runs tend to be short and costs high. Standardized machinery must await the standardization of the product into a limited number of variations. Naturally, research and development outlays, especially the latter, loom large.

During the growth phase, the proper amount of feedback between producers and consumers has been accomplished. Production becomes more rationalized as the number of variations in product design are reduced, and specialized machinery and mass production techniques are introduced. On the consumer side, price competition becomes more acute during this growth phase. Finally, a mature phase denotes a period when production has become quite routinized in that techniques are stable since inefficient methods of production have by this time been weeded out. Labor skills are unimportant as is the entrepreneurial function. Marketing and advertising strategies become important on the demand side.

However, the product life cycle theory is concerned not so much with change in patterns of demand and production in the domestic market as with a likely gradual decline in the competitive position of firms in the innovating countries. Define the 'demand lag' as the lag between consumption in the country that first introduces some good and its consumption in some other country. Similarly, as in Chapter VI, define the 'imitation lag' as the interval between the initial production of some good in the innovating country and its production in the imitating country.[25] Then, while production of new goods may begin in a high-income country like the United States, sooner or later a sequence develops that may lead not only to the transfer of new tastes abroad (after a demand lag) but also to the transfer of the production of the good itself (after an imitation lag).

As just stated, various studies have shown that the United States has been

[24] See Wells, op. cit., for a more detailed outline.

[25] The earliest study to utilize these notions was M. Posner, 'International Trade and Technical Change,' *Oxford Economic Papers*, October 1961.

highly competitive in exports in those industries that have a high propensity to develop new products.[26] In the product life cycle sequence this competitive position would be maintained and exports would grow rapidly for a time as incomes rise in foreign countries and foreign demand for American exports of new goods expands. The length of the demand lag would depend upon a number of factors. The more the distributions of income overlap between the innovating country and its potential foreign customers, the shorter this lag; the more extensive are the barriers to trade set up in the importing country the longer the lag, etc.

At some point, foreign demand for the new good would have become so large that, unless the innovating firm in the United States sets up a subsidiary abroad, local producers in the importing countries would now find that local production and import substitution becomes a distinct possibility.[27] The length of this imitation lag also depends upon the domestic demand for the good (originally produced abroad) in the same way as does the demand lag. In addition, the degree of technical sophistication involved in production has an important influence on the lag for obvious reasons. And as mentioned in Chapter VI, the extent to which barriers for importing technology are involved plays an important role. The actual success in import substitution is due partly to government intervention, partly to Linder-type factors and partly to the lower wages in the lower-income countries.[28] To this can be added a point stressed in Chapter VI; the imitating country is in a better position to borrow the best developed technology from abroad.

Finally, the product life cycle theory envisages a third phase whereby not only may the rate of growth of exports of the innovating country decline, but exports may decline absolutely as those countries who have succeeded in substituting local production for imports duplicate their success in the local market by selling abroad, even in the country that originally developed the good.

3. The development ladder

The analysis can be extended by introducing the notion of an international 'pecking order'.[29] Thus, those countries that succeed in substituting local production for imports from the highest-income country and then expand exports of the same product may themselves fall victim to the same process as per capita incomes rise over time in other countries with relatively lower

[26] See Gruber *et al.*, op. cit.

[27] The similarity between this sequence of events and that used by historians and development economists to describe the shift of an economy from the underdeveloped to the semi-industrial stage, or from the latter stage to the industrial stage, should be apparent.

[28] This process is well illustrated by Tilton, op. cit., Chapter 3.

[29] This idea is developed by G. Hufbauer, *Synthetic Materials and the Theory of International Trade*, Harvard University Press, Cambridge, 1966. See also Tilton, op. cit., Chapter 3; and R. Nelson, 'A "Diffusion" Model of International Productivity Differences in Manufacturing Industry,' *American Economic Review*, December 1968.

incomes. For example, at some point in time, new products are developed in the high-income countries and exported down the development ladder, i.e. to countries with lower per capita incomes. As incomes rise everywhere, production of these goods moves to lower relative income countries, to be followed by exports of the same goods from the latter countries. These middle countries then soon find their competitive position weakened as import substitution takes place in countries even further down the development ladder, as these latter countries find that rising per capita incomes allow for a greatly expanded local market. In the meantime the highest-income countries develop a new set of new products and the process repeats itself.

What is being discussed here is a process recognized for some time by economists concerned with determining patterns of industrialization. Starting at relatively low per capita incomes, in this view industrialization is accompanied by the substitution of local production of 'light' industries for imports from the same industries, e.g. foodstuffs and textiles, followed by their export. Imports of products of 'heavy industry,' e.g. durable consumer and producer goods, simultaneously rise. This is then followed by a period of import substitution in capital goods and eventually their export.[30]

The development ladder model borrows heavily from the product life cycle concept. It also ties together the interrelated economies in a definite ranking pattern whereby competitive advantages in certain goods are continuously being passed down the development ladder. How rapidly competitive advantages are passed down the ladder is largely a matter of how rapidly per capita incomes are growing in the relatively low-income countries compared with the industrial leaders. In Chapters VI and VIII it was argued that, other things being equal, low-income countries would grow more rapidly than high-income countries. In a situation such as this, differences in per capita income levels between countries narrow over time as do growth rates.[31] In this case the demand and imitation lags would become shorter over some period as patterns of output, especially consumption, became more similar and as income distributions increasingly overlap. Intra-industry trade in differentiated products would also rise rapidly. However, it was clear in Chapter VIII that other things were not equal between countries in the postwar period in the sense that some countries made a greater effort, measured in terms of investment ratios, to grow rapidly than others. As a result, a country like, say, Japan, by narrowing the income gap more rapidly than others, would experience shorter demand and imitation lags than some slow-growing country. Thus, not only did Japan grow more rapidly than other countries, but it underwent a relatively rapid growth and a more radical change in its exports and imports.

[30] See Kaldor, *Strategic Factors*, op. cit., pp. 29–32, and Maizels, op. cit., Chapter 3.

[31] At the beginning of the 1950s per capita income was approximately ten times as large in the highest-income country, the United States, as in the lowest-income country, Japan. By the end of the 1960s per capita income was slightly more than three times as large in the highest-income country, United States, compared with Japan, the lowest-income country.

E. The Japanese Case

The model just presented suggests that exports of manufactures at any one time are exports of goods from countries that have a competitive advantage today in certain goods but stand to lose this advantage soon. For example, the model assumes not only that import substitution is virtually automatic once per capita incomes reach some critical level in some country, but also that export success cannot lie far behind. What is clear is that the model, while useful, neglects several influences on trade and development patterns. For example, differences in relative factor endowments undoubtedly explain trade success in certain manufactures.[32] In addition, the kinds of economies of scale derived from learning processes and other barriers to entry in the production of some good are no doubt important in some cases. Thus, an innovating country, if learning economies are very strong, may well find that it is not exporting a product life cycle good but rather a sort of good whose exports remain strong even after the expiration of some sort of patent monopoly. Determining the relative importance of these factors is a subject of great importance, but it need not be pursued here.[33]

It should also be noticed that the model does not allow much scope for exporting up the development ladder. The latter can be seen as nothing more than a situation of export-led growth. Thus, the model presupposes that import substitution precedes exports of some good indicating a spillover from domestic growth to that of exports. In contrast, export-led growth visualizes a situation where, using the pecking order framework, a country exports up the development ladder by producing for export a good that is not strongly demanded at home – say only by the rich. The notion of exporting up the development ladder not only implies that the influence of learning economies and barriers to entry can be overcome, but it downgrades the importance of greater familiarity with the domestic market as stressed by Linder. The vast majority of the theoretical and empirical studies cited in this chapter would certainly assign a low probability to this kind of export success.

It is possible to cite examples of goods produced primarily for export or even groups of products whose main market is abroad.[34] For example, it is often alleged that Japan, of all the developed market economies, grew rapidly by producing a wide range of goods largely destined for foreign markets. A closer look at the Japanese performance is, therefore, helpful.

[32] See Grubel and Lloyd, op. cit., pp. 85–8. This is especially likely to be the case when the technology in some industry has become stabilized and production quite routine.

[33] It is true that a major concern in this chapter is determining the sources of competitive advantage in exports. However, the conclusions of this part of the study are that it makes no difference whether export success results from, say, dynamic learning economies or familiarity with the market. Either of these factors is the result of entrepreneurial endeavors.

[34] Belgium is often cited as a country whose export markets for certain goods are far outweighed in importance by domestic sales of the same items. See Grubel and Lloyd, op. cit., pp. 95–7.

Those who argue against the export-led position and in favor of homespun growth cite the small proportion of Japanese output devoted to exports, less than 10 per cent in current prices and approximately 11½ per cent in constant prices in 1973. Tsurumi's disaggregative study gives further support to the homespun view.[35] By tracing the behavior of exports and total production for twenty-one categories of manufactures from 1946 to 1965, Tsurumi was able to show that for only two intermediate goods (fertilizer and rayon cloth) were exports consistently greater than 40 per cent of output. For three intermediate goods (steel pipes, steel plates and tin plate) exports as a share of total production rose very rapidly during the 1960s until they reached roughly 40 per cent. But the general picture was one of the ratio varying between 5 and 20 per cent. Especially low figures (1 to 10 per cent) were found for three durable goods (machine tools, heavy electrical equipment and motor vehicles). Thus, while the picking of any percentage figure as critical is arbitrary, the evidence is that only in a minority of the cases cited is there evidence of spillover from foreign markets to the home market. The typical case is that of homespun growth.

Supporters of the export-led view can argue in rebuttal that what is at issue is why Japan experienced a growth rate in manufacturing of 13½ per cent while in the other countries growth was slower. Framed this way, the question is whether the difference in growth rates between the fast growers such as Japan and the others could be explained in terms of a more favorable export performance. Now it is certainly true that throughout the postwar period there was a positive correlation across countries between the rate of growth of exports and the rate of growth of GDP. But this tells little about the direction of causation. For example, a higher rate of growth of GDP can be expected to give rise to more rapid rates of growth of productivity, which makes a country's competitive position much stronger. Couple this with a trend towards greater liberalization of trade throughout the world, and a plausible explanation of relative export and GDP performance is available.

There are data, however, on relative rates of growth of exports and domestic sales for Japan for a wide range of goods. Thus, when fifty-five Japanese industries were classified into five groups according to the rate of increase of exports from 1955 to 1964, there was a strong positive correlation between the rates of growth of exports and rates of growth of domestic demand of the same products.[36] The same fifty-five industries were also classified into the following four categories: (1) goods with domestic demand and export sales both growing by more than 15 per cent per year; (2) goods with domestic demand increasing by less than 10 per cent and export sales

[35] Tsurumi, op. cit., Figures III-3, III-4 and III-5.

[36] See H. Kanamori, 'Economic Growth and Exports,' in L. Klein and K. Ohkawa (eds.), *Economic Growth: The Japanese Experience since the Meiji Era*, Richard Irwin, Homewood, Illinois, 1968.

growing by more than 15 per cent; (3) goods with domestic demand increasing by more than 15 per cent and export sales growing less than 10 per cent; and (4) goods with domestic demand and export sales both growing by less than 10 per cent per year. Over 40 per cent of the goods fell in category (1), almost 44 per cent in (3) and a little less than 15 per cent fell in category (4). Significantly, only one good, footwear, fell into category (2), the category where export sales grew more rapidly than domestic sales. What the study suggests is that growth in exports seldom exceeds growth in the home market, even in a country considered to be the most oriented towards realizing and exploiting the foreign markets of the future.[37]

F. Conclusions

In concluding Chapter IX it was stated that the resolution of the question of whether growth was export-led or homespun was of secondary importance. This belief was based on a more basic view that the factors that lead to imaginative and successful export drives are the same factors that spur growth rates for the whole economy. As seen in this chapter, this in turn involves a general acceptance of the neotechnology theory of trade. This theory, with its emphasis on differences across countries in technologies, on the importance of scale economies, borrowed technology and R and D, the quality of entrepreneurship and investment outlays, is the most adequate theory for explaining export patterns and success. Clearly, all these influences comprise the same catalogue of items cited in Chapter VI as being so important for determining the rate of growth of total manufacturing output whatever its destination. Once this point is accepted, it is necessary to add only a Linder-type argument about the greater familiarity local producers have with their domestic markets or the product life cycle notions of lower costs of information feedback between producers and domestic consumers (especially important during early stages of product development). The conclusion that homespun growth will be the predominant form of spillover then follows.

The case of Japan, the most dynamic economy by far in the postwar period, illustrates these views. In a country assigned the highest marks for the quality of its entrepreneurship this latter group operated with an aim to develop both domestic and foreign markets.[38] But even in this case, growth would have to be characterized as predominantly homespun. Thus, the analysis comes down to the rather undramatic conclusion that, while there is a spillover from domestic markets to foreign markets and vice versa,

[37] None of Kanamori's fifty-five industries corresponds with those industries in Tsurumi's study which showed relatively rapid growth rates of exports, e.g. steel pipes. See Kanamori, op. cit., and Tsurumi, op. cit.

[38] In one study, 'export profiles' or patterns are found to be highly correlated to the amount of licensed technology. See T. Tsurumi, 'R and D Factors and Exports of Manufactured Goods of Japan,' in Wells, *The Product Life Cycle*, op. cit.

in some long-run sense, at least, it is the former spillover that predomi-ates.[39]

When stress is placed on the common factors determining growth and export performance, an important justification for a study of growth in an age of inflation emerges, one already suggested in the Preface. If export success can be traced to the same factors that lead to success in domestic markets, then whatever speeds up the growth rate should help not only exports but the employment picture. By relieving a country of balance of payments problems, success in exports and growth allows an economy to be run closer to full employment. It might also be added that a more successful growth and export performance, because of the accompanying productivity developments, should be helpful in reducing inflationary pressures.

Having, hopefully, determined that the model developed in Chapters IV–VIII to explain why growth rates differ was not in grievous error in its neglect of the foreign sector, the analysis concludes in the remaining chapters with an analysis of the very recent past. What is suggested is that events of the last few years have set in motion certain structural changes in the workings of modern capitalism that are liable to be more basic than any considered so far.

[39] The qualification, 'in the long-run,' is intended to allow for the importance of export-led booms. In this 'short-run' situation the growth of exports allows a boom to be sustained which spills over, allowing rapid growth of sales in the domestic markets.

Chapter XI Closing Time in the Gardens of the West

A. Introduction

The earlier chapters attempted to outline and explain the dramatic character of economic events that took place on a wide scale over the postwar period. Most of the analysis was limited to a period from the early 1950s until 1973. Economic events before the early 1950s were so dominated by World War II and its aftermath that little would have been gained by extending the analysis further back in time. Similarly, as will soon be apparent economic events after 1973 were and still are being dominated by recession tendencies and other 'shocks' to such an extent that the basic features of postwar growth would have been obscured if post-1973 years had been included in the analysis. In general, the period from the early 1950s until 1973 or 1974 (depending upon the particular country) was and could be looked upon as the 'greatest boom in history' in most of the market economies with some justification.

In the eyes of the press, government leaders and, indeed, a good part of the economics profession, the period shortly before and after 1973 marked a turning point. The oil embargo; a movement of the terms of trade against the developed economies; the possibility of persistent energy shortages; the increasing importance of domestic communist power in two large market economies (France and Italy); the inability of another large market economy (Britain) to handle its major economic problems; the widespread corruption of the political and economic systems in another (the United States); the expressed lack of confidence in the 'market' by the ruling party in yet another (Canada); the beginning of what was to become the most severe recession in the postwar period – all these and other influences contributed to a general loss of confidence, even by sympathizers, in the ability of market capitalism 'to deliver the goods.' To many observers an end of a remarkable period either had come or was near at hand.

To be sure, there were those who were prepared to dismiss these events as isolated phenomena blown all out of proportion by an increasingly frivolous popular press. However, other equally if not more important developments were increasingly visible by the early 1970s that could not be written off as the mere product of journalistic sensationalism.

Thus instead of treating the period from the early 1950s until 1973 as a whole, if the postwar period is broken up into periods marked off by peak years in economic activity, some important tendencies become clear. For example, it has already been pointed out in Chapter II that the period of widespread accelerated rates of growth of output per worker overall and in manufacturing appeared to come to an end around 1969 or 1970.[1] The period from the end of the 1960s to 1973 was very mixed in this regards, with some countries experiencing a pick-up in growth rates so measured and others (typically those with good overall postwar growth performances) a deceleration. With more certainty it can be said that by the late 1960s certain employment and aggregate output trends had become very widespread and unmistakable. Finally, the period from the late 1960s until 1973 marked a transition in the official response to inflation. It is these developments that the present chapter will consider. Taken together they suggested at the time, and continue to suggest, that events to follow would and will lead to important changes in the nature and performance of market capitalism.

B. The De-industrialization of the Market Economies

Beginning in the late 1960s and continuing into the 1970s there developed on a wide scale a process of de-industrialization, i.e. a process resulting in the relative decline of employment in the industrial and manufacturing sectors in the various market economies. Diagram 11.1 shows the sectoral employment patterns for the six large OECD countries using the Cripps and Tarling method of subdividing the postwar period. As indicated in Table 4.3 earlier, Japan, Germany, Italy and France conformed to the workings of the dual model when the postwar period as a whole was considered. Moreover, Diagram 11.1 indicates that, up until the end of the 1960s, from one period to the next employment in manufacturing grows more rapidly than total employment in Japan, Germany and Italy.

However, when viewing the patterns up until 1973 period by period, the underlying trends depicted in Diagram 11.1 can only be characterized as a relatively steady process of de-industrialization for all six large economies. Over time the differences between the rate of growth of employment in manufacturing and the rate of growth of employment overall narrowed until, by the last recorded boom, overall employment grew more rapidly than that in manufacturing in all six countries. In three economies (Germany, the United Kingdom and the United States), the rate of growth of manufacturing employment in the last boom period was actually negative.

Another aspect of the same process can be seen by tracing the movements of employment in the two major subsectors of the service sector, commerce (ISIC 6 and 8 under the new definitions) and other services (roughly ISIC

[1] See p. 12.

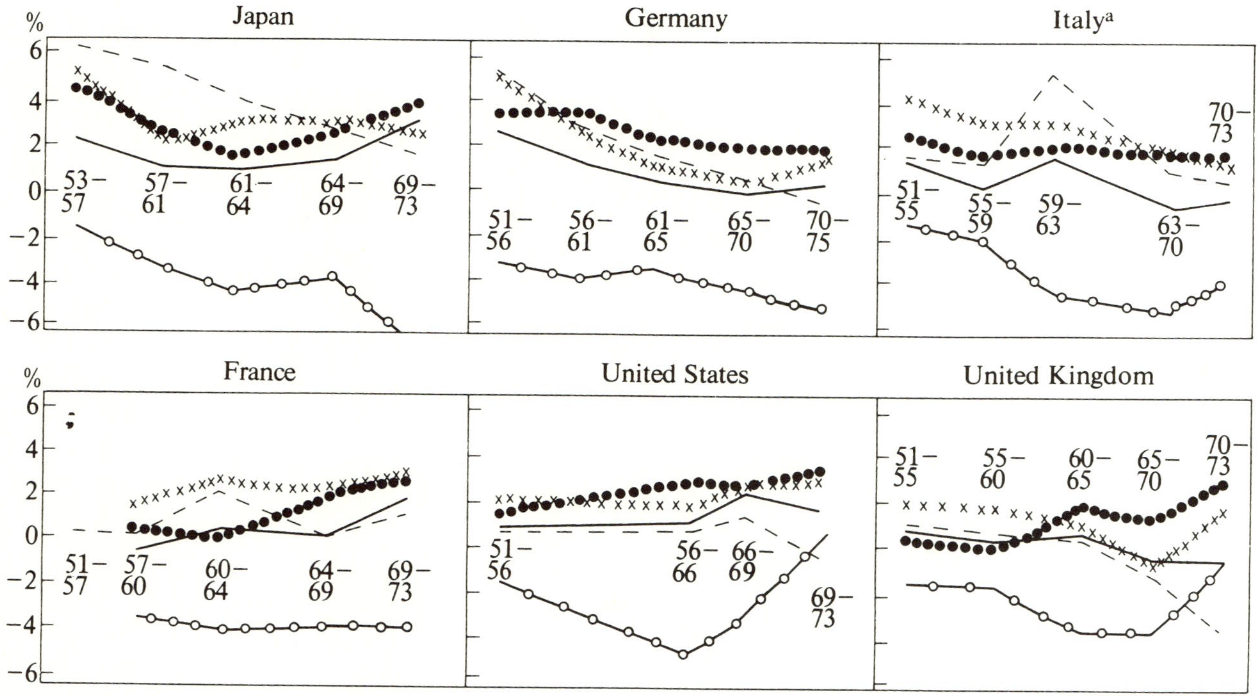

Rates of growth of employment are as follows: overall ——; in manufacturing – – –; in commerce xxxxxx; in other services ●●●●● and, in agriculture o—o—o—o.

[a] For 1970–73 it was necessary to use the rate of growth of employment in commerce and other services.

Sources: Cripps and Tarling, op. cit.; and *Labour Force Statistics, 1962–1973*, op. cit.

Diagram 11.1. Rates of growth of employment by Activities

9). Taking the postwar period as a whole, rates of growth of employment in these sectors exceeded the overall growth of employment in all six economies. Employment in these sectors also grew faster than manufacturing in five of the countries, Japan being the lone exception. However, if the patterns are again viewed period by period, what stands out is the increase in the rate of growth of employment in these sectors, absolutely and relative to other sectoral employment patterns, especially towards the end of the 1960s. The overall picture is little changed when the sample is expanded to include the six other OECD countries included by Cripps and Tarling in their sample. For example, in five of these six other countries, a similar kind of downward trend was in evidence for manufacturing employment so that employment in that sector grew less rapidly than overall employment by the 1969–73 or 1970–73 period, Austria being the lone exception.[2] And in four of the six, this inequality first developed during a period beginning in the mid-1960s (Norway and Austria being the exceptions).

C. The Underlying Causes of the De-industrialization Process

It is tempting in explaining the de-industrialization process to focus attention on the supply side of the different national labor markets. For example, by 1970 agricultural employment was less than 10 per cent of the labor force in six of the twelve countries included in Cripps and Tarling's sample compared with just two at the beginning of the 1950s. In addition, what was defined as the rate of growth of supply of labor available to the non-agricultural sector in Chapter V had declined substantially by the second half of the 1960s in a number of countries and has continued on into the 1970s.[3]

However, several things are overlooked in this concentration on the supply side of the labor market. First, as pointed out in Chapter II, low-income elasticities of demand for food and rapid rates of growth of productivity in agriculture allowed continuous reductions in employment in agriculture. To this can be added that the three developed market economies with the lowest per capita income throughout the postwar period (Austria, Italy and Japan) showed even in 1973 a relatively high ratio of agricultural employment to total employment – 16.1, 17.4 and 13.4 per cent, respectively.

[2] Both total and manufacturing employment declined in Austria from 1970 to 1973 but the rate of decline was more rapid for the former. Rates of growth of employment in industry also fell below those overall for most of the countries as well by the early 1970s.

[3] The rate of growth of the supply of labor available to the non-agricultural sector from 1969 or 1970 (depending on the date of a peak in activity) to 1973 was (in percentages):

Norway	4.2	Denmark	1.8	Germany	0.5
Canada	3.4	Austria	1.6	Netherlands	0.0
USA	2.1	Japan	1.4	Italy	−0.5
France	1.9	Belgium	0.9	UK	−0.3

A comparison with Table 5.1 indicates a decline in this growth rate in the early 1970s compared with the earlier postwar period for all countries except Norway, Canada, the United States, France and Austria.

Second, it has not been suggested that when labor shortages develop the high-wage sectors such as manufacturing suffer relatively more than other sectors, including the low-wage ones. Indeed, the discussion in Chapter V indicated that when labor markets tighten there is a general upgrading of the labor force as job openings and employment expand relatively in manufacturing and industry.[4]

If anything, the higher rates of growth of employment in the service sectors suggests a lack of demand for labor by manufacturing as the main cause of de-industrialization. What has been cited as evidence of labor shortages is a decrease in the dispersion of the wage structure as wages in the low-wage industries rise relatively to those in the high-wage industries. Thus in Chapter V it was pointed out that over the cycle the dispersion of wages varies, narrowing in booms and widening in recessions.[5] Typically, then, it would be expected that when demand pressures intensify over time the dispersion of wages would narrow. Yet, as indicated in Chapters IV and V, measures of the dispersion of manufacturing wages and the differential between agricultural wages and those for the rest of the economy over longer periods gave no indication of a general tightening of labor markets.[6] For example, the absolute and usually the relative dispersion of manufacturing wages increased over time for most of the countries treated in Table 5.7, indicating, if anything, a relative decline from one boom to the next in the degree of tightness.[7] What was suggested in Chapter V was that, in general,

[4] See pp. 76–78.

[5] See Chapter IV, Section E.

[6] See Chapter IV, Section E and Chapter V, Section G. There are comparable data on the number of job vacancies and numbers unemployed for eight market economies going back as far as the mid-1950s. Increases in the ratio of unfilled vacancies to unemployed persons is a rough measure of increases in the degree of tightness in labor markets, at least within a country. Again, using years of cyclical peaks, as determined by Cripps and Tarling, for the period up to the end of the 1960s and the year 1973 as the final recorded peak for all countries, these measures reveal the following: a downward trend in the ratio of unfilled vacancies to unemployed for the Netherlands and the United Kingdom; no noticeable trend for Belgium, France or Japan; a moderate upward trend until 1970 for Austria and 1973 for Norway; and a strong upward trend for Germany until 1970. From 1970 to 1973 the ratio declines sharply for Germany and rises sharply for Austria. See *Main Economic Indicators, Historical Statistics, 1955–1971*, and *December 1975*, OECD, Paris.

[7] It has been suggested that a general tightness of labor markets is indicated by a shift in the distribution of output from profits to labor. Write $P/Q=(P/K)\cdot(K/Q)$ where P/Q, P/K and K/Q are profits as a share of output, the rate of return on capital and the capital–output ratio, respectively. Assume that firms price in such a way as to obtain some targeted rate of return on their capital and that this rate of return is fixed in some long-run sense. Then, the behavior of profits as a share of output depends upon the capital–output ratio. Typically, the capital–output ratio rises during the early stages of industrialization, reflecting the development of a country's overhead capital. This is followed by a later period of rising average productivity of capital. The fact that by the 1960s the share of output shifted toward wages in several market economies may merely be reflecting the behavior of the average productivity of capital and not the tightness of the labor markets. See S. Kuznets, *Capital in the American Economy*, National Bureau of Economic Research, New York, 1961, pp. 78–90; and P. Deane and W. Cole, *British Economic Growth 1688–1959*, Cambridge University Press, 1967, Tables 80 and 81.

when manufacturing required more labor it could be found.

If, then, it is accepted that the process of de-industrialization that set in in so many countries towards the end of the 1960s was not attributable to some sort of labor shortage, other explanations must be sought. Recall that in Chapter VIII it was argued that a steady acceleration in rates of growth of productivity in manufacturing took place during the postwar period. This was indicated in the form of two equations, one for the rate of growth of productivity, the other for the rate of growth of employment in manufacturing. Thus from Table 8.5 write

$$\dot{\rho}_m = 0.926 + 0.394\,\dot{Q}_m + 0.071\,(\dot{Q}_m T) \tag{4a}$$

and

$$\dot{E}_m = -0.921 + 0.605\,\dot{Q}_m - 0.070\,(\dot{Q}_m T) \tag{5a}$$

where $\dot{\rho}_m$, $\dot{E}_m$, $\dot{Q}_m$ and T again represent the rate of growth of productivity, employment and output in manufacturing, respectively, and T is a time trend. As equation (5a) indicates, for any given rate of growth of manufacturing output, the rate of growth of demand for labor declines by approximately 7 per cent per period. In the same chapter it was pointed out that throughout most of the postwar period flexibility was important in the sense that expansion of manufacturing output during the period required a simultaneous expansion of employment in manufacturing. However, because of the acceleration in the rate of productivity in manufacturing, flexibility in this sense became less important over time.

For this reason alone, it would be expected that the rate of growth of employment in manufacturing would slow down, other things being equal. Furthermore, it was pointed out in Chapter VIII that the rate of growth of the ratio of employment in manufacturing to total employment, $\dot{E}_w$, was positively related to the rate of growth of manufacturing employment; i.e.,

$$\dot{E}_w = -0.716 + 0.672\,\dot{E}_m. \tag{6'}$$

From equation (6′) it is clear that a slowing down of the rate of growth of manufacturing employment must release labor for other (often lower-paying) occupations such as other services. Given a commitment to high employment by the governments concerned, and given the ability of many firms in the service sector to share work along the lines suggested in Chapter V, most of the released labor could be expected to find work elsewhere.

Moreover, there are additional forces at work reinforcing this tendency. In Table 2.2 it was shown that until 1969 or 1970 rates of growth of output per worker in the whole economy and in manufacturing were generally upward comparing peak-to-peak periods in each country. It was only in the last period, beginning in 1969 or 1970, that the trends became mixed. However, rates of growth of aggregate output and total manufacturing output had downward trends over the postwar period with peak growth rates occuring usually in the late 1950s or early 1960s. These trends could in turn be traced to rising per capita incomes, absolutely and relative to the United States. This matter will be discussed more fully in Section D below.

In summary, then, the developments in employment over the postwar period can be attributed to factors seen by earlier writers as a natural tendency in the development of capitalism.[8] An interaction between rising productivity rates and rising per capita incomes worked in such a way that, by the end of the postwar period, most market economies no longer fulfilled one condition for the application of the dual model. Most economies had by the early 1970s reached a point where the rate of growth of employment in manufacturing (and industry) had fallen below that of total employment.

Finally, the fact that employment growth in manufacturing (and industry) had fallen below total employment growth by the early 1970s does not herald the advent of the appropriateness of some other model of analysis to that employed here. Data in Chapter V indicated that, whatever the flow

Table 11.1. Rates of growth of manufacturing output in eleven OECD countries

Austria:	years	1951–57	1957–61	1961–66	1966–70	1970–73
	%	6.88	4.37	4.40	5.89	6.55
Denmark:	years	1954–57	1957–62	1962–65	1965–69	1969–73
	%	1.88	6.89	5.87	5.07	4.80
France:	years	1951–57	1957–60	1960–64	1964–69	1969–73
	%	5.0	5.33	7.11	6.43	n.a.
Germany:	years	1951–56	1956–61	1961–65	1965–70	1970–73
	%	11.97	9.05	6.08	5.64	3.97
Italy:	years	1951–55	1955–59	1959–63	1963–70	1970–73
	%	7.57	6.84	10.07	6.05	4.54
Netherlands:	years	1951–56	1956–60	1960–65	1965–70	1970–73
	%	6.63	5.14	6.04	n.a.	5.07
Norway:	years	1951–56	1956–60	1960–65	1965–70	1970–73
	%	3.95	3.63	5.59	n.a.	3.8
UK:	years	1951–55	1955– 0	1960–65	1965–69	1969–73
	%	3.83	2.85	3.33	3.18	2.60
Canada:	years	1951–56	1956–66	1966–69	1969–73	
	%	5.47	5.34	5.51	4.84	
Belgium:	years	1951–57	1957–64	1964–70	1970–73	
	%	n.a.	5.94	6.54	5.56	
USA:	years	1951–56	1956–66	1966–69	1969–73	
	%	2.91	4.37	3.41	4.50	

Source: *National Accounts of the OECD, 1950–1968, 1953–1969* and *1962–1973, Vol. I and II,* op. cit.

[8] See, for example, Clark, op. cit.

of employment, this reallocation across sectors was accomplished within the framework of a relatively stable wage structure. What does differ with the advent of de-industrialization is the existence of a labor allocative mechanism tending to give the 'wrong signals.' The relatively rapidly growing employment sectors in the 1970s tended to be the low-wage industries, at least compared with earlier periods.

D. Trends in Output

In Chapter VIII various regression tests of models developed to explain the rate of growth of manufacturing output were undertaken. For example, equation (1) from Table 8.1 gave

$$\dot{Q}_m = 0.185 + 1.09/q_r + 0.173\,(I/Q)_m$$

where q_r and $(I/Q)_m$ were, respectively, the ratio of per capita income in some country relative to the United States and the ratio of investment to output in manufacturing. Taking the postwar period as a whole, every country experienced a more rapid rate of growth of per capita income than the United States. Hence, q_r rose over time. Unless movements in relative per capita income were offset by a rising investment ratio, it would be expected that rates of growth of output of manufacturing would decline over time.

The actual behavior of rates of growth of manufacturing output for eleven countries are given in Table 11.1.[9] Peak-to-peak computations were used as before to eliminate as much as possible cyclical influences. The peak years differed, naturally, because of differences in cyclical movements across countries. The year 1973 was used as the final peak year for all countries. With the exception of Austria and the United States the trends were downward, certainly since the early 1960s. OECD data are not available for Japan although Cripps and Tarling's computations reveal a decline in the rate of growth of manufacturing output from the second half of the 1950s until the second half of the 1960s. As mentioned in Section C, these trends would have something to do with trends in employment patterns. On the basis of the engine of growth hypothesis developed in Chapter VII, it would be expected that rates of growth of total output would also decline for most countries. OECD data reveals this to be true for the same nine countries experiencing a decline in the rate of growth of manufacturing output in Table 11.1 and in Japan as well. As might be expected, the downward trend in

[9] The data in Table 11.1 are taken from different issues of *National Accounts of the OECD*. Cripps and Tarling's estimates of rates of growth of output in manufacturing rather consistently give less rapid rates of growth of manufacturing output in the second half of the 1960s for the various countries than do those estimates obtained directly from OECD sources. Because of this, the data in Table 11.1 will, if anything, underestimate how extensive and pronounced has been the decline in growth rates of manufacturing output for most countries. The trends revealed in Table 11.1 are in line with the estimates provided by D. Jones, 'Output, Employment and Labour Productivity in Europe Since 1955,' *National Institute Economic Review*, August 1976.

rates of growth of manufacturing and total output experienced by most countries was accompanied by a narrowing of the difference between the (higher) rate of growth of manufacturing and total output.[10]

It will be recalled that in Chapter VI it was suggested that the absolute level of per capita income would also influence rates of growth of manufacturing output because of a shift in relative demands towards services as income levels rose. Although this influence could not be picked up in the regressions of Chapter VIII because of multicollinearity, it very likely accounts for some of the decline in manufacturing and, therefore, total output. What seems to be involved here is a retardation in growth rates for most of the market economies. The manufacturing sector continued to operate as the engine of growth, but since rates of growth of manufacturing output were declining for most countries this pulled down the rate of growth of total output. While these trends were not as noticeable for rates of growth of manufacturing and total output per worker, events up until 1973 seemed to indicate that even these growth rates might be slowing down. As will be argued in the next section, events since 1973 are if anything reinforcing these tendencies.

E. The Transition to Stagflation

The period from 1969 or 1970 to the end of the last recorded boom of the postwar period around 1973 was a transitional period in another important sense which has been obscured somewhat by the dramatic nature of the events beginning in 1973. Table 11.2 is very helpful in this regard. It indicates clearly the remarkably (in retrospect) low rates of inflation of consumer prices over a fifteen-year period that was accompanied by rapid growth and low rates of unemployment. However, beginning with the late 1960s and early 1970s, inflation rates accelerated in every country. The period 1970–73 showed at least a doubling of inflation rates compared with 1955–70 for every country except Japan, France and the United States. Then, comparing the year 1974 with the average rate of inflation in the 1970–73 period, inflation rates doubled again, this time in every country except the Netherlands, Germany and Switzerland, with the UK a borderline case. Finally, the period from the fourth quarter of 1974 to the fourth quarter of 1976 shows a decline in inflation for every country except the UK, partially in response to the downturn in economic activity, which in turn was partially a response to

[10] Write

$$\dot{Q} = e_0 + e_1\dot{Q}_m$$

as the equation depicting the engine of growth with $e_0 > 0$ and $0 < e_1 < 1$. Then,

$$\dot{Q}_m - \dot{Q} = -e_0 + (1 - e_1)\dot{Q}_m.$$

A decline in $\dot{Q}_m$ is accompanied by a decline in $\dot{Q}_m - \dot{Q}$. It still remained true that, whatever the period, countries with relatively rapid rates of growth of manufacturing output tended to be those with rapid rates of growth of total output. The manufacturing sector continued to act as the engine of growth in this important sense even in the early 1970s.

Table 11.2. Annual average rates of inflation of consumer prices for selected market economies

	1955–70	*1970–73*	*1974*	*1974(IV)–76(IV)*
	%	%	%	%
Belgium	2.6	5.6	12.7	9.5
Canada	2.5	5.1	10.9	8.0
France	4.6	6.2	13.7	9.9
Germany	2.4	5.9	7.0	4.7
Italy	3.2	7.1	19.1	16.1
Japan	4.5	7.6	22.7	9.1
Netherlands	3.7	7.8	9.7	9.0
Switzerland	2.6	7.3	9.8	2.5
United Kingdom	3.6	8.5	16.2	19.4
United States	2.5	4.6	11.0	6.1

Source: *Rates of Change in Economic Data for Ten Industrial Countries*, Federal Reserve Bank of St Louis, September 1975 and 10 December 1976.

the various deflationary (or 'neutral') policies pursued by the various governments.

Prior to the period under discussion when unemployment trends turned upward, government officials responded by initiating stimulative policies in spite of existing inflationary tendencies, at least outside the United States.[11] During the period from the late 1960s to 1973, there was a rising concern about the acceleration in inflation rates and official intervention in the form of various kinds of incomes policies became commonplace. But because of the apparent success of the latter and for other reasons, authorities were still persuaded when unemployment rates began to rise in the early 1970s that policy measures to stimulate employment could still be undertaken on their own merits. In other words, during this period the potential inflationary impact of stimulative fiscal and monetary policies could still be given a relatively low weight in some sort of social welfare function. No such low weight was possible after 1973.

F. The Recession of 1973

It has already been remarked that in 1973 market capitalism received several undesirable shocks. The adverse affects of these shocks are still being felt today, and their origin can be traced not only to the cumulative movements set in motion by the disturbances but to some of the developments building up during the transitional period just discussed.

Taking the OECD countries as a whole, the index of industrial production

[11] During the late 1950s, the American government reacted half-heartedly to the recession of 1957–58, which had much to do with the weakness of the subsequent boom.

reached a peak in 1973 of 118 (1970 = 100), was unchanged in 1974 and fell to 108 by the end of the third quarter of 1975. While aggregate OECD industrial production had fallen in the past (in 1954 and 1958), the decline was much more pronounced in the 1970s and the period of stagnation more prolonged. Similar events were shown in the movements of GNP. The year 1974 marked the first time that the combined growth rate of GNP for the OECD countries failed to increase, and 1975 marked the first negative growth rate of this measure of economic activity since the end of World War II.

As might be expected, underlying the behavior of the aggregates was a greater synchronization in the movements of economic activity in the countries involved. For the first time in the postwar period, industrial output and GNP in constant prices were simultaneously declining by the end of 1974 in the seven major OECD countries. This in itself was considered to be some cause for alarm in that none of the major countries could be relied on, as in earlier postwar recessions, to provide a stimulus to the others through rising demand for the latter's exports. Forecasts of a repeat of the 1930s were prevalent at the time. By late 1976 each major OECD economy was still awaiting a recovery in the other economies.

The synchronization in the downward movements of aggregate economic activity was due in part to the extraordinary events of 1973. However, a more persistent and profound influence was at work during this period, contributing to the decline and stagnation over so many countries; and that was the widespread unwillingness of governments in the various market economies to reflate their economies in the face of a rising trend in the rate of inflation, a trend that had been building up since the second half of the 1960s. Table 11.2 above illustrates the developments in nine of the market economies.

The impact of the downturn and the various deflationary policies on unemployment rates is detailed in Table 11.3 for several market economies for which comparable data are available. Table 2.8 above gives additional perspective. As is clear, unemployment rates reached a postwar high in the majority of these countries. Only in Sweden and Italy was this not the case; however, based on additional considerations, Italy also can be considered a country suffering from a recession during the mid-1970s. The relatively high rates of unemployment throughout the period for the United States indicates, to a large extent, the traditionally greater cost attributed to inflation and the smaller benefit imputed to high employment in that country compared with the others.[12]

Tables 11.2 and 11.3 together illustrate the phenomenon of 'stagflation,'

[12]To be sure, the higher rates of unemployment can also be attributed to a less homogeneous labor force, the existence of dual labor markets, the lack of job training programs and poorly run employment exchanges. But to a large extent these factors loom large in the United States because of the relatively low weight given to high employment in some national welfare function.

Table 11.3. Unemployment rates of eight industrial countries after adjustment to US definitions, 1959–76

	Canada	France	Germany	Great Britain	Italy	Japan	Sweden	United States
	%	%	%	%	%	%	%	%
1959	6.0	2.4	1.7	3.1	5.7	2.3	n.a.	5.5
1960	7.0	2.2	0.8	2.3	4.3	1.7	n.a.	5.5
1961	7.1	1.9	0.5	2.1	3.7	1.5	1.5	6.7
1962	5.9	1.9	0.4	3.0	3.2	1.3	1.5	5.5
1963	5.5	1.9	0.5	3.8	2.7	1.3	1.7	5.7
1964	4.7	1.6	0.3	2.6	3.0	1.2	1.5	5.2
1965	3.9	1.8	0.3	2.3	4.0	1.2	1.2	4.5
1966	3.6	1.8	0.3	2.4	4.3	1.4	1.6	3.8
1967	4.1	2.3	1.0	3.8	3.8	1.3	2.1	3.8
1968	4.8	2.7	1.2	3.7	3.8	1.2	2.2	3.6
1969	4.7	2.1	0.8	3.7	3.7	1.1	1.9	3.5
1970	5.9	2.5	0.5	3.1	3.5	1.2	1.5	4.9
1971	6.4	2.8	0.7	3.8	3.5	1.3	2.6	5.9
1972	6.3	2.8[a]	0.9	4.3	4.0	1.4	2.7	5.6
1973	5.6	2.7[a]	1.0	3.0	3.8	1.3	2.5	4.9
1974	5.4	3.1[a]	1.7	3.2[a]	3.1	1.4	2.0	5.6
1975	6.9	4.3[a]	3.7[a]	4.7[a]	3.6	1.9	1.6	8.5
1976[a]	7.1[b]	4.9[c]	3.8[c]	6.7[b]	3.9[d]	2.0[e]	1.6[c]	7.6[b]

[a]Preliminary data [b]First nine months [c]First eight months
[d]First six months [e]First three months

Sources: US Department of Labor, *Monthly Labor Review*, June 1972 and June 1975 and; unpublished data, Bureau of Labor Statistics, US Department of Labor.

the simultaneous occurence of high unemployment (and low growth) along with high rates of inflation. It was the advent of stagflation throughout the 1970s but especially since 1973 that did as much as anything else to undermine the confidence of government leaders and economists in the future of market capitalism. For what was believed to be involved was not only a situation of high unemployment rates and high rates of inflation, but the fact that the rate of inflation would be higher still should the authorities attempt to reduce unemployment. In other words, the Phillips Curve was seen by the early and mid-1970s to have shifted so far to the right that none of the unemployment–inflation rate choices were now acceptable except in the very short run.

Two different kinds of response to these events developed, as would be expected. On the one hand, there was the view that in some long-run sense the conditions that prevailed before 1970 could be restored. The Phillips Curve could be shifted back to the left eventually so that low rates of inflation and low rates of unemployment would be a possibility again. In this view, events of the 1970s were seen as a temporary aberration. A return to the pre-1970 situation could be expected, provided something was done to 'whip the inflation psychology once and for all,' i.e. to reverse expectations that future prices must always be higher.

On the other hand, a belief arose that low, politically acceptable, rates of unemployment would in the future be permanently associated with politically unacceptable (and accelerating) rates of inflation in the absence of an incomes policy. According to this view, events of the first half of the 1970s gave support to the conclusion that relative price stability and 'full employment' such as that recorded in the 1955–70 period were no longer possible without some form of direct intervention in the market system on a more or less permanent basis, i.e. some permanent form of incomes policy. To put matters somewhat differently, if high levels of employment were to be given the high priority among the policy goals which they were assigned in the past, the market economies would have to undergo some drastic structural changes.

G. Some Consequences of Current Policies

The view that a permanent feature of capitalism of the very near future will be some kind of incomes policy is in the second half of the 1970s a minority view. A more typical view would be that which holds that the inflationary psychology built up during the 1960s and 1970s must and can be wiped out, although this may involve (usually unadmitted) Draconian measures. In any case this position argues for one or two more attempts to eliminate the inflationary psychology before even considering a more or less permanent interference with the traditional price-setting mechanisms. As a result, what has developed since 1973 is an unwillingness of governments forcefully to reflate their economies in such a way as to return to levels of employment that have been considered full in the past and the imposition in many cases of (hopefully temporary) incomes policies. The employment figures given in Table 11.3 are to a large extent the result. Moreover, given the recent forecast of a rise in inflation rates for most, if not all, market economies at least until mid-1977, a projected fall in unemployment rates of any consequence does not seem likely for some time to come.[13]

What can be argued is that, even if the view that a collection of tolerable unemployment–inflation rate choices can be realized at some time in the near future, is correct, current deflationary policies entail some costs. And these costs are in addition to the loss of output and rise in unemployment costs usually cited. Furthermore, the longer the period before the shift in Phillips Curve can be achieved (and statesmen in the United States and Canada, for example, are talking about high unemployment rates lasting into the 1980s), the greater are the risks that such a policy will lead to structural changes more drastic than those associated with a permanent incomes policy. These arise from the increased economic and political instability induced by a policy of prolonged restraint.

[13] *OECD Observer*, July/August 1976, pp. 28–32.

Consider first the impact on economic stability of high levels of unemployment that are allowed to persist. The counterpart to high levels of unemployment, low-wage incomes and expectations of long-term unemployment are low levels of capacity utilization, low profits and low investment-to-output ratios. Now it can be argued that a good deal of the economic stability of capitalism – stability in the sense of moderate fluctuations in GNP around some trend – can be attributed to offsetting fluctuations in some of the more important spending components.[14] For example, in the typical postwar boom, the growth of non-consumption expenditures has tended to be dominated by investment outlays of enterprises, while the capital outlays of other groups were squeezed. Consumer investment, in the form of housing and household durables and to a lesser extent capital outlays by local government bodies, showed a tendency in booms to grow less rapidly than enterprise investment and in many instances to suffer an absolute decline. The net effect was a kind of perpetual 'disequilibrium' situation whereby desired spending during the booms was always less than actual (non-consumption) spending.

Partly this was the result of the working of monetary policy whereby the supply of loanable funds during a boom was channeled toward the business sector. This was reinforced by the tendency of the capital goods industry to backlog orders during the boom, working them off or down to normal levels during subsequent recessions. Similarly, during the recession, non-consumption outlays by the consumer and local government sectors rose in importance as business investment plans were cut back and unfavorable profit prospects led to a lack of formulation of new plans. Easy monetary policy increased the supply of loanable funds available for the former groups. Over the cycle, the lack of synchronization of realized non-consumption spending by the different sectors led to greater stability in the above sense, compared with a situation where capacity constraints or 'ceilings' were absent.

Now, a prolonged period of high unemployment rates and low rates of capacity utilization acts to eliminate the built-in stabilizing properties of the kind of economy just discussed. First, the rapid increases in consumer investment outlays during the recession and early stages of the recovery just described are predicated on a widely held belief that recessions will be short-lived. Capital outlays of the consumer sector, whether postponed by the operation of constraints or not, will not be undertaken when employment prospects are decidedly rather poor. Much the same can be said of capital spending plans of local governments. Second, when capacity is not strained during a boom, including the capacity of the capital goods industry, backlogs of demand are not built up. This also has two aspects. On the one hand, backlogs of demand for capital goods by enterprises will not be built up to the same extent during a boom as they were during the booms of the

[14] See Cornwall, *Growth and Stability in a Mature Economy*, Chapters VI–VII.

1950s and 1960s, which results in fewer orders having to be worked off during the subsequent recession. On the other hand, diminished investment demand by enterprises during a boom will lead to less of a postponement of investment demands by the consumer sector.

In many of the market economies during the postwar period, firms in the construction industry moved in and out of residential construction depending upon the strength of demand by enterprises for industrial construction. Typically, during booms construction firms with the resources enabling them to provide either residential or industrial construction moved into the latter, imposing, in effect, a supply constraint on residential construction. Following the downturn in economic activity these same firms moved back into residential construction projects and worked off any backlog arising from postponed demands of the previous boom. In a world of high unemployment, low investment demand by enterprises and low capacity utilization rates, including those of the construction industry, the squeezing out of residential construction need never take place.[15]

Because running the economy at high rates of unemployment acts to eliminate the supply constraints just discussed, it involves serious risks for economic instability. To be sure, if recessions become more severe because of this increased instability, and unemployment rates reach levels higher even than those contemplated by the policy-makers intent on eliminating the inflation psychology, some reflation of the economy is to be expected. But given the fact that the recession will have started from a relatively depressed level of activity, the required stimulation of the economy is liable either to be underestimated or, if correctly estimated, to be considered politically unfeasible. The various lags involved in discretionary policy when the policy-makers are concerned with inflation only intensifies the difficulties. Thus, a policy of 'a slow, deliberate and balanced return to full employment' involves real risks. The likelihood of serious and prolonged recessions – recessions that themselves may induce basic changes in the economy – will greatly increase.

H. A Delicate Balance

The problems of political instability are, if anything, potentially more dangerous than those just discussed and arise out of the same set of Draconian policy measures taken up in the previous section. Assume, as before, that current and prospective profits and business investment as a share of output are negatively related to the unemployment rate. Then, according to the analysis of Chapters VI and VIII, the rate of growth of manufacturing and total output and, therefore, of per capita output will also be adversely affected by a policy to 'whip the inflationary psychology.' This

[15] Indeed, this is just what happened during the 1920s in the United States, which had much to do with the severity of the decline in activity during the 1930s. See Cornwall, *Growth and Stability*, Chapter X.

is the situation today in many countries where low investment, slow growth and even no growth of per capita incomes have become established along with high unemployment rates. As in the interwar period, growth and transformation have slowed or come to a halt largely as a result of a lack of effective demand.

Now it can be argued that until the 1970s a kind of social harmony prevailed in most of the market economies between labor and management, organized and non-organized labor, etc. This harmony prevailed in spite of the increasing commercialization of society that accompanies affluence or consumerism, a commercialization that has also acted in such a way as to undermine those traditional ties that at one time served as a source of social harmony.[16] This social harmony or social contract between, say, labor and management has prevailed in more recent times in spite of the rising commercialization of the market economies, in large measure because of the spectacular growth record described in earlier chapters. For what rapid growth allowed was not only the expansion of per capita incomes but the simultaneous preservation and even expansion of public services such as health care, old age pensions and unemployment compensation. To put the matter differently, with a rapidly expanding output to be divided up, the traditional arguments for a redistribution of output of those with an anti-capitalism orientation were blunted. The result was an implicit, if somewhat shaky, alliance not only between labor and management but also between various labor groups and different sectors of the economy.

However, a lack of economic growth introduces a 'zero-sum game' whereby the gains of one social or economic group can be realized only at the expense or loss of some other. Given a declining sense of national solidarity or 'common shared experience,' increasing class, group, occupational and sectoral antagonisms can only be expected.[17] Again, the longer it takes to eliminate the inflationary psychology, the higher is the risk that serious problems of political instability will arise.

I. Conclusions

What has been discussed above are some possible consequences of policies

[16] Even in tradition-minded Japan, a marked change has been noted in more recent times in the behavior and attitudes of younger workers. Personal gain and happiness have increasingly replaced 'duty' as a goal of life.

[17] See Bacon and Eltis, op. cit., for a discussion of the kinds of antagonisms that are intensified by the British failure to grow. What also seems clear is that a low or zero growth situation and the kinds of social problems generated by this situation also generate 'radical' solutions (both right- and left-wing) that seem capable of only making matters worse. The text conclusion is similar to that recently arrived at in M. Crozier, S. Huntington and J. Watanuki, in *The Crisis of Democracy: Report on the Governability of Democracies to the Trilateral Commission*, New York University Press, 1975. The view adopted in this study was that democracy requires economic growth. However, this conclusion was arrived at by invoking the fifty-year Kondratieff cycle with the early 1970s as its peak. The previous peak was 1921 according to this theory, and so something like the repeat of the interwar period is in store.

based on the assumption that the inflationary psychology that developed during the late 1960s and early 1970s can be largely eliminated or even reversed once and for all. The possibility that any success in combating inflation might at best be temporary was not considered. Naturally, if it is only temporary, and attempts to stimulate the economy a few years hence (say, 1980) meet with renewed inflationary pressures (in the absence of incomes policy), then the various costs and risks repeat themselves. As just stated, the position that a permanent incomes policy is needed today is a minority view.[18] This does not mean, however, that the majority view is necessarily the (factually) correct one. Various kinds of arguments have been made to support the position that the unemployment–inflation record of the 1950s and 1960s detailed in Tables 11.2 and 11.3 can no longer be achieved in the absence of an incomes policy.[19] If this view is correct, and if, for whatever reasons, the fiscal and monetary authorities persist in maintaining policies that allow the unemployment rates of the mid-1970s to continue, then even an optimist is bound to draw comparisons with the interwar period.[20] Thus, in Chapter I it was pointed out that, because of a preoccupation of leaders in the European economies between the wars with currency problems and reducing costs and prices, aggregate demand was not strong. As a result, high unemployment and stagnation resulted. A concern with an inflation that cannot be handled by managing aggregate demand (together with some form of temporary incomes policy) will, at best, lead to a similar situation of prolonged high unemployment and stagnation. And not only will these policies be wasteful and dangerous; they will have delayed the possible development of any kind of a permanent incomes policy that could minimize the losses that might arise from such an alteration of capitalist economies.

The earlier chapters attempted to document a process of transformation that transpired in the postwar period in a large number of countries. Throughout, the emphasis has been on the unbalanced nature of growth as seen by continuous and rapid changes in the composition of output, the sectoral distribution of employment and the spatial distribution of activities. The expression 'transformation' in the title of this study was originally intended to emphasize this aspect of growth. What is being suggested in this chapter is that events of the 1970s are most likely leading to structural changes in the nature of capitalism that will be more fundamental than those discussed in earlier chapters.

[18] However, the respectable London *Economist* is now a member of this minority, at least in its attitude toward the United Kingdom.

[19] See R. Gordon, 'Rigor and Relevance in a Changing Institutional Setting,' *American Economic Review*, March 1976, p. 9 for a list of structural changes that are alleged to make for persistent and accelerating inflation at high levels of employment in the absence of an incomes policy.

[20] Note that, even if some countries do succeed in shifting the Phillips Curve back to something like that which prevailed during the prewar 1970s, they may not be willing to stimulate the economy because of possible payments problems arising from a lack of foreign demand for their goods.

Chapter XII A Final Statement

A. Differences between the Interwar and Postwar Periods

The earlier pages attempted to describe and explain in some detail some of the more important macro-developments that have taken place under market capitalism since the end of World War II. A guiding principle throughout the study has been the view that if macrodynamics is of value it is so to the extent that it can explain history. One aspect of this is the ability of macrodynamic theory or models to explain why growth and transformation were so rapid in so many countries in the postwar period. At the outset it was argued that an important factor distinguishing the postwar period up to 1973 from that between the wars was the difference in demand pressures. Following Svennilson, with a general slackness in aggregate demand such as prevailed between the wars, slow growth was the only possibility. Alternatively, since growth involves qualitative change (to use Schumpeter's term) or transformation (to use Svennilson's), the reallocation of resources and efforts into the development of new production techniques and new industries was very much retarded by the large macro-risks that existed in a world of slack demand and high unemployment. At the same time, the innovations that spur cost reductions and productivity growth were lacking, resulting in a slow growth of per capita incomes.

Largely because of a commitment to full employment by the governments of the various economies, owing to the stimulating balanced budget multiplier effect arising from the expanded role of the government sector itself, and also simply to a greater desire by many groups for rapid growth and transformation, demand pressures were much stronger in the postwar period. Other factors were also involved in explaining differences in performances between the interwar and postwar period, e.g. a larger accumulated stock of technology to borrow and more highly developed technology sectors. But the differences in aggregate demand and the impact of these differences on such things as investment and the willingness to innovate and borrow technology does much to explain the more rapid growth of almost every country in the postwar period compared with any other period in its history.[1]

[1] See Tables 2.1, 2.8 and 2.11 for the relevant data.

B. Differences Across Countries in the Postwar Period

Explaining why growth rates differed across countries during the postwar period involves a difference in emphasis. All the market economies studied placed full employment high on the list of economic goals. While some economies adopted, or were forced into, more of a 'stop–go' strategy than others, differences in demand pressures between countries in the postwar period were not nearly so great as differences in demand pressures between the interwar and postwar periods for the same country.[2] Hence the need to search for additional causes.

Among the important factors stressed in Chapters VI and VIII were an aggressive entrepreneurial group keen on innovating and borrowing the technology developed earlier in other countries and a skilled labor force with the flexibility required to accept new production tasks, new work rules and new capital equipment, together with a willingness to move to new jobs and areas. All of this, in turn, would be reflected in a high ratio of investment, and therefore of savings, to output. The size of the investment ratio served as a measure of the extent to which an entrepreneurial class was committed to borrowing and implementing these new technologies. It also indicated the degree to which a labor force was able and willing, in the interests of rapid growth of output and exports, to allow these changes and innovations to be introduced on a continuous basis.

A great deal was also made of the importance of flexibility in achieving rapid growth. Here the emphasis was on the importance of growth in the stock of workers available for transfer or initial employment in the industries of potentially rapid growth of demand, as well as the importance of growth in the stock of capital. An ability rapidly to allocate labor and capital to these industries was seen as the main instrument for overcoming problems of the non-malleability and immobility of the existing employed labor force and capital stock.

For example, the agricultural sector of a country was singled out as an important source of surplus labor that could be tapped by the expanding sectors in industry and manufacturing. Lacking favorable long-term employment prospects for much of its work force, compared with those, say, associated with highly structured internal markets in manufacturing, the agricultural sectors of various countries provided a ready supply of labor for other sectors. The traditionally high birth rates in rural areas greatly facilitated this movement. Much the same can be said of foreign workers as a source of surplus labor for many of the wealthier market economies. With low wages in the home industries, foreign workers very much resembled agricultural workers in the market economies, especially those of the latter with 'peasant' agricultural sectors.

[2] As pointed out in Chapter XI, there was and is less difference in demand pressures in many of the market economies since 1973 and the interwar period.

But having stressed the importance of flexibility of labor supply, it was also argued that, if the other factors required for rapid growth were present, e.g. a high-quality group of entrepreneurs and a sizeable skilled industrial labor force, no country was denied rapid growth because of labor shortages. In other words, differences in growth rates across countries in the postwar period could not be attributed to differences in the degree of flexibility of the labor force because when the demand for additional flexibility arose, the additional (surplus) labor was found.[3]

Similarly, differences in the way in which financial institutions developed did not seem to account for differences in growth rates.[4] Germany and the United States adopted financial institutions that gave the greatest play to 'free market' forces. Yet the former achieved one of the more rapid rates of growth in the postwar period, the latter one of the slowest. On the other hand, Japan experienced the most rapid rate of growth of all the market economies. Yet it adopted a financial system of widespread controls, including credit rationing and government policies that worked to thwart the traditional market mechanisms, e.g. the use of interest rates as an allocative mechanism. Given a commitment to rapid growth, different kinds of financial structures developed to accommodate these commitments.

One end result of the process of rapid growth in so many countries has been described in different ways. The expressions 'post-industrial society,' the 'service economy' and the 'age of consumerism' all suggest what has evolved during the postwar period. By the 1970s economies were increasingly less involved in developing their industrial bases and increasingly more involved in enjoying the fruits of some such earlier development. The attitude of the Japanese government toward the type of technology that could be borrowed points this up quite well. By the 1960s foreign exchange had become fairly freely available for the purchases of patents and licenses that would permit the production of new and improved consumer goods[5] – and this in the country with the lowest per capita income throughout most of

[3] As indicated in the text, the basic factors responsible for rapid growth were a high quality of entrepreneurship and a skilled adaptable labor force. These factors would, in turn, be revealed by a high investment ratio, especially in manufacturing, and a rapid expansion of employment in the manufacturing and industrial sectors. What has also been argued is that, when there was an increase in demand for labor in the manufacturing and industrial sectors, the labor required was found. Much of the discussion of Chapters IV and V was taken up with this point. What was not considered was whether a strong demand for new capital goods would also be met on the supply side. This would involve one or more mechanisms for channeling resources away from current consumption, at least as a share of output. Kaldor has argued that there is such a mechanism in the ability of firms to raise their profit margins if they desire to obtain the internal funds for financing greater levels of investment. See N. Kaldor, 'Alternative Theories of Distribution,' *Review of Economic Studies*, 1955–56. Japan certainly suggests the workings of such a mechanism; being the country with the lowest per capita income throughout the period, it also was the country with the lowest ratio of consumption to output and the highest rates of investment to output.

[4] For a contrary view see D. Hodgman, *National Monetary Policies and International Monetary Cooperation*, Little Brown, Boston, 1974.

[5] See Ozawa, op. cit.

the postwar period. Along with this rising importance of consumer capital formation was the increased use of consumer credit and advertising and expenditures on services. Even the 'loss of the work-ethic' has been seen as related development. The extent of these developments in all the market economies was partially reflected in the rising importance of consumer durable expenditures. Table 2.4 earlier indicated their increasing importance in every country in terms of the percentage of total consumer outlays allocated to this spending category.[6]

C. The Changing Capitalist Structure and the Relevance of Economic Models

The singling out of surplus labor as an important facilitating aspect of growth was seen in earlier chapters as part of the development of a more general model of the dual economy, one that could be used to explain growth patterns in developed as well as developing economies. The stress in dual models on the importance of bisecting or disaggregating the economy was extended in Chapters VII and VIII by treating the manufacturing sector as the leading sector in the growth process of developed as well as developing economies. Rapid growth of manufacturing stimulated rapid growth overall.

The trends in employment in the postwar period indicated a definite, almost universal, process of de-industrialization whereby rates of employment in manufacturing and industry fell absolutely and relative to employment growth overall and in the services sectors. By the end of the postwar period, only one market economy – Austria – had a rate of growth of employment in manufacturing and industry greater than the overall rate of growth of employment. However, rates of growth of manufacturing output exceeded the overall rate of growth of output in all economies taking the postwar period as a whole, and did so in most economies even up to 1973.[7] In addition, economies with rapidly growing manufacturing output were typically the rapidly growing economies in terms of overall and per capita output. As a result, the dual model stress on the importance of bisecting or disaggregating the economy on the output side was suggestive for isolating one source of rapid growth in the postwar period.

This similarity in the nature of growth and transformation between countries still in a semi-industrial state and those studied here who have become modernized can be seen more clearly by recounting the various factors cited

[6] A detailed long-range study has been made of the relative importance of capital outlays by the business and household or consumer sectors for the United States. In the postwar period, the latter exceeded the former as a share of total output during the period 1946–62. Given the underlying long-term trends, the relative importance of household investment should be even greater in the period since. See T. F. Juster, *Household Capital Formation and Financing, 1887–1962*, National Bureau of Economic Research, New York, 1966.

[7] See Table 4.4. Rates of growth of aggregate output exceeded those in manufacturing during the early 1970s in Canada, Norway and the United Kingdom. In all other countries manufacturing output grew at a more rapid rate than aggregate output even during the early 1970s.

in Section B of the present chapter to explain rapid growth in the postwar period. To emphasize differences in the quality of entrepreneurship and the labor force, in the stock of technology available to be borrowed and in the investment and savings rates as factors largely responsible for differences in growth rates across countries in the postwar period is but to list the factors cited by development economists as some of the most important in determining the speed of growth during the early stages of industrialization.

The generalized model of the dual economy sought to bridge the gap somewhat between development and growth economics. In contrast, in various other writings it has been assumed that, once an economy has 'taken off' in its growth process from a state of backwardness, sooner or later, in what can be referred to as the semi-industrial phase, the classical model of the dual economy ceases to be appropriate.[8] At that point neoclassical models were thought by some to be the most fruitful models for understanding future developments.[9] What the various chapters have tried to make clear is that this assumption cannot be justified by looking at the behavior of the market economies of the postwar period. For example, there was little evidence that net benefits showed a tendency toward equalization across industries in a modern market economy any more than they did in an economy with much lower per capita incomes. Nor did the allocative mechanism at work in labor markets appear to undergo a change at some stage somewhere between backwardness and modernity. Nor for that matter did surplus labor disappear with rising affluence. The evidence that was available indicated that, whether an economy was semi-industrialized or industrialized, a situation of perpetual disequilibrium described the actual growth process better than some intertemporal version of general equilibrium theory.[10]

If anything, developments in the postwar period would lead the observer to conclude that neoclassical models were less applicable at the end of the postwar period than they were at the beginning and less applicable then than, say, prior to World War I. For example, the neoclassical view of labor markets is more appropriate for a phase in capitalist development when unions and internal labor markets are not widely developed. Similarly, the neoclassical theory of trade, growth and value applies best to a world of trade and production of staples, not manufactured goods produced by research intensive oligopolies.

But while a similar model may be used to explain the growth performances of semi-industrialized and developed market economies up until 1973, events discussed in Chapter XI indicate that something entirely different may be

[8] The dividing line between a semi-industrial and industrial or developed economy in Maizels study is whether (1) a net value added in manufacturing (at 1955 prices) is less than or greater than $150 per person, and (2) finished manufactures as a proportion of total exports are less than or greater than 15 per cent. See Maizels, op. cit., p. 10.

[9] See Jorgenson, op. cit.

[10] See Chapter III for a discussion of the intertemporal version of a general equilibrium model.

required to explain developments in developed or industrialized market economies from this point on. This is true whether the authorities choose to adopt some sort of incomes policy on a more or less permanent basis or choose to try and 'whip the inflation psychology once and for all' by running the economy at higher rates of unemployment.

In either case the institutional arrangements that are likely to emerge and evolve will be vastly different from those studied here. What has been argued in this study is that the competitive, neoclassical model, with its neglect of frictions, monopoly elements and uncertainty – all those elements that make for the market imperfections of the real world – has become increasingly less relevant in analyzing the developments of market capitalism. The structural and institutional changes now under way suggest that an even greater discrepancy may develop between the manner in which capitalist economies perform and the models of mainstream economics employed to analyze them.[11]

D. Where might we go from here?

The present study can be looked upon as an attempt to lay out in as simple a manner as possible the basic causal mechanism underlying the growth and transformation process of the developed market economies in the postwar period. It was intended that the model would function eventually as a background for another important task; designing a policy that allows economies to once again perform at high levels of employment without serious inflation. As suggested in Chapter XI, this policy must be such as to lead to rising per capita incomes if it is to have any chance of success. It is difficult to imagine any capitalist economy functioning at all well in an age of widespread and intense commercialization of social relationships if caught in a zero-sum game. However, this need not be construed as an advocacy of a return to the kind of rapid growth of the pre-1973 period. Certainly a proper concern for the environment and a need to conserve energy resources are likely to act as two important constraints on future rates of growth. The likely decline in the rate of growth of the manufacturing sector will also act to reduce growth rates.

The majority view among economists and policy-makers today is that the proper policy to achieve these different aims is basically to 'whip the inflationary psychology' by allowing relatively high rates of unemployment to persist until expectations are reversed. If this view is correct and if somehow policy-makers are able to avert some very probable adverse consequences during the course of implementing this policy, then something like the conditions preceding the late 1960s might be recreated. The model developed in earlier chapters should then be helpful in understanding future developments in these circumstances.

[11] See Gordon, op. cit.

But what if the minority view is correct (the position taken but not supported here) and price stability and full employment can only be achieved if accompanied by a permanent incomes policy? Even then the earlier chapters should be of some value in suggesting what kind of incomes policy will be consistent with the goals of price stability, full employment and a moderate rise in incomes.

For example, in Chapter IV it was argued that in the market economies, the allocation of labor across industries has taken place essentially within a relatively stable wage structure. Certainly, changes in relative wages have not been the signals used to allocate labor; rather that role has been assigned to the opening and closing of job vacancies. While this analysis requires a good deal more refinement, it does suggest that one of the more persistent criticisms of wage (and price) controls has been, at the very least, poorly formulated. Thus, if an incomes policy impairs the allocative functioning of an economy, it does not do so as the critics have argued because it freezes the wage structure thereby denying an economy its allocative signals. Rather it is likely to do so because the policy is seen by one or more of the affected groups as inequitable and intolerable. As a result industrial relations will deteriorate and neither a reasonably efficient system of resource allocation nor growth will be possible. What constitutes a 'fair' and, therefore, tolerable wage structure is the real concern of the policy-makers here.

Going further, the previous chapters cited the importance of high rates of investment, growth of the manufacturing sector (especially the technology sector), high quality entrepreneurship and a skilled, cooperative labor force in the interests of growth of output and per capita incomes. Affluence may lessen the importance of the manufacturing sector in the future as demands shift more to services. But certainly all the remaining factors cited should remain as much if not more important for achieving growth in economies adopting a permanent incomes policy.

This means, for example, that if investment is to remain high and to be carried out primarily by the private sector, then a workable incomes policy must incorporate a rewards system that encourages a high quality level of entrepreneurship. Similarly, if flexibility is to be maintained in the sense that new techniques, new work rules and new industries are to be readily and quickly developed, a successful incomes policy must incorporate rewards to encourage labor to accept change as it did in those economies that grew rapidly in the past. The earlier chapters contain other more detailed suggestions that should at least provide a start in formulating an endurable incomes policy.

The record of incomes policies in the postwar period has certainly not been one to inspire confidence that the relatively harmonious industrial relations of the pre-inflation period would be carried over into a period of permanent interference with the traditional wage and price setting mechanisms. But, if anything, this only makes more urgent the need to explore alternative policies to see which are consistent with growth and can minimize the costs involved. In the Preface an apology was extended for undertaking a study of why growth rates differ in an age of double-digit inflation and its aftermath. One justification offered was that too little was known of the workings of market capitalism in an age largely free of serious inflation, roughly 1950–70. It is to be hoped that, by gaining a better understanding of capitalist development in its transformation prior to the age of stagflation, some light has been thrown on how to begin to resolve the serious problems of today.

Author Index

Subject Index